Reframing Bullying Prevention to Build Stronger School Communities

James Dillon

CORWIN
A SAGE Company

CORWIN
A SAGE Company

FOR INFORMATION:

Corwin
A SAGE Company
2455 Teller Road
Thousand Oaks, California 91320
(800) 233-9936
www.corwin.com

SAGE Publications Ltd.
1 Oliver's Yard
55 City Road
London EC1Y 1SP
United Kingdom

SAGE Publications India Pvt. Ltd.
B 1/I 1 Mohan Cooperative Industrial Area
Mathura Road, New Delhi 110 044
India

SAGE Publications Asia-Pacific Pte. Ltd.
3 Church Street
#10-04 Samsung Hub
Singapore 049483

Acquisitions Editor: Jessica Allan
Associate Editor: Kimberly Greenberg
Editorial Assistant: Cesar Reyes
Production Editor: Amy Schroller
Copy Editor: Janet Ford
Typesetter: C&M Digitals (P) Ltd.
Proofreader: Rae Ann Goodwin
Indexer: Jean Casalegno
Cover Designer: Michael Dubowe
Marketing Manager: Amy Vader

Copyright © 2015 by Corwin

All rights reserved. When forms and sample documents are included, their use is authorized only by educators, local school sites, and/or noncommercial or nonprofit entities that have purchased the book. Except for that usage, no part of this book may be reproduced or utilized in any form or by any means, electronic or mechanical, including photocopying, recording, or by any information storage and retrieval system, without permission in writing from the publisher.

All trademarks depicted within this book, including trademarks appearing as part of a screenshot, figure, or other image, are included solely for the purpose of illustration and are the property of their respective holders. The use of the trademarks in no way indicates any relationship with, or endorsement by, the holders of said trademarks.

Printed in the United States of America.

Library of Congress Cataloging-in-Publication Data

Dillon, James (James E.)

Reframing bullying prevention to build stronger school communities/James E. Dillon.

pages cm
Includes bibliographical references and index.

ISBN 978-1-4833-6527-5 (pbk. : alk. paper) 1. Bullying in schools—Prevention. 2. Educational leadership. I. Title.

LB3013.3.D58 2015
371.5'8—dc23   2014048624

This book is printed on acid-free paper.

SUSTAINABLE FORESTRY INITIATIVE
Certified Chain of Custody
Promoting Sustainable Forestry
www.sfiprogram.org
SFI-01268
SFI label applies to text stock

15 16 17 18 19 10 9 8 7 6 5 4 3 2 1

Contents

Preface	v
Acknowledgments	ix
About the Author	xi
Introduction	1

SECTION I: THE NEED FOR REFRAMING BULLYING PREVENTION — 7

1. Bullying: From a Prank to an Outrage — 9
2. The Frame Determines the Game — 25
3. Bullying in the Frame/Game of Schools — 51
4. How the Frame/Game Shapes Student Identity — 65
5. The Promise of Reframing — 83
6. Reframing Bullying Prevention: Building Community Spirit in Schools — 113

SECTION II: THE PROCESS OF REFRAMING BULLYING PREVENTION — 153

7. Guidelines for Reframing Bullying Prevention — 157
8. Heart Strategies for Reframing Bullying Prevention — 191
9. "Who" Strategies for Reframing Bullying Prevention — 215
10. "Do" Strategies for Reframing Bullying Prevention — 241

11. Checklists for Reframing Bullying Prevention: Building Community Spirit in Schools	277
12. Questions and Answers	285
Bibliography	299
Index	307

Preface

> "The truth knocks on your door and you say, 'Go away I am looking for the truth,' and it goes away."
>
> —Robert Pirsig, *Zen and the Art of Motorcycle Maintenance.*

Five years ago, I retired as an elementary school principal. Since that time I have read and written a lot, and I am fortunate to still spend some time in schools, allowing me the great opportunity to be among students and dedicated educators.

Every time I visit a school, I recall what my first supervisor many years ago told me: "Never forget that the people who know the most are the people who are the closest to the students." That single piece of advice guided my professional career before retirement and it continues to guide me today.

As a result, when I present to educators or write something for them to read, I do not pretend to know more than they do, because I don't. I engage with them because I have something that I didn't have for thirty-five years—more time to read, think, and reflect.

What I discovered from all my reading wasn't surprising; it didn't tell me anything I didn't already know from my experience with students and educators. Yet, what it did was to help me get the *right words* to understand what I had learned. So, when I stand in front of a group of educators I confess that since I don't have the daily experience of being in school with students, I know less than they do. I add, however, that because of the time I now have, I can offer them some ideas that just might help them reflect on and understand what they already know from their experiences. I ask them to take advantage of me, or to use me in a good sense, knowing that I can share some ideas or research that they probably would have eventually discovered, if only they had the time. I extend that same invitation to anyone who reads this book.

I share these thoughts, not out of any great humility, but because I am disturbed by the trend in education policy and practice to tell the people who know the most—the ones who work every day with students—that somehow they don't know enough. To convey to them that they have been doing things the wrong way and they need to do what other people, the experts, have determined is correct. Educators in schools who are closest to the students are now told to let others do the thinking for them. Unfortunately, too many educators believe that message and have accepted the idea that doing their job requires them to follow a program, a protocol, or a script that will make certain that they get it right. Consequently, time must be devoted to doing what others tell them to do, which leaves little or no time to do their own thinking.

Time constraints have always been and will always be a problem for any educator, but I am also disturbed by another current trend. This development was summed up by one school administrator who honestly admitted that because of all the mandates and regulations and the little time allocated for implementation, it was harder and harder to be kind to students and teachers. Today, not only do educators have no time to think on their own, now they have no time or freedom to do what their heart tells them to do.

These disturbing trends remind me of that quote about truth knocking on your door. After almost forty years of reflecting on that quote, I can step back and reflect on what is happening in schools and state what "truth" would say if you stood long enough at the door to listen to it. It would tell you that the truth is indeed inside and you were right to look for it, but the problem was that you were wearing the wrong glasses, somebody else's glasses, glasses that prevented you from finding your own truth. It would tell you that you can really only find the truth, when you look for it with your own eyes because it is in your own heart and mind.

Regardless of these trends and the mandates to change or *else*, I am convinced now more than ever that the **truth** for how we need to educate our students is already right inside the hearts and minds of the people who work and live in the schools: the students and the educators who serve them.

The truth in our minds is what we find when we think, reflect, share, and listen to ourselves and to our colleagues. The truth in our hearts is what we find when we act toward others with empathy, compassion, and kindness. I have written this book to help educators find their own truth about what it means to educate students.

This book is practical because it is *not* a program, protocol, or a set of procedures to follow to change or fix a school. It *is* a guide for thinking, reflecting, and sharing with others. It is practical because I believe that meaningful and lasting change requires people to change people. It is practical because it supports the type of change that happens when people's hearts and minds connect, the type of change that affirms people and brings them closer together.

What I offer in this book is what I discovered when I looked into my mind and my heart using forty years' experience in education as my database. It is filled with stories that helped me make sense out of what I have seen, heard, and felt in schools. It is meant to help you use your own eyes and to use your own database of experiences to help you make sense out of the truth in your own heart and mind.

I hope it encourages you to explore your stories and those of your colleagues, but even more importantly to create new ones that your school community can write and tell every day. I hope and believe that your school community can create new stories filled with good times together and filled with enough time to think and to share and to be kind.

Acknowledgments

I am extremely grateful to Corwin for publishing two of my books; it is a special honor and a privilege to be given the opportunity to share my words and ideas with readers. I greatly appreciate the help and support that I received from the staff at Corwin in the process of bringing this book to life. Corwin consistently demonstrates a high degree of respect for its authors and their voices.

I especially want to thank my editor, Jessica Allan, who continues to offer support and encouragement, not just for my writing, but for all the work I do.

I am fortunate to still have frequent opportunities to work in schools on a regular basis. I continue to grow and learn from each interaction I have with students and with educators. I thank all of the principals, teachers, and students who have welcomed me into their schools.

I offer a very special thank you to my friend, colleague, and vice president of Measurement Incorporated (MI), Tom Kelsh. His unwavering support and encouragement has allowed me to continue to learn and grow as an educator and to be able to translate my work into two published books.

My other colleagues in the Albany office of Measurement Incorporated have created an ideal environment for professional dialogue and collaboration. I owe a great deal to all of them for welcoming me, listening to me, and sharing with me.

I am part of team at MI that provides professional development for the Regional Special Education and Technical Assistance Centers of New York State. Many of the key concepts offered in this book grew out of the work I have done as part of this team, so special thanks go to Kelly Valmore, Diana Straut, Vince Tarsio, and Tina Tierney for being such great teammates and colleagues. Each one of you does tremendous work and each of you is a model for openness and professionalism.

Sometimes developing a book proposal is almost as difficult as writing the book itself. Carla Corina, a colleague at MI, took the time to read my many draft proposals and offered insightful feedback, which helped me clarify and sharpen the ideas in my proposal.

Casey Bardin is currently a school administrator at Shaker High School, who previously worked as a physical education teacher in the school where I was a principal. Casey has always been a "sponge" for new and exciting ideas in the field of education, psychology, and leadership, to name just a few subjects. Our conversations have been a tremendous help to me in developing many of the concepts I share in this book. His leadership and professionalism is great source of hope and optimism to remind me what is possible in schools.

My friend and colleague, Corrine Falope, continues to be an inspiration for me. Her deep love of learning and commitment to education continues to grow well after her retirement as an active teacher. She has shown me how a true educator never "retires," but just grows wiser.

My work and friendship with Nancy Andress continues to guide everything I do professionally. Her support and belief in me has always given me the confidence to feel as if I have something to offer others beyond my own professional circle. Everyone should be so blessed to have this type of colleague and friend in their lives.

A key theme is this book is community. Some communities are so strong that they are more like families, however, not all families are always strong communities. I was fortunate to marry into a family that is also an extremely strong and nurturing community. I know firsthand the influence that someone of faith, generosity of spirit, and an optimistic outlook can have on generations of people. That person is my mother-in-law, Antoinette Lombardo, who raised 10 children (number four became my wife), twenty-five grandchildren, and four great grandchildren. I thank her for showing me the power of faith, hope, and love and how it can transform the lives of so many for the better. She is ninety years old and still going strong!

My four grown children, Ernie, Tim, Brian and Hannah are also my good friends. Their unconditional support and encouragement are always there for me in everything that I do. They manage to find the time and patience to listen to me talk (sometimes too much) about what I have written about or just read.

Finally, nothing I do or achieve is possible without the constant love and support of my wife, Louisa. She has the biggest and most giving heart of anyone I have ever known. Every day she teaches me what it means to value, care for, and love the people in your life.

About the Author

James Dillon has been an educator for more than 35 years, including 20 years as a school administrator. While he was the principal of Lynnwood Elementary in New York, he developed the Peaceful School Bus Program that was designed to prevent and reduce bullying; he subsequently wrote *The Peaceful School Bus* in 2008, as a guide for implementing the program.

Jim was named Principal of the Year in 2007 by the Greater Capital District Principal Center. He received recognition for administrative leadership in character education. In 2010, Lynnwood Elementary was recognized by the Association for Supervision and Curriculum Development (ASCD) in New York State with the school designation of Educating the Whole Child for the 21st century. Jim was an invited participant and presenter at the first National Summit on Bullying Prevention sponsored by the U.S. Department of Education in 2010 and is a certified Olweus Bullying Prevention Program trainer.

Jim is currently an educational consultant for Measurement Incorporated and presents at many local, state, and national conferences. Measurement Incorporated is a company that provides assessment and evaluation services, professional development, and technical assistance to a number of different educational organizations. His presentations and workshops are conducted on a variety of educational topics, including instruction, classroom management, leadership, supervision, and bullying prevention. He consults with schools, districts, coaches, teachers, and administrators.

He has four grown children, Ernie, Tim, Brian, and Hannah. He and his wife, Louisa, a school social worker live in Niskayuna, New York.

Introduction

> "The only thing we have to fear is fear itself."
> —Franklin Delano Roosevelt

The question caught me off guard and stopped me in my tracks. I was at the end of a retreat for school administrators on bullying prevention based on my book *No Place for Bullying*. After two days, we had all grown more comfortable with each other and people were opening up about some of the real issues that they faced in their schools, and many dealt with issues that went far beyond the problem of bullying. Maybe that was why this particular principal shifted from the professional to the personal when she asked the following question: "What was it that brought me to where I was at the moment—doing a workshop on bullying prevention?"

I hadn't thought too deeply about why bullying prevention was now at the center of my professional life and why I was so passionate about helping school leaders address this problem in their schools. My current status was a progression of decisions that I had made as a school leader, and in "retirement" as a writer, trainer, consultant, and now to some as a perceived "expert" on the topic. I didn't really have an answer for her, but said something about how my experiences as a student must have given me a desire to ensure that kids didn't get treated the way I had been treated in school. I had some vague connection between my experiences as a student and my mission and values as an educator.

However, that question and my fumbling attempt to answer it planted a seed for a lot of reflection, which when added to the time that "retirement" afforded me, did eventually lead me to the truth of why I did what I did and why I was standing in front of that group. In fact, that question and all that it subsequently triggered in me, led me to write this book about bullying prevention and to probe deeply into this issue and why it persists in our schools. Accordingly, I think it is fair that I share the story that I recalled in my reflection when I answered the question posed to me; the story that reveals why I do what I do now and how this book came to be.

Ironically, reflecting on that basic and personal "why" question transported me back in time to a different type of retreat almost twenty years earlier, one where I was a participant and not the leader. It was a two-day weekend spiritual retreat for the men of my parish church. It was led by a young, but very wise priest from Ireland who approached the Catholic faith very differently from any other priest I had ever met. It was for this reason that I decided to give up a weekend usually devoted to the paperwork I had to do as a relatively new elementary principal.

This priest, Father M., much to the chagrin of some others on the retreat was not interested in having us reflect on our sins and asking forgiveness, but rather in having us reflect on the times when others had "sinned" against us and how that mistreatment had affected us. Being raised in a faith (one I still practice and greatly value) that had emphasized *what I had done wrong*, this retreat gave me the opportunity to think and reflect on how people had treated me—especially when I was younger and more vulnerable.

Being a wise leader, instead of lecturing or preaching, Father M. simply told us this story:

He attended an all-boys Catholic school in Ireland. There was a teacher, a brother, who was very strict and could be harsh in his discipline with students. Very often, he embarrassed students in order to get them to stop misbehaving or to motivate them to work harder. One day when Father M. was in the fifth grade, this teacher went a little too far in ridiculing a student. Father M. decided that he had to speak up or do something in response to what was happening to his classmate. Finally, he raised his hand and when called on offered his opinion that what the teacher was doing was wrong and hurtful and that it should stop. The teacher didn't say anything in response and just went on teaching.

That event happened early in the morning and the day continued as normal. All the students in the school went to lunch at the same time and following lunch all had recess outside on the schoolyard. When recess was over, all the students lined up in formation and stood at attention until the headmaster, their principal, dismissed them with their teachers to return to their classrooms. This time, however, they weren't dismissed as promptly as they usually were. The headmaster called Father M.'s name and asked him to come up to the front and stand before him. Then, with the entire school watching, he verbally reprimanded him for disrespecting his teacher and promptly pulled down his pants and whacked him several times on his bottom. Afterwards, he was told to return to his class and the students were dismissed from recess to return to the building for their lessons.

When Father M. finished this story, I was stunned and sat motionless. I don't really recall anything else after he finished the story because that final scene remained so vividly in my mind. His story flipped on a light switch in a forgotten room of my life that had been dark for many, many years. Suddenly, my entire twelve years of education in Catholic schools replayed itself in my heart and in my mind. My past that I thought was *past* was still very much present inside of me. I thought that I had put all of it behind me. I had lived and learned and it was just part of growing up. Not so! His story revealed my story; one, I know now, that I had tried to forget.

What was it in his story that touched me so deeply and brought my story into the light? I didn't know that answer right away; all I knew was that I had to talk to Father M.; I had to tell him that his story had connected with my story. As everyone left to go to dinner, I asked Father M. if I could talk with him. We waited until the room was empty, and then he nodded and said, "Go ahead."

As the first words were about to come out of my mouth, a wave of emotion swept over me and I began to cry. I felt I was releasing something deep inside of me and when I finally stopped and took a deep breath, suddenly I knew what I was crying about—it was very clear in both my heart and my mind.

I wasn't crying over being hit or humiliated like Father M.; I was crying because I hadn't been.

I thought my story of twelve years in school was pretty simple: I did what I was told to do, got very good grades, and ultimately got into a good college. I had friends, enjoyed my summers, and viewed school as just something everybody had to go through and at times endure. Most people would say I had a good education and that the sisters and brothers did a good job by keeping students on the straight and narrow, out of trouble, and on the road to success.

What I didn't know about my story was that during all those years in school I *lost* something important along the way. That was what Father M.'s story revealed to me. That was why I cried. I was grieving the loss!

Father M.'s story was the same as mine, up to a point. We both witnessed many acts of mistreatment or bullying. We both witnessed classmates and friends being shamed and humiliated at times. He couldn't be silent anymore, finally spoke up, and paid a severe and painful price for doing so. I never spoke up and had no price to pay, or so I thought at the time. That was where our stories parted ways. I stayed safe and made sure that I avoided what some of my classmates couldn't avoid. Nevertheless, his story showed me that I ultimately did pay a price by not speaking up. His story changed how I looked at my story, and I grieved what was missing from it or what was taken from me without my knowing it.

I wasn't grieving over my lack of courage or failure to speak up or help others. The loss went deeper than that—I was grieving because *I had never even considered for one brief moment* in those twelve years, the *possibility* of my speaking up or doing anything in the face of this mistreatment of others. I just accepted it as part of how things were done in school; it was all perfectly normal. It was just a way for the teachers to keep things running smoothly and keeping the kids who broke the rules in line. I had internalized the idea that the kids who were mistreated deserved it, that they had it coming to them. They were being punished "for their own good." Looking back, I realized just how well my fears had worked; it was so much a part of me and of my experience of going to school that I couldn't see it or even know it existed. How could I know what it was taking from me?

On some subconscious level, I made the decision that I had to protect myself and ensure that I stayed safe. I felt bad in some way for those kids who got in trouble, but not bad enough to think of doing or saying anything to help them—certainly not by challenging or questioning my teachers! In retrospect, I didn't blame myself for this attitude, I was only doing what most kids or people do: stay safe in the face of danger.

However, when the danger and the fear it generates isn't a onetime event or emergency, but is spread out over the years cleverly disguised as a normal routine, then it ends up producing long-term consequences. The people who endure it, who learn to live with this silent and visible fear, lose a part of themselves—they lose some compassion, empathy, and courage. Consequently, they become more of what those who have the power over them want them to be, and less and less of who they really are. That was the loss I was grieving. That was the true and high price I ended up paying.

Looking back now, I realize that it was this invisible silent fear that made me stay in school and become an educator; I learned to be successful in school, but had very little confidence that I could be successful anywhere else. Nevertheless, as an educator I did know that somewhere deep inside of me, I knew that school could be different than my experience, had to be different for the students I served. I didn't want school to take away from them what it took from me. The driving force for me as an educator was to make school a safer place, a place without fear, a place where students could be themselves and feel at home. That mission, my mission, continues to this day. It is the true answer to the question posed to me at the end of that retreat for principals. It is the reason that I wrote this book.

This book is a different way of telling my story, a way to shine a light on a problem that has remained hidden for too long. The act of bullying, using fear to change others or as a means to an end is sadly woven into the fabric of how schools function, and until it is exposed to the light, it will persist despite all of our attempts to address it as a separate and distinct problem.

In this regard, this is an ambitious book that I hope contributes to addressing an issue greater than bullying alone. Currently bullying in schools remains a persistent symptom of a deeper problem that disguises itself using the nomenclature of *standard operating procedure*. Despite the best intentions and the hard work and effort of so many people, and despite the fact that most people don't bully and don't approve of bullying, it continues to be a problem that negatively affects the entire school environment. This book is designed to help educators step back and view bullying in its complete context and not as a separate problem to fix.

The first section of this book, Chapters 1 through 4, explains the relationship between the problem of bullying and the current structure and operational framework of most schools. Chapters 5 offers promising research on how organizations can positively change their culture and climate. Chapter 6 articulates a new vision for understanding the problem of bullying, and offers a positive way to not just address the problem, but to improve the learning environment for all members of the school community. As it is described in the book, reframing bullying prevention should support the work of competent and caring educators, students, and parents in creating and sustaining the type of school community they want and need.

Key concepts of Section II of this book, the *how-to* of reframing bullying prevention, can be traced back to another story that points the way for how to remove fear from schools and make them safer places for learning.

This story is very brief one, but it sheds a light on what schools can do about bullying. The story offers wise advice that has been right in front of all of us for as long as we can remember; a basic truth, which is probably why we have so much trouble seeing it and putting it into action.

My friend and mentor Dr. Barrie Bennett was conducting a workshop for our school district. (Barrie works in a stream of consciousness manner, so knowing this, I stay on the alert for any of his stray thoughts that depart from the main topic of his workshop. They can often be as valuable as anything else he says.) So, one day in the middle of some point he was trying to make about instruction, he just stopped and said the following: *"It's pretty simple with kids, never treat them in any way that you wouldn't want to be treated."* And then he just moved on the next part of his workshop. For me, however, I knew that he had boiled down into one simple sentence exactly what I knew was missing in most schools; the one thing that many teachers either forgot and/or thought didn't apply to them because they were teachers.

If Barrie's *simple* advice borrowed from the wisdom of the ages were followed in schools, so many seemingly intractable problems would move toward positive resolutions. If those in power and authority acted with more kindness and empathy toward those who have less power, the problem of bullying would be more visible and less camouflaged. Students would have a clear and positive example to follow if they could see and hear adults consistently treating all students with respect and care on a daily basis. In such an environment, bullying would stick out like a sore thumb, it would attract people's negative attention and it would go away because it would know it was not wanted and it had no place to hide.

The way to reframe bullying prevention and to create stronger school communities can be found in Barrie's seemingly stray thought, stated in the middle of a workshop in a summer many years ago. That simple advice is the counterbalance, the alternative path, the remedy, to the story by Father M., my story, and sadly the story of too many other people; a story that continues to this day in too many places.

Section II of this book is translating Barrie's advice, the "golden rule," into a variety of guidelines and strategies that support those who want to transform schools into optimal and safer places for learning. Since changing hearts and minds is a process, a human process, I offer resources and activities for people to share and experience together as a way to reframe bullying prevention and to build community spirit in our schools. To paraphrase a saying about peace, "There is no way to community, community is the way."

Although the challenge of transforming our schools is very daunting, I have great hope that we can change the *story* of our schools so that our students and staff can experience and live a better *story*—a more human and kinder story. *I am hopeful because I know that my story would have been a lot different, a lot better if I had been educated in a school with less fear.* I am hopeful because I know from my reading, my research, my interactions with others, and my experiences in school as a student and as an educator that the following is true:

- People are basically good and want to have positive relationships with others.
- People are easily frightened and need to stay safe.
- Sometimes the need to stay safe prevents them from doing good and helping others.
- Sometimes situations arise and good people find themselves mistreating others, yet think that they are really helping them and are doing what they believe to be "right."
- When people feel safe and supported, the good in them comes out. They help others and discover that they are also helping themselves.
- When you change the conditions of people's environments and give them alternative and more humane ways of meeting their needs, they will ultimately do what they originally wanted to do in their hearts: do good and help others.
- Once people believe that they can change their circumstances by working together, they will do so and create the type of environment where everyone can feel safe and supported and where everyone can thrive.

My hope is that we can join together to make our schools places where each student, each person is cared for and valued. My hope is that this book can help us achieve this goal.

> "Never doubt that a small group of thoughtful, committed citizens can change the world. Indeed, it is the only thing that ever has."
>
> —Margaret Mead

SECTION I

The Need for Reframing Bullying Prevention

1

Bullying: From a Prank to an Outrage

> "Our tendency to see and explain the world in common narratives is so deeply ingrained that we often don't notice it—even when we have written the words ourselves."
>
> —Daniel Pink, A *Whole New Mind*

TWO STORIES

In the spring of 2012, there were two stories of bullying that received a lot of media attention and provoked a strong public reaction.

THE BOARDING SCHOOL

The first story originally appeared in the Washington Post on May 5, 2012 (Horowitz, 2012).

In a prestigious boarding school in Michigan, a high school senior had just returned from spring break. He was a popular student, manager of the hockey team, and belonged to over eleven school clubs. He noticed another student, a junior, who didn't look the way most of the students looked. This student was relatively new to the school, but already had been teased for being different; he acted effeminate and was thought to be a homosexual. After returning from spring break, his appearance was even more unusual because his hair was bleached blond and styled to drape over one eye. His decision to make his differences even more prominent must have bothered the popular student who decided that something had to be done about it.

He gathered some friends together to complain, "Who did this student think he was anyway?" A few days later, he recruited them to help him cut the junior's hair as a way to teach him a lesson. This senior and his friends marched into the junior's room, tackled him to the floor and held him down. The senior then proceeded to cut his victim's hair. Stunned and terrified, the junior screamed out for help and when none came, he just lay there and cried. When the senior and his classmates finished the deed, they congratulated themselves and walked away. They certainly had taught that junior a lesson.

Years later, when the five friends of the senior who participated in the incident gave their accounts of what happened, they exhibited great remorse commenting "What a senseless, stupid, idiotic thing to do," "It was a hack job," "It was vicious," "He was just easy pickin's." One of them remembered being guilt ridden and avoided associating with the senior for a while. He waited to see if they would be disciplined for their actions, but what they did was never reported to school authorities. Those students were never held accountable for their actions, but went on to graduate and lead very successful lives.

THE SCHOOL BUS

The other news story happened on June 21, 2012.

On one of the last days of the school year, a group of four middle school boys, over the course of ten minutes, mocked and ridiculed a sixty-eight-year-old bus aide with vile, nasty, and hurtful comments. For most of that time, the bus aide sat there and ignored what the boys were saying. At one point, one student touched her ear and another student took a textbook and touched her arm. A different student recorded a video of the incident and posted it on the Internet on *YouTube* hoping that it would eventually be shown on the Comedy Central show *Tosh 2.0*. The video ended up receiving over a million views across the world.

Very quickly the news outlets discovered the video and broadcast it on network and cable channels. The bus aide was interviewed on all the major news outlets. The students who tormented her were universally and publicly condemned. The parents of these students were also severely criticized for raising such mean children. One TV host called the students, "narrow-minded little monsters" while another commented that "if they are this rotten as this age, just wait until they are grown-ups." The incident generated so much sympathy for the bus aide that she received free airline tickets and an all-expense paid vacation to Disney World. A website was created to solicit donations for her and within a month's time over $700,000 was raised, which ultimately allowed her to retire and establish an anti-bullying foundation.

The outrage against the students who bullied the bus aide also quickly grew. The students and their families received hundreds of death threats. The local police had to guard their homes for several days. The students had to go into hiding for a significant period of time.

When interviewed by the media, the bus aide who wears a hearing aid initially reported that she didn't hear everything that was said until she actually viewed and heard the video. She gave varying reports on how often that type of bullying had occurred. In one interview, she said that it had never happened before; in another she said that students had been teasing her for a while. When asked how she withstood the barrage, she responded that it took a lot of willpower.

When she was asked if the students who bullied her were bad kids, she replied that they weren't; she said that she thought they were just trying to impress each other, to try to outdo each other with their comments. She also commented that something different happens when students are grouped together. When she interacted with them individually, she didn't have these types of problems.

The students eventually were suspended from school for the entire following school year and were required to complete fifty hours of community service. The bus aide decided not to press criminal charges against the students. When asked what should be done to make sure that incidents like this weren't repeated, she suggested the school initiate a class to teach students not to bully and how to be respectful.

Although these stories appeared weeks apart in the media, they couldn't be more different; they represent different times, attitudes, and values—different worlds. However, taken together they illustrate how the concept and the perception of bullying has evolved in our culture and our collective consciousness.

FOLLOW-UP AND ANALYSIS OF THE BOARDING SCHOOL STORY

Although the report of the first story appeared in 2012, the actual event itself occurred in 1965. The reason why an event that happened almost 50 years ago was finally made public was because the senior who had enlisted his friends to pin down his victim so that he could cut his hair was Mitt Romney, who in 2012 was running for president. An investigative reporter felt that this event that happened in 1965 might be relevant in helping people decide how to vote in the election. The appearance of this news story in 2012 was a clear sign that the issue of bullying was deemed important enough to impact the decision of whether a candidate who had bullied someone in the distant past should be viewed as lacking the moral character to be president.

The article in the Washington Post added the following postscript to the incident:

> In the mid-1990s, David Seed noticed a familiar face at the bar at O'Hare International Airport.
>
> "Hey, you're John Lauber, and I am sorry that I didn't do more to help in the situation," he said.
>
> Lauber responded, "It was terrible. It's something I have thought a lot about since then."
>
> Initially after this story was reported, the Romney campaign tried to use this incident to his advantage.
>
> "Romney's campaign even went as far as using the incident as evidence of his capacity for harmless, humanizing pranks as an indication of his looser, less wooden self."

Eventually in response to public criticism, Mitt Romney made the following comment (Davidson, 2012):

> Back in high school, you know, I did some dumb things, and if anybody was hurt or offended, obviously, you know, I don't remember that particular incident. I participated in a lot of hijinks and pranks during high school and some might have gone too far, and for that I apologize.

This story raises some troubling questions:

> In 1965, how could these good students (who later led successful lives) physically hold another student down and cut his hair against his will, even while he was screaming and crying?
>
> Why didn't the student who was hurt and humiliated tell anyone?
>
> How could such a hurtful, physical act be interpreted as hijinks or a prank even in retrospect?
>
> How could these students learn from their mistakes without ever being held accountable for them?

These questions defy easy answers and challenge all of us to reflect more deeply, not just about bullying, but about how good people can commit terrible and hurtful acts toward others.

In 1965, being gay or homosexual was not just being different, it was being immoral and sinful. When Mitt Romney and his friends held that student down and cut his hair, he was less than human to them. He was someone who "got" what he deserved because of *what* he was. *Who* he was mattered less than *what* he was. Perhaps in some twisted way they thought that they that were helping him; that this painful act would cause him to change his behavior and make him act the right way—the way most of the students acted. They probably assumed that almost everyone else in their school, possibly even their teachers, would also view what they did as justified. This does not excuse what they did, but sadly they were like many others who felt justified for committing hurtful acts: the student who was gay deserved what he got.

This is the view of homosexuality they inherited from their society and culture. They were taught that those people who were different *had to be taught* not to be different and they should be punished for that difference. It was the prevailing view of the world that they internalized and acted on. They felt the way that the majority of people felt at that time, so their actions were easily justified and rationalized.

The victim of that act probably reasoned that reporting it would do him little good. He knew only too well that those in authority shared the same attitudes as the perpetrators, so why mention and confirm the fact that he was gay? Why should he risk having those in authority tell him that he shouldn't have provoked them in the first place? The victim might also have felt that in some way he deserved what he got, since he was the one who was different. (In 1965, people who were *different* often assimilated these prevailing misguided attitudes of the culture and condemned themselves.)

What Mitt Romney and his friends did was very wrong and possibly criminal, but they were not "little monsters" whose "rottenness" only grew as they aged. They were people who sadly did great harm to another in the process of learning right from wrong. Some of those students who participated in bullying, however, realized what they did was wrong without having to be punished by those in authority. These students as they grew older could look back and feel genuine remorse about what they had done. Their moral consciences, developed through living more years and interacting with different types of people, *told* them that their justifications and rationalizations did not exempt them from adhering to higher standard of behavior.

What happened in 1965 demonstrated again that individuals who are thought to be *different* enough, deserve the negative treatment they receive. This is just another example of how people can commit harmful acts and then justify and rationalize them; this is the deeper more troubling phenomenon that is the root cause of bullying and all mistreatment of people who are considered *too* different.

Although it is a sign of progress to view bullying as a serious offense (not a prank), simply proclaiming it as is unacceptable behavior is not enough to stop it from happening. As this story showed, the real roots of bullying reside in people thinking that their hurtful acts are justified because others are just *too* different. This is what we need to understand

and address. As a result, this story shows that it will take more than just telling people what not to do to effect change.

FOLLOW-UP AND ANALYSIS OF THE BUS STORY

Author's note: Since I wrote the book *Peaceful School Bus*, I was asked by my publisher if I would be willing to be interviewed as an expert on school bus bullying and I agreed. As the story unfolded in the media, I watched as many news reports as possible and read many news articles. I took notes to ensure that I was prepared to answer questions posed to me in case I was interviewed.

As the more current story of the middle school boys and the bus aide proves, bullying is no longer ignored or culturally sanctioned; it is rightfully viewed as unacceptable behavior, peer abuse, and a violation of a person's human rights.

However, the bullying that occurred on the school bus did not happen in secret only to be retold years later. It occurred at a time when almost every human act has the potential for not only being recorded, but also instantly shown to the world. "Witnessing" bullying on video as opposed to hearing about it after it has happened, rapidly intensifies our emotional response and the judgments we all make about the incident and the people involved. While our collective emotional outrage against acts of bullying has been one of the reasons why bullying is no longer ignored or excused, we also must be cautious about how that reaction affects subsequent actions and decisions we make in addressing the problem. This story provides a vivid illustration of what can happen when bullying becomes a media story that attracts the attention of millions.

This 2012 story is so recent that it can easily be researched and relived. Go to *YouTube* on the Internet to watch the interviews and read the reactions of people and their comments on the videos.

In reviewing all of the videos pertaining to the bullying on the bus, the aide's perspective on the incident provided a more accurate and insightful version than the story the media told. It should come as no surprise, however, that someone who works directly with students every day is better qualified to comment meaningfully on bullying than commentators or pundits on the sidelines.

Here is what the aide had to offer about her own experience of being bullied.

- She didn't think that the kids who bullied her were bad kids. In fact, she said deep down that they were good kids.
- She thought that what they did was wrong and disrespectful.
- She attributed their behavior, even the mean and hurtful things said, as being less about her and more about impressing each other.
- She has been around kids for a while and knows that good kids say and do stupid and even hurtful things, especially on the bus.

- She knows that kids are not at their best on the bus, so she does cut them some slack.
- She liked the kids on the bus (even the ones who said those things to her), or else she wouldn't have stayed in the job for as long as she did.
- She really didn't know what an appropriate consequence would be at first, but she knew it wasn't a criminal act.
- She didn't condemn their parents, she knew that kids do and say things that they would never say at home.
- She realized that the kids needed more help in learning better ways of interacting socially.
- She also couldn't understand what all the media fuss was about initially, but ultimately took some of the money she got and invested it in preventive efforts.

The bus aide's perspective on what happened is closer to the truth than the story that was told in the media, but is obviously less dramatic. It doesn't instantly create villains and victims nor does it allow viewers to easily cast judgment on the students and their parents. It is to her credit that despite the prompting and the leading questions from those in the media, that she refused to press criminal charges and refrained from condemning them or their parents.

Nonetheless, what those students did was wrong and hurtful, but explaining the reasons and circumstances behind the incident is not tantamount to condoning the behavior. Using the bus aide's perspective on the incident as a starting point, the following circumstances can shed some insight into why the students acted that way and why there was such a strong and emotional public response to the incident.

1. The bus aide was hearing impaired, and as she admitted heard very little of what was said. The students also knew she was hearing impaired and probably thought that she did not hear their comments.

2. Their comments about her were not directed toward her with the intent of hurting her. The comments were delivered toward each other in a one-upmanship manner, as the bus aide herself explained in subsequent interviews. In a very crude way (not untypical of middle school boys), they were trying to be funny not mean.

3. The comments heard on the video that was posted on the web and subsequently viewed by millions were recorded on a smartphone with the microphone located closer to the boys rather than the bus aide.

4. Most viewers incorrectly assumed that what they were hearing on the video was what the bus aide was hearing. This would also explain why the bus aide seemed to be able to ignore the comments for most of the time; it is easy to ignore comments that you don't hear clearly or hear at all.

5. Although the content of the comments were crude and disgusting, the tone of the students was not mean or hurtful. They were joking with her like she was a peer, just the way that boys direct crude and disgusting comments toward each other.

6. It appeared that at the end of the day when they were tired and their inhibitions were lower, they got carried away with their crude and disgusting joking.

7. When the bus aide appeared not to be bothered by the comments, the boys probably misinterpreted this an indication that their behavior was okay. There was one moment when they touched her with a textbook and she glared at them and told them to stop. They picked up on that signal and the touching never happened again. Presumably, if she had responded to the crude comments in a similar way, the boys also would have stopped their remarks.

8. It is possible that the aide's apparent lack of response to their comments indicated to them that she knew that they were just kidding and was okay with what was happening. In their minds, when someone in authority doesn't stop them, it is a sign that they can keep doing what they are doing. Sometimes middle school kids can be pretty oblivious to social cues unless they are dramatic ones.

Although what these boys did was wrong, hurtful, and mean spirited, it might not be categorized as bullying, depending on the definition of bullying.

Bullying is when someone repeatedly and on purpose says or does mean and hurtful things to another person who has a hard time defending himself or herself. (Olweus, 2007, p. 11)

Bullying is unwanted, aggressive behavior among school-age children that involves a real or perceived power imbalance. The behavior is repeated, or has the potential to be repeated, over time. Bullying includes actions, such as making threats, spreading rumors, attacking someone physically or verbally, and excluding someone from a group on purpose. (United States Department of Health and Human Services, 2014)

Typically an adult in a supervisory position does not have *less* power than students, therefore, the power imbalance, which is an essential element of the act of bullying, could be missing from this incident. When the bus aide defended herself, the boys stopped, so she could not be viewed as defenseless. It is not clear if the boys deliberately wanted to hurt her, especially if they thought she couldn't hear them. It is also unclear if this incident was part of a regular pattern of behavior or a onetime event.

These explanations are not meant to diminish what the boys did, but only to illustrate how bullying situations can be ambiguous and unclear for many reasons. Putting what happened on the bus that day in context by examining the circumstances and the definition of bullying, those students should have been given some benefit of the doubt, at least enough to avoid condemning them as people. Ironically, it should have been the same benefit of the doubt that the bus aide herself gave them.

Putting the incident on the school bus in context raises some questions:

Were these boys "little monsters"?

Would they continue to grow more "rotten" as they got older?

Were they justly condemned?

Were the death threats justified?

Were they the products of irresponsible parenting?

Did they need to be suspended from school for an entire year in order to not act that way again?

Even without firsthand knowledge of the boys on the bus, my best analysis of the incident would be a clear "No" to those questions. They were typical middle school kids trying to outdo each other in being gross and cool. They got carried away and did something wrong and hurtful; something that they would probably never do again, even if they weren't punished for it. This is similar to how most of us behave. If we make serious mistakes, and once we understand our actions as mistakes and see their consequences, we learn not to make them again. It is possible to learn and grow without external pain or consequences being imposed on us. (If there are doubts that this is possible, refer to the story that happened in 1965.) At the time of the incident, there were no voices heard anywhere in the media and in the public that would support answering "no" to those questions. The story was another source of public outrage that quickly faded away for everyone except for the students who had to attend an alternative school for a year and for the bus aide who was able to retire with the donations she received from a sympathetic public. However, it is highly doubtful that the incident deterred any other group of middle school students from repeating other versions of similar scenarios.

COMPARING AND CONTRASTING THE INCIDENTS

Incident	Boarding School 1965	School Bus 2012
Description of events	Group of students physically attacking one student.	Group of students verbally mocking and ridiculing a supervisory, elderly adult.
Relationship to definition of bullying	Definitely bullying, but could also be considered assault or possible hate crime.	Might not meet the criteria of some definitions of bullying.
Perpetrators' intent	Deliberately planned the attack on one individual as a way to "teach him a lesson" because he was acting in an unacceptable way.	Doubtful that it was planned, even though it was targeted at an individual person who was used as a target of the jokes to impress peers.
Social context	Occurred outside the classroom. Adults were not present in a supervisory role.	Outside the typical school structure. A paraprofessional with minimal authority was the target of comments and insults.
Targeted person's response	Probably never told anyone in school. Accepted and/or resigned to mistreatment.	Never reported it, but didn't have to because a student posted the video online. Didn't want students to be charged with a crime. Stated belief that students were basically good, but showing off for each other.
Effects on targeted person	Immediate signs of distress and hurt; lingering psychological pain and distress.	Some immediate signs of being emotionally bothered. Aide admitted to not hearing all of it. Received public support and monetary donations in response to incident.
Public awareness and response	Happened without any public awareness until over forty years later with some negative public response.	Immediate negative public response and outcry. Perpetrators and parents condemned. Some death threats made to them.
Consequences for perpetrators	No accountability for actions, no punishment.	Perpetrators received negative labels from public media. Received yearlong suspensions from school.

Incident	Boarding School 1965	School Bus 2012
Public perception of bullying and those who bully	Actions often dismissed as rite of passage; perpetrators excused as being young and unaware of the damage done.	Bullying is not acceptable behavior and perpetrators deserve and need punishment in order not to do it again.
Long term consequences for perpetrators	All participants had successful careers, some as leaders.	TBD

THE "INVISIBLE CHARACTER" IN BOTH STORIES

No summary of these stories is complete without acknowledging a central and invisible character present in both stories. This character played a critical role in driving all the action in both stories, yet the characters in both stories were unaware that this invisible character affected what they did and said. This invisible character is described in the following two statements:

> Research using functional magnetic resonance imaging has demonstrated that adolescents actually use their brains differently than adults when reasoning or solving problems. For example, they tend to rely more on these instinctual structures, like the amygdala, and less on the more advanced areas, like the frontal lobes, which are associated with more goal oriented and rational thinking. They also tend to misread social cues, such as the emotions associated with facial expressions. (Fassler, 2012)

> The rewards centers of the adolescent brain are much more active than those of either children or adults. What teenagers want most of all are social rewards, especially the respect of their peers. The reward systems of their brain lighted up much more when they thought another teenager was watching what they did—and they took more risks. (Gopnik, 2012)

This invisible character in these stories and in many other instances is the adolescent brain in the process of maturing. It explains (without condoning) why good students could do mean and hurtful things to others. In the boarding school incident, it explains why a student's different outward appearance could provoke such strong reactions from peers. It also explains how those peers can easily convince themselves to physically attack that peer in order to suppress that expression of individual difference. In the bus story, it explains how the students can be oblivious to the content of their comments about someone they probably liked, the bus aide, in an effort to outdo each other.

Without seeing or understanding how the adolescent brain influences words and actions, it can be easy to attribute student behavior to poor parenting, character traits, or a willful defiance of authority. It can explain how easily the *group* changed each *individual's* perception of the situation. It also explains why over time the students in the boarding school incident could develop genuine remorse for their actions without having been punished for what they did.

This invisible character explains how students can be indifferent to what they know to be right and wrong and to the feelings of others. It explains how they perceive the world differently from adults and why they should be viewed as "works in progress" and held to a different level of accountability than adults. Our interpretation of the stories is dependent on whether we are aware of the invisible character or not. Understanding how the adolescent brain affects what students say and do can help us to make sense out of both stories and lead us to temper our emotional response to them.

THE ROLE *REACTION* PLAYS IN THE STORIES

Echoing these two stories, Emily Bazelon in her excellent book *Sticks and Stones* recounts in detail other stories of bullying. This is how she summarizes some of the unintended results of how we respond to incidents of bullying:

> In its extreme form, the rush to punish can lead to overreaction. We can forget that kids are kids and shouldn't necessarily be held to the same standard of accountability as adults. But, when a bullying incident blows up in the media frenzy and one teenager comes to stand for malice writ large, we lose sight of our own standard for giving kids a second chance. Instead, we indulge our primal urge for revenge; . . . The problem is that when you dig into the facts and the context, stories of bullying become more complicated. The key to remember is that almost everyone has the capacity for empathy and decency—and to tend that seed as best we possibly can. (2013, p.14)

The quick and intense response to the bus story illustrates how easy it is for observers to forget what it was like to be an adolescent and therefore make quick moral judgments about others. As the aftermath of the bus story illustrated, those quick condemnations were built into a chorus led by the media causing many people to wish great harm on the students. This phenomenon is now a central element in how bullying manifests itself in our culture. This outrage and outcry against those who bully only seems to produce attitudes and behaviors that are more deplorable than the bullying itself. This is part of the story that must also be understood: How is it that reactions to bullying often mirror bullying?

Although it is easier and comforting to judge others, we must be open to examining how the roots of bullying reside in our culture, our schools, and in ourselves and not just in those individuals who get caught bullying others. What Bazelon called "our primal urge" for revenge is really just another way of describing how we as a society initially respond to any problem by trying to use force or power to stop it. The more we try to *bully* our way to *bullying prevention*, the farther away we get from actually preventing and reducing it.

MORAL OF THE STORIES

Although the two stories presented in this chapter seem very different and have very different outcomes, they illustrate an essential element of all bullying situations and all acts of mistreatment: *the judging of others as being less worthy or even less human than oneself.*

Our perceptions of bullying may have radically changed, but unfortunately some of our more basic thoughts and beliefs about human beings have not changed. These two stories have an odd reversal, but reveal a similar pattern. The perpetrators of bullying, the boys on the bus, who without thinking had their fun at the expense of another person's feelings, then became those who deserved and needed harsh treatment in order to change. They are condemned as people, which is determined by their bullying actions. Because they made that mistake, their lives were threatened. In the eyes of too many people, they didn't just do something wrong and hurtful; they were bad people who deserved harsh, violent treatment. Ironically this is the same type of thinking that precipitated the attack on the student who was gay—he was also just getting what he deserved or needed. *The belief that any of these acts are somehow justified because the victims were different or immoral is the deeper problem and one that sets the stage and creates the conditions for bullying and violence.*

If bullying prevention has *evolved* to the point that the young people who bully now become the ones labeled as morally deficient or deviant (as was the case for gay individuals in 1965) maybe our collective view of bullying hasn't progressed as far as we think.

We know that people continue to be mistreated every day and that those who mistreat them have readily available reasons and justifications for their actions. The root cause of bullying is connected to our tendency to find justification and rationalization for acts that we would not want to happen to ourselves, our family, friends, or to people who are similar to us. Acts of bullying emanate from something deeper and basic to how we as human beings view other people and our response to those who are not the same as we are.

This book explains bullying in the broader context of how people interact and are influenced by the cultural values and norms of their schools and communities. It attempts to answer these questions raised by the stories and to illustrate how schools have addressed bullying to date:

- Why do incidents of bullying become *the type of stories* that they do?
- Why are people so quick to label and condemn students who bully without having all the facts or understanding the context of their actions?
- What does that reaction say about our culture, about how we view the world?
- Is there something to be learned about why we so easily "lose sight" of forgiveness?
- Why does our approach to bullying fail to recognize what we know about human development and social interaction?

These questions, though difficult to answer, can lead us on the path to empathy and ultimately greater progress in not just stopping bullying, but improving how we treat each other in our schools and in our culture.

A NEW DIRECTION

"We must develop and maintain the capacity to forgive. He who is devoid of the power to forgive is devoid of the power to love. There is some good in the worst of us and some evil in the best of us. When we discover this, we are less prone to hate our enemies."

—Martin Luther King, Jr.

To significantly prevent and reduce bullying, we need to view bullying in a way that doesn't easily define "good guys" and "bad guys" and trigger behaviors that mirror the original act of bullying. Although our emotions should be stirred by all acts of bullying, they also should be tempered to better understand what it is, to help us act in accord with that understanding, and to bring people together to address this important issue. Without condoning their actions, students who bully also have some important and necessary things to learn about respecting and caring about others. We must help them learn about themselves and others by doing more than just providing consequences for their mistakes. All students, even the ones that bully need our empathy and guidance, not just our discipline.

Our "primal urge for revenge" does not have to be an immutable fact, or become a driving force in how our institutions respond to bullying. We should be capable of replacing this urge with the better parts of ourselves:

our capacity for wisdom, understanding, compassion, and caring. To begin that process to change our approach, we must start by believing that our students cannot be expected to change unless the schools and the adults who work with them change first. Our schools must reflect in word and deed the positive changes we want our students to emulate.

We must analyze and understand the current culture of schools and practices that might unintentionally contribute to and promote our tendency to negatively judge those who are different and to inhibit the tendency to help and support others. This means examining the often hidden assumptions and paradigms that govern or frame what we perceive and define as school. We first must explore that how we feel, think, speak, and act is governed by how we *see* the world—how we frame it.

Only when we see and understand our current frame of schooling and all that emanates from it, can we begin the process of reframing it in a way that will not just stop bullying, but also ultimately make our schools stronger communities. This is the process that can ultimately transform our schools into places that reflect the words of Dr. King.

2

The Frame Determines the Game

"Your moral feelings are attached to frames, to descriptions of reality, rather than to reality itself."

—Daniel Kahneman, *Thinking, Fast and Slow*

MAKING SENSE; BEING WRONG

While searching on *YouTube* to review the news coverage of the school bus bullying incident, I found a homemade video by a father who felt compelled to comment on the reasons why the students bullied the aide. He presented a reasoned argument that it was because they had not been disciplined or spanked enough by their parents. However, nowhere in the coverage was there any indication of how the boys were raised by their parents. Apparently a statement made by one of the boys' father that his son might need counseling was taken to mean that he was excusing what his son did. Nevertheless, the father who made the video interpreted it to mean that the boy lacked discipline, which explained why he bullied. He spoke calmly and with certainty; he was making the video as a public service to contribute to the ongoing discussion occurring in the media about bullying.

He extended this reasoning to our permissive society and how as a country we needed to crack down harder on children who misbehave.

The word "bullying" and the video showing it certainly activated this father's view of the world—what was wrong with it, and what was needed to right it.

This simple commonsense interpretation of the school bus story accompanied by a stated prescription for correcting the problem reveals a great deal about current approaches to the problem of bullying and their ineffectiveness.

Just as in the case of this well-intentioned father, people need to make sense out of the world and do so quickly without regard to how much they know or don't know about the problem or the situation. This father had no knowledge of how the students on the bus were raised by their parents, yet he assumed that they were raised without being spanked and therefore had not learned right from wrong.

This way of thinking is what contributes to making rationalizations and justifications for mistreating others or treating them differently from the way we want to be treated. In the father's mind, bullying others is wrong and should not be ignored. Students who bully others need strict and often harsh discipline (that was probably lacking at home) in order to learn right from wrong. This approach suggests that punishing those who bully or break any rule is really a way of teaching what has to be learned. Not punishing offenders only ensures that those who break the rules will continue to do so.

Many people observing this man's video will readily agree with him. His argument makes "sense" and resonates with other perceptions about what is wrong with our world today. Many people reflect back to their own upbringing, which might have included corporal punishment, and conclude that since they turned out okay, it then stands to reason that all children need the type of discipline they received. They are moral and good people so if corporal punishment "worked" for them, why wouldn't it "work" for those bad or immoral students who bullied the bus aide. Since the world is out of control and bullying is everywhere (as presented in the media), the only solution that makes sense is to impose stricter and even harsher discipline on children to make certain that they don't bully others. So pervasive is this view of the world that the students in the boarding school in 1965 were probably applying this reasoning when they physically attacked their victim: it was their corporal punishment for his immoral, wrong behavior. They might have thought that they were helping him not hurting him, or that they *had to hurt him in order to help him.*

THE SOLUTION THAT'S THE PROBLEM

As discussed in Chapter 1, the bus story and the boarding school story both included an invisible element—the adolescent brain in the process of maturing. The father who advocated for stricter discipline as the solution to the problem of bullying didn't recognize this invisible component in the story—it was not a factor in his reasoning. He determined that those students acted the way they did because they were lacking something (discipline) that should have happened years before; their actions were in a sense predetermined and were not influenced by their peers or their desire to gain approval from them. He was guilty of this common perspective: getting the facts or gathering as much information as possible, sometimes only gets in the way of figuring out troublesome problems.

His reasoning, therefore, for why the students bullied the aide would have difficulty explaining how these students as individuals, removed from peer influences, would probably act civilly toward the bus aide. He also probably forgot what it was like to be an adolescent with a strong desire to fit in and be accepted by his peers. In proposing his solution to the problem of bullying, his "primal urge for revenge" disguised itself as commonsense and took precedence over his empathy or any knowledge about human development. He would also find it difficult to acknowledge that it was his emotions that led to him to the "right" solution to the problem. His solution made sense to him, just as it would to many others.

I offer this analysis not to criticize this particular father, but to illustrate how commonsense solutions, even if they are held by a majority of people, are not necessarily the best ones to follow. In fact, this tendency we all have to "jump to solutions" to problems is a problem itself. If policy and practice embraced the father's solution, as many people might propose, not only would the problem of bullying persist—it would get worse: increased use of corporal punishment in childhood, is NOT the solution to bullying, it *causes the behavior it seeks to stop*.

The research on corporal punishment has revealed the following:

This study adds to the growing body of literature suggesting that parental use of CP (corporal punishment) may lead to increased child aggression. This evidence base suggests that primary prevention of violence can start with efforts to prevent the use of CP against children. (Taylor, Manganello, Lee, & Rice, 2010, p. 1063)

The study goes on to add this additional comment:

Efforts to teach nonphysical discipline to parents in general in general pediatric office visits have met with mixed results. (Taylor, Manganello, Lee, & Rice, 2010, p. 1063)

This is not just a problem with parents: nineteen states permit corporal punishment in school and 223,190 students in the 2005-2006 school year received it (The Center for Effective Discipline, 2010).

This commonsense solution to problem misbehavior is shared by many states, the same states that also have laws prohibiting bullying in schools. This is a troubling fact that shouldn't be ignored. When our solutions to problems become counterproductive to achieving worthwhile goals, we need to understand how that relationship happens before we can expect to solve the original problem.

A DEEPER PROBLEM: THE NATURE OF CHANGE ITSELF

Imagine this scenario: Polio is a disease with a cure. This cure has been translated into medical practice and delivered across the world. Imagine a place where the knowledge of that cure hasn't been applied; a place where medical practitioners for various reasons continue to treat patients the way they did before the cure was discovered. What is then the problem? It isn't polio. The problem is whatever is preventing those practitioners from using the treatment that is proven to work, and failing to understand *why the necessary change didn't transpire*.

This analogy is applicable to the bullying that occurs in schools today. The research is readily available that tells us what we need to know to significantly reduce and prevent bullying in schools. We know about the social dynamics that create the conditions that promote and sustain bullying. Many books, articles, and resources containing this information are available at little or no cost. Bullying is recognized and accepted as a serious problem that few people condone. Laws are passed to formalize this universal agreement that it is something that should not happen in schools. The people who work in schools are competent and caring people who also don't approve of this form of abuse and don't want it to happen. With all of this data in place, the most recent government statistics indicate that the reported rates of bullying have remained at approximately 28 percent from the years 2005 to 2011 (National Center for Education Statistics, 2014).

However, in our discussions as educators, both professionally and personally, we continue to say that the problem is bullying. As long we do so, our solutions won't work because they are directed at the wrong problem. Just *as polio wasn't the problem in our analogy, bullying isn't the problem in schools. The real problem is change: what is preventing or impeding schools from applying solutions that are already known to be effective in preventing and reducing bullying?* This is what we should be talking about, even if commonsense solutions to this deeper problem don't come readily to mind.

SOME ANSWERS TO WHY CHANGE IS COMPLEX

Perhaps part of the reason why we seemed stalled or stuck in our bullying prevention efforts is because the questions regarding change are hard ones to answer; it is easier to keep the focus on bullying alone.

However, social psychology has begun to explain how and why we respond to complex and baffling questions the way we do. The best extended summary and synthesis of this research can be found in the book *Thinking, Fast and Slow* (Kahneman, 2011). It provides an answer to the following question:

> What happens when a person or an organization has to solve a problem or answer a question when they don't have the answer?
>
> Answer: They tend to turn it into a question or a problem that they *can* answer.

This tendency is referred to as heuristic judgment. Daniel Kahneman (2011) describes it this way:

> A remarkable aspect of your mental life is that you are rarely stumped.... The normal state of your mind is that you have intuitive feelings and opinions about almost everything that comes your way.... Whether you state them or not, you often have answers to questions that you do not completely understand, relying on evidence that you can neither explain nor defend.... The technical definition of an heuristic is a simple procedure that helps find adequate, though often imperfect answers to difficult questions.... Furthermore, you may not realize that the target question was difficult, because an intuitive answer came readily to mind. (p. 97)

Heuristic judgment is part of our "system one" or fast thinking response to the world. Kahneman (2011) says that there are two ways of thinking and processing information: "system one" or fast thinking and "system two" or slow thinking. System one is an everyday operating system for most of our typical or repeated experiences. This fast thinking doesn't require a lot of thought or reflection as we encounter familiar experiences—it is like being on automatic pilot. We make judgments and decisions instantaneously to live and function efficiently. Most of this type of thinking is the product of past experiences shaped by our culture and the prevailing and conventional ways of thinking about the world. This type of thinking doesn't favor complexity or doubt precisely because we need to think and act quickly and efficiently in life. Humans also have an unconscious preference for this fast thinking and response pattern as there is a part of us that wants things to remain the same and run smoothly. We like things that are familiar and that we can easily understand. Conversely, we can be dismissive and leery of the unfamiliar or anything that disrupts the pattern of business as usual.

Slow thinking or "system two" thinking is when we stop generating quick answers to problems and stop to gather more information. It is when we listen to others, reflect, question, probe, and collaborate. Slow thinking requires us to listen to different perspectives, to empathize with others and to put our own thoughts on hold while we explore new ideas. It allows us to tolerate uncertainty, to accept the uncomfortable feeling of being wrong and to admit mistaken thinking. Slow thinking helps us to realize that our fast thinking was not accurate; it allows us to step out of our familiar and comforting frame of reference and realize that there are other legitimate frames to explore.

This system one/fast thinking tendency explains why someone could think corporal punishment is the answer to the problem of bullying. Fast thinking *has to make* sense of things and provide answers that are consistent with our previous experiences and limited personal knowledge. As a result, fast thinking is why we can make sense of something yet our solutions to the problem can end up being counterproductive. Fast thinking is neither right nor wrong, but it is limited because more complex questions or problems require additional information and knowledge from sources beyond our own experiences. Fast thinking keeps processing old information and produces little new knowledge or creative thinking. If we believe we already know the answers and are certain of them, then there is little reason to look outside of what we already know for the answers.

Fast thinking is effective at maintaining the status quo and resisting substantive changes; it impedes creativity. Fast thinking can make thinking outside the box almost impossible because it fools us into thinking that there is only one box, or that the one box is all that exists. Since this type of thinking manifests itself in so many ways in his research, Kahneman (2011) refers to this as WWSIATI or "what we see is all there is." Other writers and researchers have other names for this thinking fast phenomenon. Cialdini (2001) refers to this as the "click and whirr" approach to problems in order to emphasize how certain situations trigger a response that we think makes sense, but in reality doesn't. He explains how these "click and whirr" (automatic and unconscious) responses are exploited by advertisers and those in the business of influencing people's buying habits.

Heath and Heath (2013) refer to fast thinking as the "spotlight effect" or giving too much weight to a narrow range of information and ignoring information that could be helpful in making better decisions. They restate Kahneman's WWSIATI this way:

> What's in the spotlight will rarely be everything we need to make a good decision, but we won't always be able to shift the light. Sometimes we'll forget there's a spotlight at all, dwelling so long in the tiny circle of light we forget there's a broader landscape beyond it. (Heath & Heath, 2013, p. 3)

This tendency to apply simpler solutions and answers to complex problems is further exacerbated by other factors:

> Sometimes the issues may be so complicated, the time so tight, the distractions so intrusive, the emotional arousal so strong, or the mental fatigue so deep that we are in no cognitive condition to operate mindfully. Important topic or not, we have to take the shortcut. (Cialdini, 2001, p. 9)

That internal process of taking a mental shortcut is to apply the familiar and comfortable approaches that might have worked with other problems to all problems no matter how different they might be. With a limited amount of time and energy, our minds, our ways of thinking are strongly biased toward sticking with what we know and are used to rather than admitting that the problem might require more thought and examination. Those factors described above by Cialdini are so prominent in schools today that no educator can be faulted for wanting to rely on any shortcut available to them. Unfortunately, the shortcuts used are not leading them in the right direction.

This type of automatic response to problems is also further complicated by another tendency people have to find information to strengthen their initial reactions or opinions. It is easy to find evidence to reinforce current ways of thinking. Heath and Heath (2013) refer to this pattern as confirmation bias:

> Our normal habit in life is to develop a quick belief about a situation and then seek out information that bolsters that belief. . . . When people have the opportunity to collect information from the world, they are more likely to select information that supports preexisting attitudes, beliefs and actions. . . . We often pretend that we want truth when we are merely seeking reassurance. (pp. 11–12)

This research in social psychology has clearly shown that change is not a rational process, even though we keep thinking that it should be (i.e., our fast thinking at work). Humans are very vulnerable to self-deception or feeling certain when doubt and questioning would be the better state of mind. The more perplexing and complex the problem appears, the stronger our tendency is to let our preconceived ideas (and their accompanying commonsense) override more accurate information gained from research and knowledge of human behavior, thus preventing our slow thinking. We have a need to be right and to know the answers, when in most situations our personal knowledge is both limited and constrained by preexisting attitudes, biases, and invisible emotions disguised as rational thought.

If we use the understanding provided by social psychology, we can draw the following conclusions about how the father in the video could make so much sense and be so wrong in his assumptions and how we all can make similar mistakes in our approaches to bullying prevention:

- **People project their own beliefs into situations and then think that they objectively understand it.** This father believed that children needed strict corporal punishment in order to learn right from wrong, so when a child did something wrong it was because he or she wasn't properly disciplined.
- **The more certain people are of their interpretation, the more they think that it's not an interpretation, but the truth.** This makes it difficult for them to see any alternative way of understanding the world. It would be very hard to argue with this father's interpretation of what happened on the bus or what should be done about it. Those who might suggest an alternative to harsh punishment would be easily accused of being indifferent to the problem, or even worse, contributing to it.
- **How people view or understand a problem determines how they think the problem should be solved.** This father's solution to the problem of bullying didn't require too much thinking or reflection. The cause of the problem and the solution to it were simple and obvious to him.

Not only do individuals easily get stuck in *fast thinking*, so do organizations, including our schools.

IMPLICATIONS FOR BULLYING PREVENTION

If bullying persists as a problem in our schools and in our culture, we shouldn't fool ourselves into thinking that knowledge alone about bullying and the rational solutions we derive can be readily embraced and implemented by people. Bullying is an emotional issue and does not exist in isolation from the attitudes and cultural norms that have played a role in creating and sustaining it. Bullying is a problem that we want to solve because it violates our sense of right and wrong. We want answers, so we quickly (using our *fast thinking*) create solutions that might have worked for other problems and then hope they work with bullying. When they don't work, instead of embracing some useful doubt or uncertainty (switching to *slow thinking*), our tendency is to double down on tried and true solutions that might have worked for other problems. When we discover that those solutions aren't working, we then attribute the lack of progress to the improper design and implementation of the solutions, or we just develop slight variations of those tried and true solutions.

Well-publicized incidents of bullying stir people's emotions and opinions (e.g., when *fast thinking* occurs on a collective basis) and can drive policy and practice. This book explains why our current solutions to bullying (in the form of policies and practices) are manifestations of organizational fast thinking that is impeding the development of more creative and effective approaches.

While our emotional reaction to bullying should compel us to do something about it, it shouldn't determine what we do about it. Before we can start going in the right direction, we first need to recognize some *warning signs* in many of our current approaches to addressing the problem of bullying that indicate that we are going in the wrong direction:

- Any solution to a problem that fixes blame to any group of people.
- Reactions that label, judge, and condemn people instead of their words or actions.
- Solutions that use power to force people to change: *bullying* others in order to get them to stop bullying.

To ensure that we effectively address the problem of bullying, we must examine how we perceive that problem and how our perception affects all that we do in response to it. Understanding the tendency that we all have to individually and collectively fool ourselves into thinking we know the answers is essential to ultimately finding solutions that do work. We must know what shapes our *fast thinking* and provides the basis for our easy answers to questions and solutions to the problem. In other words, the preexisting frame of how we perceive and interpret the world.

MENTAL FRAMES AND THEIR IMPACT

The reason that people (e.g., the father whose advocated increased corporal punishment) react to many bullying incidents with strong feelings and accompanied with certain explanations/solutions is because they view the incident through their preexisting mental or cognitive frame. A mental frame filters, limits, and shapes how any problem is understood, and subsequently the response to the problem. Frames can explain why making sense and being wrong happens so frequently and why many of our solutions to problems not only don't work, but also are counterproductive.

George Lakoff (2004) has written extensively about frames and their political impact, explains how frames shape the world as we experience it, and govern how we respond to it:

Frames are mental structures that shape the way we see the world. As a result, they shape the goals we seek, the plans we make, the way we act and what counts as a good or bad outcome of our actions . . . to change frames is to change all of this. Reframing is social change. (p. xv)

The concept of mental frames explains why so many incidents of bullying seem to be instantly transformed into stark dramas of good versus evil, perpetrator versus victim. Frames are the reason why so many people make such quick judgments without having all the available information. Frames are the reason why people can be so wrong, even when they are so convinced that they are right. Frames are the reason why facts, appeal to reason, and even the best ideas almost always fail to change people's hearts and minds.

In sum, mental frames create the path that our *fast thinking* follows in response to any problem or experience.

Summary of research and theory on the mental frames (Edmondson, 2012; Lakoff, 2004; Schwartz & Sharpe, 2010)
Frames organize the information we receive from our experiences.
Frames help us use this information to interpret and make sense out of the world. They contain basic assumptions about life, people, and the nature of the world.
Frames filter out some information that doesn't fit or is inconsistent with the frame. Some information can be rendered irrelevant or ignored as a factor in thinking and understanding.
Frames can be easily confused with the world or reality itself—such as confusing a map with territory or a lens with the object viewed.
Frames are invisible and ever present and are influenced by past experiences, attitudes, and biases.
Frames affect how we view people and interact with them.
Frames can be a real source of conflict that is hard to resolve especially when those in conflict are unaware of how frames have influenced how they think and act.
Frames can change through respectful and trusting relationships and conversation. They are more resistant to change when someone deliberately appears to want to change another person.
Frames are neither right nor wrong, but some frames can be more inclusive and open to new or different types of information.

MENTAL FRAMES GOVERNING SCHOOLS

To understand why our schools are not making progress in reducing and preventing bullying, we need to analyze the current mental frames that govern the *fast thinking* that occurs in our schools today. There are two steps to developing a more creative approach to the problem of bullying:

- Realize that we perceive and interpret bullying through a mental frame.
- Understand and analyze what the frame is and how it influences our thinking and response to the problem of bullying.

Some mental frames have a particularly strong influence on our politics, our culture, and our schools. George Lakoff (2006) refers to this type of mental frame as a "deep frame" because it encompasses so much of how we view and understand the world. One such deep frame is the dominant/strict father frame. Here is a table describing its key features:

Key Elements of the Dominant/Strict Father Mental Frame
We live in a dangerous world with constant competition and inevitable winners and losers.
Children are born bad. They just want to do what feels good, not what is right; therefore, they have to be made good.
Morally there are absolute rights and wrongs.
The father is the moral authority that knows right from wrong.
This moral authority should not be challenged.
Obedience to this moral authority determines what is moral (right) and what is immoral (wrong).
Children are born undisciplined and need to be taught right from wrong.
A father is obligated to punish when a child does something wrong in order to teach that child and to provide an incentive to do what is right.

It is easy to see how this mental frame created the path for the *fast thinking* that governed the thoughts and actions of

- the boarding school students' treatment of the student thought to be gay;
- the public in their demand for criminal charges to filed for a group of middle school boys on the school bus; and
- the father who thought that the cause of bullying was the lack of corporal punishment in the students' childhoods.

This mental frame not only justifies punishment it almost requires it in order to insure that a child learns right from wrong. Punishment becomes progressively more severe, if milder versions fail to teach the required lesson. Within this mental frame, not only is our knowledge of human development or the adolescent brain not considered important, it is irrelevant since right and wrong are absolutes and wrong decisions ultimately reflect character flaws. What children have to learn is pretty simple: follow the rules determined by the dominant parent. Do what is right and don't do what is wrong because the higher moral authority has the power and license to inflict pain and/or offer approval and reward. This is done in the service of teaching the difference between right and wrong. External, harsh consequences are often necessary for controlling and teaching children what they need to know.

Although a more enlightened view might replace severe punishment with less intense consequences for violations of the moral code, nonetheless, the basic justification for inflicting some type of mistreatment on those who do wrong still remains. (I define mistreatment as any experience that causes physical, emotional, or psychological pain with the intent to have the person feel badly about himself or herself as a way to correct the behavior. To put it in simpler terms—not following the "golden rule" or treating another in a way you would not want to be treated.) This mistreatment is still considered a necessary action: some type of negative experience is needed as a consequence for those who made the mistake or were wrong. Within this frame, "bullying" or forcing others to stop bullying makes a lot of commonsense. Power or force is justified when those who are more moral and knowledgeable are using it to teach those with less power and knowledge to become moral. In this mental frame, "might does indeed make right."

Consequently, keep in mind that within this mental frame gaining power becomes a way to gain control and to stay safe at the same time, which becomes a very powerful incentive for moving into positions of higher status and authority. This frame creates the conditions that can foster bullying, especially for those who need to stay safe and feel in control. It not only models a way to solve problems, it fosters a type of thinking that justifies mistreatment. It probably also explains why a person in a greater position of power who mistreats others seldom thinks he or she is wrong and usually blames the victim who deserved the mistreatment. This is also probably why the research shows that children who receive corporal punishment are more likely to bully other children: they are not only imitating what they have seen modeled, they have assimilated the mental frame that justified their own mistreatment.

However, there is another frame that has and continues to have a profound and lasting influence on schools and therefore on how schools view and respond to bullying: the factory frame. This frame fits neatly with the dominant father frame and when combined, these two frames withstand many attempts to change them.

FACTORY FRAME OF EDUCATION

In his 2011 book *Out of Our Minds: Learning to Be Creative,* Kenneth Robinson provides this description of the influence of the factory frame on how our schools are organized and governed:

> Like factories, schools are special facilities with clear boundaries that separate them from the outside world. They have set hours of operation and prescribed rules of conduct. They are based on the

principles of standardization and conformity. Students with the academic system are taught broadly the same material and they are assessed against common scales of achievement, with relatively few opportunities for choice or deviation. The day is organized into standard units of time and the transitions are marked by the ringing of bells or buzzers. (p. 57)

Paulo Freire in *Pedagogy of the Oppressed* (2000) describes this dominant parent/factory frame this way:

(a) the teacher teaches and the students are taught; (b) the teacher knows everything and the students know nothing; (c) the teacher thinks and the students are thought about; (d) the teacher talks and the students listen-meekly; (e) the teacher disciplines and the students are disciplined; (f) the teacher chooses and enforces his choice, and the students comply. (p. 59)

Although there might be exceptions to this description, most schools still retain this basic organizational structure. My purpose is not to analyze why this factory frame is no longer relevant to the type of education that our students need; there are many excellent analyses available and they are important to know. Instead, I focus on understanding the impact of this frame related to school discipline and bullying prevention. Exploring the key features of the factory frame sheds light on how the factory frame negatively impacts bullying prevention efforts.

The Key Features of the Factory Frame Applied to the Structure/Organization of Schools
A command and control structure: Higher levels of authority are required to manage and control the work of those below them.
An organization designed to manage and control the work of large groups of people: Having many people all in the same place and at the same time requires standardization and routine.
Order and efficiency as essential elements for productivity of large groups: Those within the organization need to comply and conform to rules and regulations designed to maintain the efficiency of the organization.
Work completion and performance must occur within standardized time frames and adhere to well-defined tasks: Learning is evaluated based on performance within the standards determined by the organization.
Individual performance for completing required work is the main focus of the organization: Social interaction is incidental to the goals of the organization and could be a distraction and/or a problem.
Individuals are evaluated and ranked according to their performance: This creates a competitive atmosphere and stratification among schools, teachers, and students.

> **Historical Roots of the Factory Model on Public Education**
>
> "F.W. Taylor's thinking so permeates the soil of modern life we no longer realize that it's there." (Kanigel, 1997, p. 7)
>
> Frederick Taylor was not an educator, but the scientific management system he developed in the 1900s to improve the manufacturing industry had a profound and lasting impact on our education system. The goal of his management system was to provide greater efficiency and standardization, which in turn would lead to increased profits for businesses. His approach proved to be very successful and spread to other types of organizations including schools.
>
> In an excellent analysis of Taylor's impact on education, Friesen and Jardine (2009) in their report, *21st Century Learning and Learners*, describe the reasons why this approach was applied to education.
>
>> Given the burgeoning numbers of immigrant children into large East Coast American Cities, and the equally burgeoning need for minimally educated workers in industry, schools had become overwhelmed early in the 20th century, and the prospect of a more manageable efficient organization of schooling became irresistible.... Specifically in regard to education, we have the words of Ellwood P. Cubberly, Dean of the School of Education at Stanford. In his text he considers that "schools are, in a sense, factories in which raw products (children) are to be shaped and fashioned" and that "it is the business of school to build its pupils according to specifications laid down." In order to accomplish this, a principle of Taylor's work is not only desirable but indispensable. (pp. 10–11)
>
> Central to this system of management was the control of students and teachers. Frederick Taylor made the following statement: "In our scheme we do not ask for the initiative of our men. We do not want any initiative. All we want of them is to obey the orders we give them, do what we say and do it quick" (p. 11).
>
> In this system, compliance and conformity were essential and mandatory. This approach also fit neatly with a behavioral approach that rewarded such conformity and punished any behavior that was out of line. Schools were organizations that had to control students (and teachers) first in order to educate them.
>
> Children, workers, students didn't need to worry about what they were learning or why they needed to learn it, they just needed to do what they were told in the way they were told.

THE CURRENT "GAME OF SCHOOL"

I present these fundamental structural aspects of our schools in order to connect them specifically to the problem of bullying and why schools have difficulty in effectively reducing and preventing its occurrence.

My contention is that based on the dominant parent/factory frame the structure and organization of schools today creates the conditions that unintentionally promote and sustain bullying behaviors. Using power and authority to consistently get people to do things without their volition, or simply because they are told to, mirrors the essence of bullying. The *game of school* that is an outgrowth of the dominant parent/factory frame has the three basic rules for students to follow:

- Do the work given to you and get good grades.
- Follow the rules—do what those in authority tell you to do.
- Mind your business—don't let the social world distract you from following the first two rules.

Those who play the game well are rewarded, gain status, and attain higher degrees of safety and control. Those who don't play the game well are more vulnerable and targeted for mistreatment. Consequently, this basic game of school is effectively what students learn in school more so than the content or subject matter presented to them.

CURRENT EXAMPLES OF THE "GAME OF SCHOOL"

The frame/game of school blurs the distinction between learning in school and performing in a workplace. It follows this basic sequence:

- What should be learned is determined and defined by authority.
- Students must be taught by someone in authority in order to learn.
- Teaching requires organization and management.
- Student must be managed in order to learn.
- Students are managed and motivated by those in authority using the right system of rewards and consequences.

Although schools have progressed from the days of strict punishments and blatant mistreatment of students, they still operate within the dominant/parent and factory frame, albeit a more positive manifestation of it.

Here are two recent experiences of mine that illustrate this fact.

Story One

It was the fourth day of kindergarten and already Benjamin was having a hard time. He walked through the school door wanting to do well as evidenced by his wearing a nice shirt and tie and having a smile on his face—motivation was not an issue for him. However, he had not attended preschool, so kindergarten was his first experience of learning with twenty-four other students around him and taking directions from one adult. By the end of his first day, he had already demonstrated that he couldn't consistently do everything he was told to do in the way he was supposed to perform. (His teacher had already complained about him, so that was why the principal asked me to spend some time in this classroom to see if I could support the student and his teacher.)

I observed Benjamin in music class, and although he sat in a chair while his classmates sat on the carpet, he enjoyed singing and the movement and he did okay in that class. I followed him back to his classroom and got a brief chance to meet him and talk. Since I was wearing a tie just as he was, we had something in common and ended up getting along well.

At the end of the day the teacher let the children play. However, she determined what table played with certain sets of toys/materials and unfortunately, Benjamin's table was assigned to play with the farm animals and not the cars and the parking garage. In addition, the farm animal toys were placed on the carpet just a few feet from the cars and the garage toys.

At first, Benjamin couldn't understand why he had to play with toys he didn't want to play with and I was at a lost to explain the reasons for this situation.

Benjamin started to get agitated and I quickly tried to come up with a solution to the problem when a little girl suggested that the two sets of toys be combined so that both groups could play together. "What a great idea!" I told her. I leaned over and repeated that suggestion to Benjamin and told him to go ask his teacher if they could do that. As he walked over to her, I was silently wishing and hoping that she would see this as an opportunity to acknowledge both the problem solving and communication skills of Benjamin. I watched her closely and was so relieved when she nodded yes. Benjamin ran back and played successfully with the other kids and consequently had a good end to the school day.

After school, I commended the teacher for her flexibility and told the principal that I thought a positive step had been made in helping Benjamin adjust to kindergarten. I went home feeling optimistic about what Benjamin and his teacher might have learned from their positive interaction.

As I returned to the classroom the next day, the teacher approached me. I thought she would comment positively on what had happened the day before, but what she said left me speechless: "I went home last night and thought a lot about what happened with Benjamin. I realize now that I was wrong to allow him to play with the cars. I was starting a bad precedent that would only lead to trouble in the future by letting him and the other students think that they don't have to follow my directions. This would not be teaching them what they really need to know."

She had reviewed the incident through her mental frame of school and realized that she had made a serious mistake. Control and compliance need to be established and took precedence over problem solving, communicating, and probably trust. *The frame once again determined the game that had to be played.*

Story Two

I was assigned to coach another kindergarten teacher later in the school year. This teacher had established clear routines and her classroom was well organized. The children had learned to respond chorally to many of her routine questions. It was very clear that the students were well managed and that this teacher was very much in control of her classroom.

In my own interactions with the children, I observed that many of them had trouble expressing ideas or answering open-ended questions. Overall, I was concerned with the lack of time allotted for the students to think and talk to each other. Although I was assigned by the principal to help this teacher, I didn't think that this teacher thought she needed any help.

Close to the last day of school, I revisited the classroom and observed a completely different environment. The students were moving all over the room doing all sorts of different things. The teacher who was assessing individual students looked at me apologetically and said that she had to suspend "school as normal" to finish her assessments and therefore let the rest of the class have free play for an hour. There was no teaching occurring in this room, but it was bursting with learning—more than I had observed in all of my previous visits and observations. Some students had created a pretend restaurant and came to me asking how to spell various items that they wanted on their menus. Some students had created a beauty salon and were giving each other all different types of hairdos. Some were constructing imaginative buildings out of Legos and creating dramatic scenarios that they acted out with play figures. Some were making beautiful drawings and went around showing them to their friends. Overall, there was more thinking, talking, and learning in that one hour that I had observed in all my time in the room.

Unfortunately, the teacher couldn't *see* what was happening in the room at that time as learning because she wasn't teaching the children and the typical routines of the day weren't followed. Her school frame filtered out those experiences of learning because they didn't fit what school really was to her—that type of learning didn't exist within her mental frame.

TEXTBOOK EXAMPLES

What I observed in both of the preceding stories is further reflected in the following statements in a current handbook for behavior management (Lane, Mensies, Bruhn, & Crnbori, 2011):

> Good classroom management is what makes it possible to teach effectively. Without an orderly, purposeful environment, educators cannot establish a classroom climate that fosters learning and collaboration. (p. 14)

> We use the term discipline to refer to a teacher's system of establishing expectations, helping students to understand those expectations, and using consequences and rewards. (p. 24)

These two statements are presented as basic fundamental truths of education. From these *givens*, the authors do an excellent job in describing an approach to teaching and managing that make the classroom environment predictable, positive, and under control. Who could argue that such an environment is preferable to one that is chaotic, negative, and out of control? So strong is the argument for adopting the recommendations put forth in this handbook that it is almost impossible in most educational settings to even offer a differing thought or perspective on what the authors so carefully explain and advocate.

Adherence to the dominant parent factory frame ensures that any alternative approach to teaching and learning is seen as chaotic and untenable. What these authors propose would indeed make schools work more efficiently with the current frame/game of school remaining firmly in place, but there are consequences, usually unseen, when our vision doesn't include what we know about human development and learning. Schools may operate more smoothly, but do so at the expense of meeting the needs of the *whole* child. Many *effective* behavioral controls in school are designed more for the management needs of the teacher and less for the learning needs of the students. This is a hard premise to accept unless we have the courage to step out of the frame and explore what it has blocked from our awareness.

WHAT'S MISSING FROM THE FRAME/GAME OF SCHOOL?

An important part of understanding any mental frame is to examine what ideas, information, or concepts that the mental frame filters out of our awareness. For example, how the learning in the kindergarten classroom was invisible to the teacher, or how the invisible character (the adolescent brain) was missing from the father's understanding and interpretation of bullying on the school bus. Considering new ideas that might conflict with preexisting ones is necessary to switch from *fast thinking* to *slow thinking* and to develop more creative approaches. (Always remember that there is usually reluctance and often a resistance to acknowledging the existence of alternative ideas or even facts.)

As cited in detail in Section II of this book, here is a list of some statements and/or assumptions that are currently supported by empirical research that conflict with the assumptions of the current frame governing most schools today:

- Children are born to learn and need the right conditions for this learning to flourish.
- Children learn from everything around them, not just from a teacher.
- Learning is not just an intellectual act, but involves emotions and is dependent on the social context.
- Learning to navigate the social world is not a simple thing that can be instilled in childhood and left alone. Children need support and guidance and the right environment to learn to accept differences among others.
- People learn more deeply when they can exercise some control over their learning.
- People learn more when they feel socially connected and supported by others around them.
- People make mistakes in the process of learning and growing. These mistakes are not signs of bad character or poor upbringing, but are influenced by the social context where they occur.
- People learn more and learn more deeply when they understand the purpose, value, and meaning of what they are learning.

Schools that are reframed using these assumptions would have a very different type of structure and organization than most schools in existence today. Learning and the way people treat each other in schools would look and sound a lot different.

As I explain in this book, these assumptions should no longer be filtered out of the vision of how we organize and operate our schools. Educators should not ignore these assumptions or worse yet, pretend they do not even exist. When schools are reframed in this way, everything changes for the better—which is what bullying prevention should really be about. Progress in bullying prevention is directly linked to making progress in changing how we educate our students.

BULLYING IN THE CURRENT FRAME/GAME OF SCHOOL

The problem of bullying has always existed in schools; what has changed is the awareness of it as a serious problem and a public demand that something be done about it. Pressure has been put on schools to eliminate it as soon as possible. Unfortunately, our institutions of authority from the state governors, to legislatures, to districts and to the schools have reacted to the problem in a similar way as with other problems: their solutions have stayed within the dominant parent/factory model frame and simply tightened it as the answer for fixing the problem.

Rather than using *slow thinking* to examine the problem and how it might differ significantly from other school problems, this urgency to solve the issue combined with the many other pressures and demands placed on schools has triggered a collective *fast thinking* approach that relies on established ways of solving other types of school problems. This *fast thinking* approach has also avoided any analysis of how the current structure and organization of schools might actually contribute to the problem. The best way to describe this current approach to the problem of bullying is this joke found in the 1996 book *Revisiting "The Culture of School and the Problem of Change" by* Seymour Sarason.

> It is midwinter and a man feels ill. He goes to his physician who after examining him carefully says, "I want you to go home, take off all of your clothes, open all windows, stand in front of one and breathe deeply." The man is aghast. "But if I do that," he says, "I'll get pneumonia." "That I know what to do about." *There is a difference between doing what you know and doing what needs to be done.* (p. 339)

Schools are in a bind. They have to do something about a problem they really don't understand (but think they do understand), so like the doctor in the story, they want to turn bullying into a simple rule infraction that can be treated like other rules infractions, such as running in the hallway or hitting someone. When the rule infraction conversion doesn't work, they stay within the frame and take the next logical commonsense step, they up the ante and convert bullying into a crime and those committing it into potential criminals. As a result of all of these influences on our schools, our approaches to bullying prevention appear to be new, but are really familiar manifestations of how other school problems have been solved in the past. The current features of bullying prevention stay consistent with the features of the dominant parent/factory frame governing most school practices:

- Bullying is wrong and needs to stop. It is against the rules and now the law.
- It is an individual act of defiance against authority.
- Too many people, students primarily, have been doing it.
- Schools haven't been successful at solving this problem because they haven't controlled student behavior.
- Stricter laws and the enforcement of them will help schools do a better job in controlling students and stopping bullying.
- Clear and consistent consequences are necessary to deter students from bullying.
- Clear and consistent consequences are necessary to make sure school staff enforce the laws.
- Schools need to be monitored and evaluated to make certain that they comply with the law and the designated procedures for addressing bullying.

The Legal Frame Added to the Current Frame/Game of School

"The operation was a success, but the patient died."

—Old saying

A local attorney who specialized in education law and worked for several school districts was scheduled to follow my presentation on bullying prevention to an audience of school administrators. He was kind enough to sit in the audience to hear what I had to say while he waited his turn to present. His presentation was on the Dignity for All Students Act (DASA), which was a new anti-bullying law for New York State. As I approached the end of my presentation, I indicated that I had not covered all the material I had planned. The attorney raised his hand and indicated that it was fine with him if I took an extra ten minutes from his time. I accepted his offer, finished my talk and then stayed to hear what he had to say.

When he finished, I immediately went up to thank him for giving me extra time. He responded by thanking me for what I was saying to these administrators. He said that what I had to offer would hopefully help schools avoid calling him in to address bullying issues. "It's really all about the learning environment for students; it shouldn't be a legal issue," he said shaking his head. He proceeded to share his concerns about the issue of bullying prevention in schools based on his recent experiences.

Here are the main points that he shared:

- Although it was a good thing to address bullying through legislation and school policy, he observed that too many administrators were more concerned about following procedures and making certain that they weren't legally liable.
- The time required to follow the regulations took the focus off actually trying to reduce and prevent bullying.
- He regretted the increased tendency for parents to seek legal remedies to problems that should be resolved through ongoing dialogue based on trusting relationships.
- The legal system in his view was probably the worst place to address bullying because it was based on one party winning and the other losing. Most bullying situations he thought could be resolved with parents and school staff working together to communicate the right message to all the students involved.
- The students who bullied should not be viewed as criminals or be condemned. They had lessons to learn and schools could be places where they should learn from their mistakes.
- He said that he warned the educators with whom he worked to resist the temptation to delegate authority for addressing incidents of bullying to

(Continued)

(Continued)

- law enforcement officials whose primary concern is not maintaining the learning environment, but finding evidence and affixing blame.
- Legal concepts like "hostile environment" were created for the workplace to address harassment and are very difficult to apply to schools. It is like trying to fit a square peg into a round hole. Employers can terminate employees who consistently act in a way to make the environment hostile for others. Employers can also hire people they judge appropriate for the workplace. Schools cannot terminate students, nor select new ones from a host of candidates. They have to work with the student population and help them.
- It was very important for students to feel safe and have trust in the teachers and staff, so that they felt comfortable in sharing what was happening to them. The same held true for those students who witnessed bullying; they needed to trust the adults in the school in order to report it.

Although I was initially concerned that the attorney would only increase the administrators' attention to procedural issues regarding bullying, his perspective turned out to be enlightening. He knew what the law and the legal system was designed to do and he knew its limitations in addressing social problems.

A law is a way to highlight a problem, to demonstrate concern and send a message to the public about what actions are not acceptable in our society. Public pressure is put on government officials to do something about a serious problem and as a result now almost every state has some type of law related to school bullying.

Many schools that previously might have ignored the issue now attend workshops and presentations about bullying prevention because they have to be in compliance. Hence, they show up at presentations like the seminar I gave with the school attorney hoping to learn what they need to stay in compliance. Most educators are very diligent about adhering to laws and regulations.

Compliance with the law should not be equated with actually preventing and reducing bullying. Since compliance itself is a challenge for most schools, when they finally achieve it, educators can easily settle for that type of success rather than actively seeking greater improvement in preventing and reducing bullying.

In most cases, the legal mandate on schools to address the problem has only prompted schools to tighten the controls already in place on student behaviors as a way to stop bullying. This tightening of controls on schools makes them more likely to tighten their controls on students. Viewing bullying as a crime has not improved bullying prevention efforts nor has it achieved positive results.

In my 2012 book, *No Place for Bullying* I explain how the criminal justice approach toward bullying (with its reliance on evidence to prove criminality) present an almost impossible situation for school administrators and parents who call to complain about their child being bullied. Since many students who bully learn to do it under the radar of adult supervision, administrators rely on students who witness the bullying to "testify" or tell on students who are much more popular than the students who are bullied, so the evidence they seek is very often hard to find. Key points about bullying as a *crime*:

- Bullying can be done in subtle and undetectable ways. For a student who is already vulnerable because of their status, even the slightest intimidating gesture can be very painful and damaging.
- Students know that many other things distract adults, so it is relatively easy to bully others even with adults present and supervising.
- Students can be carefully selected as targets because they have few allies and defenders. These students might not be well liked by teachers. Students who bully know that complaints from these students can easily be ignored or dismissed by those in authority.
- Bullying becomes a crime that is easy to commit, deny, and get away with. For students who might otherwise feel powerless, bullying can feel very good and powerful.
- Schools can easily appear to be safe and well-functioning environments—crime free. Everything can appear to be "under control" to even the most vigilant and caring adults, yet bullying can persist and be a daily painful experience for a minority of students.

Administrators often report back to parents that since they are unable to find evidence that there is nothing they can really do about the bullying. Parents then become angry, frustrated, and fearful for their child's safety. The law and the legal mandate for stopping bullying only tends to strengthen a parent's desire to solve the problem through harsher disciplinary measures and punishments. When administrators fail to gather sufficient evidence and therefore cannot punish the student(s) they believe guilty, then parents can view administrators as uncaring, incompetent, or both.

Without readily available alternatives, school administrators tend to rely too much on school discipline. This limits what they are able to do and probably frustrates them as much as it does the parents. Using traditional school discipline to address bullying is like trying to build a house with just one tool. That one tool can be used, but it needs many others to get the job done. Bullying prevention requires many tools and skilled and knowledgeable educators who know how to use them.

This chart describes the limits of the legal approach within a school setting and recommends an educational approach.

(Continued)

(Continued)

Bullying: Criminal Justice Mind-set	Bullying: An Educational Mind-set
Discipline alone is the main method of addressing the problem. Rules and consequences properly and consistently used should sufficiently address the problem.	Discipline one part of a larger comprehensive approach with strong emphasis on climate and culture as key elements.
Responds to bullying primarily after it happens.	Much can be done preventively by teaching and learning about bullying in the context of all social relationships.
Administrators are the ones responsible for dealing with bullying.	All staff need to be involved in addressing the problem and promoting positive skills and attitudes.
Accepts status quo of the school environment.	Assumes growth and change in the school environment as part of the solution.
Primarily concerns perpetrator and target.	Concerns everyone including bystanders.
Event specific. Case opened and closed.	Ongoing process of learning about how people treat each other.
Most reports involve severe cases that have escalated over time.	Greater likelihood of minor incidents being reported.
School leaders limited in responding and often on the defensive.	School leaders are key people in changing the culture and school climate.
Doesn't involve knowledge and skills needed to deal with the problem.	Acknowledges that students need social and emotional skills.
Ideally violations "should" never happen	Students are "works in progress" and learn through trial and error.
Parents can think that the school doesn't care if no action (consequence) is given out.	Parents are educated about the problem. They can see the school's commitment to addressing the problem even if a particular situation is unclear. Much can be done and said to students without overreliance on consequences.
If students know that consequences are the main response, it decreases the likelihood of bystanders reporting.	Students can be taught the importance of reporting and how it is a responsibility of everyone.
Goal of stopping bullying.	Goal of improving how people treat each other.

Source: Dillon, *No Place for Bullying*, 2012

Another Dilemma

Schools are left with the dilemma of now having to accept bullying as a problem even when staff never actually see or hear most of the bullying that is occurring. Many staff privately feel that the laws and policies against bullying are a solution in search of a problem. They are already doing their

> job in keeping students safe and they resent public criticism that they are not doing so. Privately they feel that it is the responsibility of the parents to raise their children to know right from wrong, therefore they should accept responsibility when their children do wrong. Legal mandates, therefore, can actually decrease a staff's commitment to creating a safer learning environment because they are more focused on following the regulations and avoiding the negative consequences for being out of compliance.

NEW PATH TO TAKE: WISDOM OF UNCERTAINTY AND SLOWING DOWN

I would feel a lot more confident about the state of bullying prevention in our country if I heard more educators say things like "This is a tough problem. I am not sure what to do about it. We need to learn more before we can come up with a plan or a solution to it." With the high visibility and attention given to the problem in the media almost every day, school leaders seem to have fewer options available to them because they must comply with prescribed rules and procedures. Sadly, the safer route for many schools is to appear confident and decisive without actually being effective in addressing the problem. Compliance with the laws, however reassuring it may be to some, is a weak substitute for the commitment needed to make schools truly safe for all students.

Even if a school leader wanted to significantly change the approach to bullying prevention, he or she cannot impose it on the community as that would only reinforce the current dominant parent/factory frame. Instead, it requires the wise collective leadership of the entire school community to step outside the frame to try alternative and potentially more effective approaches. Moving in this direction of change is becoming more and more difficult in the highly charged atmosphere of intense public feelings about bullying as an issue.

Accordingly, our school communities need a new path to a more effective way of addressing the problem of bullying, one that is not a shortcut or a solution that quickly converts a perplexing question into a simpler one.

This alternative approach (*slow thinking*) is characterized by

- awareness of the tendency to make quick, automatic judgments and how they are often inaccurate or incomplete;
- awareness of how the influences of prior experiences on the frame through which we perceive the world;
- understanding that a problem is more complex than originally thought and that there are no quick fixes or easy answers;

- understanding that a process, including dialogue with others, is necessary for understanding a problem and making quality decisions;
- embracing doubt, confusion, and uncertainty along the way to solving a problem and admitting to past errors;
- knowing that time, effort, and reflection (i.e., learning and unlearning) is central to this process; and
- knowing that a better, more complete frame and inclusive frame is possible for this learning.

Consequently, bullying prevention needs to be reframed so that members of the school community who are rightfully concerned about it can develop the creative responses necessary to address its complexity and its relationship to the structure and frame that governs our schools. The rest of this book continues to examine the current school frame and its effects on bullying prevention, but then offers an alternative approach that can lead to more creative solutions and improvements to the learning environment.

SUMMARY

This chapter describes the first steps in a new more creative approach illustrating a *slow thinking* alternative to the challenges facing schools. The key concepts about frames and their influence are essential to the process of understanding the problem of bullying and to ultimately reframing bullying prevention in a more creative, positive, and effective way. This chapter

- explains what frames are and how they govern what we perceive and how we think and act;
- articulates the dominant frames governing our schools;
- explains the reasons why frames are hard to see and therefore hard to change;
- describes how frames govern even our understanding of learning;
- presents the concept of *fast thinking* to explain why we rely on the familiar in the face of complex and challenging problems;
- analyzes how the current frame of schools limits our understanding of the problem and impedes more creative and effective approaches to addressing it; and
- articulates the assumptions now supported by empirical research that have been filtered out of our vision and definition of schools and our understanding of teaching and learning.

The next chapter describes how bullying manifests itself in the current frame/game of school by using examples of how school problems arise and are addressed. It describes how many current school practices actually create conditions that promote and sustain bullying and limit more creative approaches to effectively addressing this issue.

3

Bullying in the Frame/ Game of Schools

"Schools are places in which relationships of domination are played out extensively everyday between teachers and students, and always this domination is justified in the best interests of the students."

—Seth Kreisberg, *Transforming Power*

THE STORY OF A MISTAKE

A principal told me this story about a first grade teacher. While teaching a lesson, she stopped periodically to ask questions and subsequently then called on a boy who responded with a wrong answer. Hearing the wrong answer, a little girl started to chuckle. The teacher immediately and sharply reprimanded this girl and told her how rude it was to embarrass a classmate who made a mistake. She told her that it was okay to make a mistake, and it was wrong to laugh at someone who did. The girl immediately put her head down on her desk. The teacher directed the girl to look at her to make sure that she learned this important lesson about respect. When the girl refused to comply with the direction, the teacher grew more impatient and upset with the girl's refusal and defiance. Eventually the girl was sent to the principal's office.

This situation is not atypical of problems in our schools. It's a scenario that happens every day and passes unnoticed as business as usual. Too often the mistakes that students make are subject to public reprimands and consequences. Many teachers would have handled this mistake differently, but not enough do! Children *have to make* mistakes as part of the learning process, even if the mistake is a social lesson about laughing at another student's mistake. When mistakes in school become unacceptable behaviors, learning is compromised and replaced with compliance. The following questions help us explore what happens when a teacher responds negatively to a mistake:

- Why did the teacher react the way that she did?
- What did the student who laughed learn from the experience?
- What did the other students learn from the experience?

The answers to these questions provide insight into how schools unintentionally and inadvertently create the conditions that promote and sustain bullying behaviors and therefore make these behaviors so hard to distinguish from sanctioned mistreatment of others.

WHY DID THE TEACHER REACT THE WAY THAT SHE DID?

The simplest answer: she was only doing what she thought was her job. She was not a bad teacher or a mean person. She probably loved and cared for her students. If this happened in a different environment and she wasn't acting in the role of teacher, she might have gently called the girl aside and talked to her about why it's important to respect others. Although no one can know for certain what was going on in her mind, here is a possible chain reaction of thoughts and feelings about the social context (the classroom environment and her perceived role in it) that might have precipitated her response to the girl's chuckle:

- Her instruction was disrupted by the girl's laughter, which interfered with her job of teaching the content of the lesson.
- The girl's laughter showed disrespect to the student who made the mistake.
- It is her job to maintain the right environment of respect in her classroom.
- If she didn't react immediately, she would be letting the girl think that what she did was appropriate.
- She also needed to teach a lesson to the other students: it was wrong to laugh at another student.
- The girl's refusal to look at her was an overt sign of disrespect to her authority and her ability to control her classroom.

- Allowing any student to defy her would weaken her authority and her control of her classroom.
- Not being able to control her classroom or her students is an indication of incompetence, making her vulnerable to being judged so by her principal.

Consequently, this relatively small incident reinforced the overriding school frame and reverberated with issues, such as how she perceived her role and responsibilities as a teacher, maintained her authority to control the students, and managed the environment. As a result, hidden, but very present in that chain reaction was a quiet fear and anxiety related to her identity as a teacher.

The teacher probably thought that if she didn't respond that way, she would not be doing her job. This is an example of *fast thinking* in action as it traveled through her mental frame of school; it determined how she perceived the incident, interpreted it, and reacted to it in a way that made sense and was right to her. She was probably only reacting the way that she had seen her teachers react when she was a student. It would be difficult for her to interpret what happened in any other way. Also, it would be difficult for her to admit that her response was influenced by fear and emotion.

In the jumble of all of these thoughts and feelings that instantaneously resulted in the quick reaction and its aftermath, something very important was missing: empathy for the girl who made the mistake. I don't blame this teacher for this lack of empathy; when you are fearful and concerned about yourself (even if you are unaware of that fear), it is very difficult, almost impossible, to think about or feel for others around you.

Here is my hope for this teacher (and others like her): In her heart of hearts, if you asked her if she would want to be treated the way she treated the student if she were in that student's shoes, her answer would be "no." And, if you then offered her another way to respond that allowed her to avoid treating the student that way and removed any fear from the consequence of trying a different unfamiliar way, her answer would be "yes."

WHAT DID THE STUDENT WHO LAUGHED LEARN FROM THE EXPERIENCE?

The simplest answer: never to make that mistake again. If we ignore what happened on a deeper level, we could easily conclude that the teacher made the right decision—end of story. The teacher's response achieved its goal. If our sole criteria for success is maintaining authority and order, and the only other alternative is letting the girl "get away" with her mistake and invite disorder, the discussion has to end at this point. There is, however, much to learn from analyzing the situation, as there is a lot more to this story.

If asked what she learns in school, she would probably answer the way most students do and reply that she is learning her school subjects of reading, writing, and math. The actual truth that she doesn't realize is that what she is really learning is *who she is* or more accurately *who she needs to be* in the school environment.

Here are some of the lessons from that incident that tell her who she needs to be in school:

- She learned that she would be judged on how well she followed the three key rules of school: do the work assigned to her, follow the rules, and mind her own business.
- She learned to make certain that she gained her teacher's approval or face consequences designed to not make her feel good about herself.
- She learned that it was her role to accept the reprimand and that there was not much she could do to change this situation.
- She learned that she had one basic choice: follow the three rules of school or not.
- She might learn to figure out what gains her teacher's approval and to adjust her behavior to obtain that approval.
- She learned to accept being confused about rules, or in this particular case, why one student's mistake was okay, but her mistake wasn't.
- She learned that she *shouldn't* make mistakes in the first place. Mistakes and problems are not good primarily because the teacher doesn't like them.
- She learned that her attempt to protect herself by putting her head down on her desk only made things worse for her.
- She probably learned that she deserved the consequences she received, because teachers are people who don't make mistakes—they determine what is right and wrong.
- She learned that if she got her teacher mad enough then she would be removed from her classroom; she learned that her membership in the group was conditional and not a given.
- Finally, she probably learned the effects of her mistakes on how her classmates viewed her and treated her.

There was a lot that she didn't learn. She didn't have any idea of why she laughed in the first place. She learned what she shouldn't do, but nothing about what she could have done differently. Consequently, she would enter new situations without much confidence in being able to stay out of trouble. Therefore, her future school experience would be filled with more anxiety and fear.

She also didn't learn the lesson that her teacher wanted to teach her—to respect her classmate. When she was reprimanded and the situation escalated, her emotions were more about self-protection, shame, and fear, which in turn made it impossible to think about anyone but herself, least of all the boy who incorrectly answered the teacher's question. Just as it did for her teacher, fear easily cancelled empathy.

WHAT DID THE OTHER STUDENTS LEARN FROM THE EXPERIENCE?

Simplest answer: just about everything the girl learned. They didn't have to directly experience what the girl did; they could learn the same lessons just by observing. They did learn one extra lesson: not to do what the girl did and to make sure they don't become like her. They learned that this girl was different from them and being different is not a good thing. As they learned not to be like the girl, they might have also learned not to like her as a person. They might focus on what is wrong about her and be blind to any positives. They might also see her as being different or even a person of lesser value.

They also learned not to say or do anything when they witness bullying, since *what the teacher did to the girl was sanctioned bullying*. They couldn't be expected to see their teacher's mistake, even if on some level they intuitively know that it's not right to be mean to other people. They learned to be silent. The longer they are in school, the more they become habituated to other acts of bullying by interpreting them as just a normal part of the school experience. They learned that if you have enough power and authority, you don't have to be accountable for your actions. They also learned that some people, if they are different enough, deserve to be mistreated.

THE GAME BOARD OF BULLYING

As a consultant asked to observe in a first grade classroom, I saw firsthand how the social dynamics of bullying are set into motion very early in elementary school. I joined a class as they were walking in a line down the hallway with apparently no problems. As we reached the classroom door, in a matter of fact way one of the boys said to me, "Joey kicked the wall." He looked eager to see my response, and I presume I let him down when I replied with a non-committal, low key, "Okay."

Joey was the boy that I had been asked to observe and help in the room. He had been having some difficulty following directions and on many occasions his behavior produced a trip to the principal's office. His teacher was clearly exasperated by him and interpreted his misbehavior as disrespectful and interfering with the learning of the rest of the class.

Joey was not very different from the little girl who laughed at the mistake. His kicking the wall was most likely a sign of nervous energy not any attempt to damage property. Why would another student notice or even care about it? Why would a student tell me, an adult visitor, about it and be eager for my response?

His classmates had already tagged Joey as the troublemaker in the class. They knew that he caused problems that the teacher didn't like. In their minds, maybe the teacher didn't like Joey and she had good reason not to like him. Since the other students wanted and usually got the good feelings that came with teacher approval, they viewed Joey's behavior as making their teacher unhappy. Since I was an adult, this boy who reported the kicking to me must have thought that I needed to know what Joey was doing so that I could know what type of student he was and how he was different from the rest of the class who didn't kick the wall. This boy was signaling to me that he and his classmates were on the side of the teacher and Joey wasn't. It was a brief yet accurate assessment of the social dynamics of the room: there was Joey and then there were the rest of the students and their teacher (him versus us).

After further observations, I could see how Joey was caught in a vicious cycle. He was anxious in the room because he didn't feel accepted by his peers. This anxiety made it harder for him to behave appropriately, which unfortunately precipitated more impulsive behaviors and more trips to the principal's office. He knew he was the troublemaker, the outsider, the one who was different from everybody else. Joey was in a hole and kept digging himself deeper into it. His subsequent behaviors only cemented his status as a troublemaker, someone who didn't belong in the same way that everyone else did. Unfortunately, in the eyes of the teacher and the students, Joey didn't just have problems, Joey was the problem, and so everything he did was scrutinized and used as evidence against him. His outsider status was something he brought on himself, something he deserved.

In many situations, students who bully students like Joey are acting as proxies for their teachers. They are getting revenge for what these students did to their teacher who they like and from whom they want approval. How could they be wrong for excluding or mistreating students like Joey? This pattern is set early on and is hard to change.

This scenario illustrates the game board of school bullying—an outgrowth or consequence of the frame/game of school. The research is conclusive that students bully other students for a variety of reasons, not simply because they want to be mean or hurtful to another (Salmivalli, 2010). Most of these reasons concern social status and the perceptions of their peer group. The act of bullying Joey and students like him can become simply a means to an end for students who bully. Students who are the target of bullying are used to getting laughed at, which further improves the status of the student doing the bullying. Although most students won't bully students like Joey, they also won't defend him or befriend him because this action risks guilt by association or increases their own social vulnerability. Even as students become less concerned about teacher approval, this early "tagging" makes students like Joey easy targets for students seeking to gain peer approval.

This story about the typical social dynamics of schools illustrates and identifies the following extracted elements that create a *game board for bullying in schools*:

> **Social stratification:** Students, depending on how well they play the game in school and gain approval of those in authority, can fall into social groups of differing value and status. In most schools, even before they learn their sight words and number facts, most students can tell which classmates are the smart ones, the good ones, and the ones who are not.
>
> **Fear of being in the wrong group:** A student's psychological and emotional safety is dependent on being in the right social group. This is an invisible driver of student behavior where self-protection is a powerful incentive that makes empathy an emotion hard to access. Some students bully other students to gain higher status, safety, and a sense of control that is not available in the normal course of school life.
>
> **Lack of acknowledgement of the social world by those in authority:** This is the world that students live in and as they grow older it becomes more prominent in their lives. In school, the focus is primarily on academics and adults can seem disinterested in what is really going on in the lives of their students. As a result, students are left to fend for themselves in the complex, shifting, and confusing web of relationships found in schools, yet still suffer negative consequences imposed by the adult world when they make mistakes navigating this social world.
>
> **Bullying is simplified as rule infraction:** Bullying occurs when social interactions cross a line that violates a principle or value about the right way to treat people. It can be subtle, ambiguous, and full of conflicting unseen and misunderstood emotions. When students are simply told not to bully as if it were a rule infraction like running in the hallways, then they can easily become confused because this message conflicts with what they experience in their social interactions with peers.

In order to illustrate how bullying can function in the social world of schools, I created this table with three tiers of social status. I also describe how students' behaviors and self-perceptions are affected by their position in these tiers.

Top Tier
- Students are successful in many ways: academically, socially, and in valued activities like sports. They also might be physically attractive and well-liked by peers and teachers.
- Students in this tier are perceived as the preferred group. Every student is judged in comparison to these students.
- Students well established in this tier feel safe and usually have little need for bullying others.
- Some students in this tier might need to "flex their muscles" or demonstrate their power by being able to control or manipulate their audience by bullying others. They might be tempted to emulate and achieve comparable status to the adults in charge.
- Some students in this tier might bully others in response to any perceived threat to their sense of entitlement or superiority.
- For most students, this tier is very difficult if not impossible to achieve on their own. Some students can be resentful of the students in this tier and/or the school that created it, certifies it, and perpetuates it.
- Students have little need to be concerned about the bullying that happens with students in the lower tiers because most of their friends are in this same tier. They would need a compelling reason to think or care about those people in a lower tier.
Middle Tier
- Some students bully others as a way to achieve some degree of comparable status to those in the top tier.
- Some students find non-school-sanctioned ways to achieve status or impress peers, even those in the top tier. They can be funny at the expense of lower status peers; they can demonstrate their ability to outmaneuver adults by circumventing rules; and/or they can highlight their physical strength or attractiveness in comparison to those who are weaker or less attractive.
- Some students use bullying to separate themselves from those labeled in the lower tier.
- Students can bully as a way to feel in control or powerful because they feel powerless to reach the top tier on their own.
- Students bully, go along with bullying, or remain indifferent to bullying as a way to remain as distant and distinct from anyone perceived to be in the lower tier.
Low Tier
- Students are painfully aware of their low status in the eyes of both teachers and students.
- Students often feel powerless about controlling anything that happens to them in school.
- Students might bully to raise their status or lower the status of someone more vulnerable.
- Students bully to feel some control over something, but often are not clever enough to get away with it.
- Students receive a double whammy by being victimized and unprotected by adults, but they get caught bullying when they impulsively attempt to retaliate or defend themselves. They see those who bullied them getting away with it, while they get punished.
- Students don't trust adults to help or support them because the school helped create their status in the first place and continues to fail in offering protection.
- Students do not feel that school is good place for them to be.

ANALYZING THE GAME BOARD

Philip Rodkin in his excellent article "Bullying—And the Power of Peers" (2011) presented research conducted in prewar Germany where ten-year-old boys were placed in two different types of clubs. The research explored how the social context of the clubs affected their behaviors. He related this research to the social context of schools today.

> Victimization and scapegoating were highest in groups with an autocratic atmosphere, with a dominant group leader and a strongly hierarchical structure. Victimization was lowest in groups with a democratic atmosphere, where relationships with group leaders were more egalitarian and cohesive. It's well worth asking whether today's schools are characterized by a democratic or autocratic social climate and whether differences in school climate are related to bullying. Classrooms with more egalitarian social status hierarchies, strong group norms in support of academic achievement and prosocial behavior, and positive social ties among children should deprive many socially connected bullies of the peer regard they require. (pp. 10–16)

Rodkin is pointing to the frame/game of school and telling us that bullying cannot be viewed as a separate or distinct problem that can be extinguished or fixed while leaving the culture and climate of school unexamined and untouched.

If schools continue to operate using a frame that filters out and blocks a more complete, human, and complex view of learning, then the *adult world* (focused on order and control) and the student world (focused on relationships) will continue to coexist in the same time and space, but remain separate and isolated from each other. In this split environment, most students will learn the simple rules of school success (the few who don't fall by the wayside), while all students who try to apply this same set of rules to their social world and the world outside of school soon discover just how inadequate and ineffective those rules are. As long as this current situation persists, schools continue to operate in a smooth and orderly fashion, but students experience a *"Lord of the Flies"* type of social environment that exists in plain sight, but remains invisible to most adults. Conversely, when schools are designed to promote the type of learning that encompasses the whole human experience, students can develop the moral compass and the social skills that better equip them, not just to adapt to the world they encounter, but to join with adults in creating a better one.

THE FRAME PROTECTS THE GAME BOARD

Not only does the current school frame create a game board (the conditions and context) that provokes bullying behavior, it also makes it very difficult for the people in the schools to see or understand what is happening right in front of them.

> Even bullying prevention programs find it very difficult to avoid the tendency to use power to teach students not to bully and to get teachers to cooperate.
>
> *As part of the training I once received in a bullying prevention program, we did a role-play of how to intervene with students who bullied. In addition to the script I was given, the instructor informed me that when I was disciplining the student who bullied I had to make sure that the student was sitting. I was instructed to deliberately stand over the student to emphasize my power and authority over him and that this would be more effective than sitting across from him. I was also told to use a stern and slightly angry voice and expression to make sure that the student understood that I was serious. In the course of the training, I was also told that in order to ensure that the teachers implemented the program, I could use the threat of a poor evaluation as a way to get their cooperation in using the program. If I wanted to try a more positive approach, I could reward the teachers who implemented the program with an opportunity to get a parking spot closer to the building.*

The dominant parent/factory frame of schools is disguised as a host cell that provides camouflage for the bullying action. Comparable to a virus that mimics the host cell and attaches to it in order to avoid detection, bullying can be insidious. This ensures that it can exist as long as the host cell exists. The host cell and the virus share the same DNA: the desire to control and manipulate others as a means to an end.

In a healthy system, an infection is something foreign to the host cell. When it is detected, it attracts the attention of antibodies that naturally attack it to restore the health of the system. Until the power and control frame begins to change, bullying will continue to find safe and hidden spots to thrive because the conditions it needs exist in today's schools.

As long as the current frame of schools and bullying prevention remains entrenched, providing camouflage for acts of bullying, the immune system (our human empathy and compassion) becomes compromised because it cannot see what it needs to see and feel in order to restore us to health. Similar to the way that a person with healthy vision can go blind if kept in the darkness long enough, the empathy of all students will eventually fade the longer the students stay in a system that devalues the diversity of human experience and elevates the greater value of conformity, consistency, and efficiency.

How can empathy—the action of understanding, awareness, and sensitivity—work when the school system almost forces people to be more concerned about their own safety and status and less concerned about the condition of others?

How can empathy work in a system where those in power practice sanctioned bullying all in the name of helping others?

When students see sanctioned bullying disguised in most schools as standard operating procedures, then the rules against bullying become at best meaningless terms, or at worst symbolic of adult hypocrisy. They see a set a rules for them and not for everyone else in the school. Ironically, the persistence of bullying by students only convinces those in authority that they need to tighten their control of students. Effective bullying prevention is dependent on how school leaders use their power and how they treat those who have less power. School administrators and educators need to understand that tightened controls are counterproductive and therefore decide to find more creative and effective ways of addressing the problem.

REDEEMING MISTAKES

The story of the little girl's mistake at the start of this chapter is merely one story of many about mistakes that seem to be difficult to correct and even more difficult to prevent in the future. Mistakes are part of learning, but only when those who make them can admit they were wrong and let go of their insistence on being right. However, the more power and authority a person has, the harder it is to perceive one's actions as ever being wrong. In a structure and organization predicated on power and control, the insistence on being right is driven by the invisible and unspoken fear of losing power and control. Like the teacher in the story, any sign of weakness could lead to losing control of the class.

Although it's difficult to let go of that fear, when those in leadership positions admit to their mistakes, they actually gain respect and admiration from those they lead. Collins (2001) provides this important insight on the nature of leadership: "True leadership exists if people follow when the have the freedom not to." A true leader is not afraid of letting go of the power conferred by status or authority, and instead leads by the example of acting in accord with a moral value or guiding principle.

A door is opened for change, when leaders who are in a position or status that exempts them from the accountability they impose on those they lead, can admit to being wrong when they bully others; this change provides a great opportunity for everyone involved to learn better ways of interacting with each other based on empathy and compassion.

Returning to our first story, here is how the teacher's mistaken response to the student's mistake can be redeemed as a positive opportunity for learning.

> The teacher could admit to herself that she made a mistake and that it was bullying. This reversal could happen in the moment when she stopped thinking about controlling her class and looked at the incident through the eyes of the little girl she publicly reprimanded.

She could act on this insight by returning to her class and accepting responsibility for mistreating the girl. She could also talk about how empathy changed her and how it can change everyone. The class could learn that everyone makes mistakes, including their teacher. They could talk about how they can support each other in learning from their mistakes.

This story of the mistake then becomes a very different story, a story of responsibility, empathy, forgiving, and getting along with people who might be different.

This alternative ending to the story can be the beginning of learning a better more humane way of treating everyone, including students. This new story is dependent on the realization by those in positions of power that they must accept responsibility for changing how they treat others. If the teacher accepted responsibility for her bullying, her leadership could start the process of transforming an autocratic environment into a true community—a process that Rodkin (2011) identified as essential to preventing and reducing bullying in schools.

THE BIGGEST MISTAKE–THE GREATEST OPPORTUNITY

Just as the teacher's mistake offered a redeeming opportunity for her classroom to become a true community, schools have that same opportunity if they can identify, articulate, and accept responsibility for their biggest mistakes. The current stucture of schools can be compared to the game of Jenga, a game that uses similar-sized rectangular blocks to construct a tower. In the game each participant removes one block at a time, until a block is removed that causes the tower to collapse. Likewise, in schools, there is *one central assumption* at the heart of how schools are defined and governed, that is *mistaken*. This assumption is like the final Jenga block that once it is removed causes the structure to collapse. Schools can be redesigned when this assumption is brought forth and examined and questioned rather than remain hidden in the existing structure. (Perhaps it is because this assumption is so intricately a part of how schools are understood that questioning it can be very threatening, especially for those firmly entrenched in positions of authority.)

There are many ways to articulate that final Jenga block in our schools, that *key mistaken assumption* that currently props up our current structure of schools, but here is the best way I can find: *our students have to be controlled in order to learn and behave.*

That key, yet mistaken, assumption explains why many actions that are considered unfair, unkind, and unacceptable in a different context are routine occurrences in schools today. However I am convinced that adults act that way because they have not been exposed to other ways of treating students, especially students who fail to meet the expectations of the school. Many adults in schools have learned to resist acting in accord with the frame of power and control. Others would like to, but either don't know how or fear repercussions from their supervisors. Therefore, the current school frame, based on that mistaken assumption, not only controls students but also everyone who operates under or within the school structure.

The belief that students must be controlled in order to learn is only a belief; it doesn't have to turn into a reality. There are many educators who believe that students want to learn and know that when students are engaged in authentic and meaningful learning, controlling them becomes a non-issue. Ironically, I believe that most educators are truly waiting to be given permission to drop the power and control frame and to embrace a different frame that allows them to be educators, not managers.

STUDENTS: THE SOURCE OF HOPE

Empathy, compassion, and a desire for genuine learning do not have to be created or instilled in students. They already have it when they walk through the doors of school on their first day. Once educators realize that schools as they currently function *don't believe in or trust the students they are supposed to serve*, then reframing bullying prevention becomes part of changing how students are viewed and treated.

Students want and need to be trusted; they want educators to believe in them, so when that happens they no longer need to be controlled. Educators must shift from devoting their energies to controlling students to serving them by helping them become the people they are meant to be, not just standardized versions of themselves. Educators can have a powerful influence in guiding and supporting students as they learn. Schools can and should be redesigned to facilitate student learning rather than just managing and controlling their behavior. Section II of this book offers specific guidelines and strategies for shifting from controlling and managing to guiding, supporting, and positively influencing students based on the assumption that students want to learn and grow.

Education should not be a process defined by a difference in power and the assumption that students need external motivation to learn. It should be a shared experience of learning with the educator and the student playing different roles governed by the recognition and respect for each other's desire to learn and grow.

Reframing bullying prevention really means reclaiming that belief in students and creating an approach consistent with this more inclusive frame of education. This reframing supports educators who believe in their students and their own ability to empower them to act with compassion and empathy.

Students are the solution to the problem of bullying not the cause of it. The next chapter explores what prevents students from helping others and what can be done to truly empower students as bystanders and people.

SUMMARY

- Analysis of how a teacher disciplines a student reveals how schools can inadvertently create the conditions and perceptions that promote and sustain acts of bullying among students.
- The typical school environment has certain elements that create the game board for how acts of bullying manifest themselves on a routine basis in ways that mirror many accepted school practices.
- The current frame of schools creates a social three-tier stratification that can lead to bullying that functions as a way to provide safety, status, and control for many students.
- The problem of bullying cannot be viewed as separate from the type of organizational structure in which it occurs.
- The current frame and organization structure of schools also protects itself by making it difficult for those in schools to see or understand the connections between the school frame and the bullying behavior.
- Schools can change when those in positions of power can accept responsibility for their actions rather than justifying them or refusing to admit their mistakes when they mistreat those with less power.
- The most important mistake made by schools that they need to take responsibility for and change is the assumption that students need to be controlled in order to learn.
- Reframing bullying prevention is intimately connected to reframing how students are viewed by basing education on positive assumptions that students want to learn and succeed in school.
- The most important belief driving positive change and reframing bullying prevention is that students are the solution to the problem not the cause of it.

4

How the Frame/Game Shapes Student Identity

"We can often predict the way an adult will treat children simply from knowing what she believes about them."

—Alfie Kohn, *Beyond Discipline: From Compliance to Community*

During our February winter recess breaks, I used to go to the baseball spring training camps in Florida. One year I visited two camps on consecutive days that resulted in two extremely different experiences. On the first day, I visited the Mets training camp in Port St. Lucie. It was filled with excited Mets fans eager just to see the players throw the ball around. Anchor fences surrounded each field and there were security guards located throughout the facility. Whenever a player finished a workout and approached the fans waiting on the other side of the fence, there was a huge mass exodus to where that player was standing, so much so that I was worried about someone being trampled. That was a typical pattern that I had seen in other training camps as well.

The next day I went to the Dodgers' training camp in Vero Beach. This facility had no anchor fences, just string or tape stretched between some temporary posts just to delineate where fans should stand to allow the players the space they needed. There were lots of fans in attendance that day, but I never saw any fan disrespecting the space of the players. When a player did agree to sign autographs, fans did not rush the player, they politely waited their turn.

Why the difference? It wasn't because Mets fans are more aggressive than other fans; Dodger fans love their players as much as the Mets fans love theirs. Think of the *message* that the anchor fence sent to the fans: you are the type of people who might interfere with the players if we let you, so let's put up this fence to make certain that you don't. The fans absorbed this message and acted accordingly.

At the Dodgers' camp, the lack of anchor fences and security guards also sent a message to their fans: you are the type of people who respect the players need for space and don't want to interfere with their training. We expect you to be reasonable and when the players are available, they will come over to you. If everyone respects everyone, we will all be okay.

The difference was the frame through which each organization viewed their fans. This frame didn't just affect how the team management treated the fans; it affected the people's response. In both instances, when the fans reacted in accordance with the frames selected, both teams had the evidence they needed to support their decision for how to manage their fans.

When fans perceived the fence as the reason why the players were safe, then they no longer had to make a conscious decision to be responsible. They let the *fence* do the work for them; it was now the team's responsibility (and not theirs) to keep everything and everyone safe. They didn't need to control their behavior because the fence automatically assumed that control. As this control is external, if and when the external control is removed, the fans are at a loss for how to behave, and therefore prone to following the majority of people. When there are no fences, the fans have to decide how to behave and when they act responsibly they attribute it to themselves and not to an external control. Their decisions reflect a value of safety and respect. They act in accordance with their identities as responsible and trustworthy people—identities that the open environment confirms and reinforces. When people are in new situations without external controls, their identities (that are based on their personal values) guide them toward similar responsible decisions. In their minds, they are responsible people, acting responsibly.

The Dodgers did take a risk by not having fences. They trusted their fans and their fans proved them correct. The fans lived *up* to those expectations. If some fans forgot and charged ahead, their behavior was then seen as out of place and violating the social norms. The critical mass of responsible fans would likely signal to the few who forgot that they needed to correct their behavior. This is how a healthy culture self-corrects or governs itself. People's behaviors are governed by positive feelings of respect, responsibility, and internalized values that guide decision making in situations not covered by rules or supervised by authority.

When people act from values, they set a strong tone and establish positive norms that are not easily broken. Ironically, the silent norms that emerge from internal values have a stronger and more lasting influence on people's behavior than external controls. The Dodger management avoided *fast thinking*, therefore avoiding the trap (e.g., the chain reaction in the teacher who publicly reprimanded the first grade girl) that fear triggers in the quick decision-making formula: risk = bad, control = good, fence = necessary.

The Dodgers thought through the situation and realized that fences didn't have to be an automatic choice, there were other ways, even more effective ways, to keep their fans safe.

In a similar comparison, schools send messages to their students, which they in turn absorb, and subsequently act in a way that justifies the messages and methods chosen to manage their behavior. The way that schools decide to treat their students sends a message to the students about who they think they are and how they need to be treated—in the same way that the fence sent a message about the expected behavior of the fans.

This chapter explores the messages that the dominant parent/factory frame sends to all students and how these messages affect how they view themselves, and consequently how they think and act. These *fences* (i.e., the apparatuses of school control) give the appearance of regulation and safety, however in reality, they only serve to separate students from each other and impede their ability to help each other.

FEAR AND THE MISTAKEN ASSUMPTION

The fence and the security guards were external manifestations of the mistaken assumptions that the Mets management made about their fans and their behavior. At the heart of those assumptions is the fear of losing control of the people and the situation: the worst-case scenario is quickly envisioned followed by a reaction designed to guarantee that it won't happen. When it comes to keeping even mistaken assumptions in place, fear can easily drive out reason (*fast thinking* preventing *slow thinking*).

Research into how our brains are wired provides insight into why we adhere so strongly to certain ways of thinking and responding to the world. Rick Hanson in *Hardwiring for Happiness* (2013) explains how our "brain has a hair-trigger readiness to go negative." Originally a protective device for our survival, we are still wired to pay more attention to the negative than the positive. As a result, we tend to overestimate threats and underestimate opportunities. We are prepared to think that unpleasant or unwanted things will get worse instead of better.

As I principal, this was a phenomenon that I observed during the first six weeks of every school year, when panicked teachers would approach me about students who initially appeared to have difficulty adjusting to the new classroom environment. What happened was a vicious cycle of student anxiety affecting teacher anxiety.

The students' anxieties often triggered some acting-out behaviors that alarmed the teachers, which, in turn, increased their apprehensions about the entire school year. Some teachers became fearful and anxious during this adjustment time further exacerbating the situation. The last thing that an anxious student needs is an anxious teacher, but that is usually what happened.

After a while, I learned to suspend judgment about many of the behaviors of these students, since I could see that the teachers overestimated the disruptions that these students were causing. My goal was to lower the anxiety in the teacher as the first step in helping the students calm down. In most cases, once the student made the adjustment and calmed down, the situation improved. However, this negativity bias often caused many teachers who had previously experienced success working through this adjustment period to forget their past successes and to project a school year that would only get worst.

Teachers also tended to underestimate their ability to engage these students. I learned that this was a process: I couldn't just tell the teachers to calm down; I needed to provide significant support to the students and the teachers. I learned that I needed to suspend drawing conclusions and making long-term decisions about what the students might need. I knew that if I could somehow make the situation work as best it could until mid-October, then the problems that seemed so overwhelming to both the teachers and the students would rapidly diminish in perception and reality.

In reality, teacher concerns about these students almost always decreased as time went on because the routine, predictability, and trust that developed over those first weeks helped the students settle down. The fear and the negativity bias that the teachers had overestimated the actual needs of the student and underestimated their own ability to solve problems.

The tight disciplinary controls that schools use are much more a function of this fear/negativity bias overestimating the difficulty of a situation than it is based on the students themselves. School staff have a tendency to think that most problems are worse than they are in reality, so they have a strong desire to make sure that the problems never happen in the first place.

The goal of keeping students safe is an essential role of school, but schools have a choice in how they go about meeting that goal. Unfortunately, the fear of *not meeting that goal* results in the automatic choice of reliance on external means of control to maintain safety rather than the awareness or deliberation that other choices are possible. Once again, this is a mistaken assumption by the adult authorities, which is held in place by the overestimation of the negative, and conveys the wrong message to students about who they are and about how adults view them.

School staff interpret a student's uncooperative behavior or lack of compliance as a lack of motivation and forget that all students really want to do well in school. In the majority of situations, students are motivated to avoid situations where they might fail in the eyes of the adults they want to please. Unfortunately, the false identities that adults impose on students by their mistaken interpretation of their behaviors, undermines and eventually negates students' original positive identities. Because students look to adults to tell them who they are and are taught to defer to adult authority, then they assimilate the *false identity* (i.e., someone lacking motivation) and act in way that confirms this identity in the eyes of the adults who created it and imposed it on them.

When schools accept the wrong assumption about students, the students are the ones who suffer the consequences of that mistake. Students want to connect and cooperate and need guidance and support in navigating the social world. They are waiting for schools to recognize that and give them what they really need: to put into practice the knowledge and skills to positively connect and empathize with others.

THE OTHER (RIGHT) ASSUMPTION ABOUT STUDENTS

> Human communities are only as healthy as our conception of human nature. It has long been assumed that selfishness, greed, and competitiveness lie at the core of human behavior, the products of our evolution. It takes little imagination to see how these assumptions have guided most realms of human affairs.... But, recent scientific findings forcefully challenge this view of human nature. We see that compassion is deeply rooted in our brains, our bodies and in the most basic ways we communicate. (Keltner & Marsh, 2010a, p. 15)

Research at the Yale Infant Cognition Center demonstrated that babies, before they can walk and talk, show a preference for good acts over bad acts. They seem to be born with a rudimentary sense of justice or an instinctive sense of right or wrong. However, very early in their development they also demonstrate a preference for people who are similar to themselves.

> In fact, our initial moral sense appears to be biased toward our own kind. There's plenty of research showing that babies have within-group preferences: 3-month-olds prefer the faces of the race that is most familiar to them to those of other races; 11-month-olds prefer

individuals who share their own taste in food and expect these individuals to be nicer than those with different tastes; 12-month-olds prefer to learn from someone who speaks their own language over someone who speaks a foreign language. (Bloom, 2010, p. 44)

This research demonstrates two important points that should influence how we educate our students:

- They don't have to be shaped or controlled in order to be good; they are born wanting to connect with others and prefer good and kind acts to negative or neutral ones.
- They are wary or fearful of those who appear to be different. They need support and guidance in their learning in order to respect differences and to discover commonalities among people.

Keltner and colleagues (2010b) summarize this responsibility, as "we must make room for our compassionate influences to grow" (p. 15).

Ironically, schools are investing more time and energy to keep students from doing "bad" things when they should be focusing on helping them develop more positive and inclusive attitudes toward all people, including those who might initially appear different. Schools should cultivate the "good" that is already there rather than try to control the "bad" that they assume is there.

If research on child development is not enough reason to change approaches to bullying, there is another compelling reason: the imposed controls are not controlling what they are supposed to control—bullying. Additionally, these controls might be limiting and preventing students' innate proclivity for good from manifesting itself in school.

HOW TIGHTER CONTROLS DON'T *CONTROL* BULLYING

Focusing on rules, compliance, and consequences reduces bullying to an individual act that either complies with or defies authority. This separates the act of bullying from its social and moral context: social responsibility toward others and the greater good. When rules and consequences predominate the messages that are sent to students, then schools remove the opportunity to teach students about hurtful words or behaviors that may be within the rules, or moral behaviors that ask them to go beyond the rules.

When students in school learn that behavior is primarily controlled externally, they have difficulty acting responsibly when they are not supervised or monitored by adults in authority. This inadvertently sends them the message that if they can get away with breaking the rules, then what they are doing is not really wrong. It is only wrong to get caught. If they do happen to get caught and the school's primary response to their actions is to impose consequences, then the best course of action is to lie and deny the action.

When bullying is the offense, imposing consequences on students who bully makes them more concerned about what is happening to them and less about the student they bullied. It is hard to fault a student or anyone who seeks to avoid the certain pain or hardship of negative consequences. This is especially true when little or no time in school is devoted to discussing why a behavior is wrong and how it affects others, combined with the fact that the student being bullied may not be someone well liked. The more that bullying is treated as a crime, the more students become invested in avoiding the label of criminal. This consequence only makes their denials more emphatic and makes them less likely to take responsibility for their words and actions.

As a result, students who bully can view themselves as victims of a system that unfairly imposes rules and consequences. They also focus on the other students who might have done what they did and suffered no consequences. It is possible that these students might decide not to bully again, but it is more likely that they will just be more determined than ever to not get caught.

The students who are bullied gain little solace or protection from these tough policies and tight controls because they don't work and are counterproductive. Ironically, these vulnerable students know what the adults don't know that their best source of protection and support comes from their peers, the students who don't bully, and not from any external rules and controls.

Despite the failure of the controls to actually stop the practice of bullying, the fact remains that most students don't bully others and don't approve of bullying. These students retain a moral sense of right and wrong that extends beyond rules and consequences. Why is it that these students are not viewed as resources and change agents to address the problem of bullying?

The answer is that the same regulations that fail to control bullying also have an effect on the students who don't break the rules. Paradoxically, these same controls send a message to this empathetic group of students, a message that controls and limits their ability to exercise the positive influence that they might have to stop the bullying.

HOW CONTROLS LIMIT THE RESPONSE OF BYSTANDERS

Those students who don't break the rules and generally conform to the expectations of the school are usually ignored when schools approach the problem of bullying. In a system that seeks to prevent deviations from expected behavior, these students who normally conform can be taken for granted. In the dominant parent/factory frame, the goal for them is to maintain that expected behavior and continue to do what they have been doing; it is the school's job to take care of the rule breakers. The message is that preventing the negative from happening is what is most important and almost everything else fades in significance in the eyes of both the students and the staff.

Effective bullying prevention requires the students who don't regularly bully others to be responsible and caring. This can be a confusing message to them since most of these students naturally assume that as long they are following the rules and creating no problems that everything is fine and working.

What is not given much if any attention in schools are the skills, knowledge, and attitudes that students need to be responsible and courageous when encountering bullying. The controlling messages about what it means to be a "good" student prevent and limit the positive influence that these good students can have in stopping bullying. If students are not given the support, guidance, and ability to use empathy and compassion toward others, it becomes almost impossible and unfair to expect them to act in a way that is very different from how they have been taught in school.

Compliance and conformity are incompatible with empowerment and assertiveness. If schools are to be effective in preventing and reducing bullying, at some point they have to make a choice about the messages they give to students. Mixed messages only favor the status quo or the default behavior: compliance and conformity will stay in place unless schools choose empowerment and assertiveness.

When some interactions between staff and students are sanctioned forms of bullying, all staff, even if their own interactions are respectful, are neutral bystanders if they fail to intervene with a colleague or even a supervisor who is bullying a student. Accordingly, these neutral staff appear hypocritical to students when they tell them to *stand up* to bullying.

Educators and all staff need to understand the difficulties that students experience when they witness acts of bullying or any mistreatment of others. Empathy alone is not always enough for students to take the risk of helping someone being mistreated or in need.

Here are some critical ways that schools inadvertently limit and disempower students in the face of bullying. Such schools

1. **Give students a vote of no confidence and set the bar low for moral behavior.**

    If most students don't bully other students and don't approve of bullying, then telling them over and over not to bully others conveys mistrust. Tightening the rules and increasing the consequences for something they don't do only serves to tell the students that the school must be worried that they will bully in the future. Not only doesn't the message fail to recognize and affirm their responsible behavior, it reinforces the notion that all students are the source of the problem of bullying and not part of the solution to the problem. This also creates a double standard that adults who might use their power to bully students are exempt from the same rules and consequences that students must accept. It also tells the students that the most important thing they can do is not break the rules.

2. **Promote a *Me* culture more than a *We* culture.**

    Students who get good grades, follow the rules, and mind their own business are considered to be successful in school. In many classrooms, students still face forward with their attention on the teacher. When individuals don't consistently face each other and work together on tasks, the social element of learning is devalued. In this type of classroom structure, talking to peers is a distraction from listening to the teacher and absorbing real learning. Instead of being a place where students can discover each other and build connections, the classroom is a place to compete for individual achievement and teacher approval.

3. **Create a very risk-adverse climate.**

    Sometimes helping others requires risk taking. When schools value efficiency and view problems as aberrations to be fixed, students become more concerned about staying out of trouble. Students who take risks, make mistakes, or cause problems receive a great amount of negative attention and disapproval; therefore, playing it safe becomes a strong cultural norm for students.

4. **Necessitate that students figure out the social world on their own.**

    Why should students bother teachers with any social world issues? Often students might want to help a peer, but they don't know what to do. Teachers can appear exclusively concerned with academic learning; their availability for advice or guidance seems very limited; therefore students don't get the advice or help they need. Hence, the student response is that if adults don't seem to be concerned about what happens in the social world, why should they. Also, since bullying is framed as a rule infraction, then words or actions that have any degree of ambiguity can be easily interpreted as not bullying.

5. **Reinforce the belief that change is not possible.**

    When students have little influence over what happens in school and most decisions are made for them, they can overgeneralize to the point that they cannot change anything in schools. If bullying persists and they don't approve of it, they have learned that there is little if anything they can do change it or anything else in school.

6. **Don't view students as resources nor respect them as positive influences.**

    A lawyer informed me that in a particular school district, the standard direction to students if they witnessed or knew about bullying was that it was their responsibility to report it to an adult. According to the attorney, this directive made the school less liable and left no doubt in the minds of the students about their responsibility to the incident. He was concerned that this directive might actually increase the amount of bullying because he believes that there are many things that students can do or say to their peers to defuse situations before they become serious bullying. Students want to feel that they can handle situations and not always defer to adult authority. Students need to feel that they can intervene on their own and if necessary seek advice from adults on how to do so. They need to see reporting as one option when their own efforts fail, and not to see it as the *only* option that those in authority allow them to use.

7. **Make bullying just another *adult problem* they have to contend with or ignore.**

    Bullying is a serious issue involving how people treat each other. It is a moral issue that requires discussion and reflection. When it becomes just another rule to follow imposed on students by the school, then students can too easily dismiss it. Combined with everything else students are told to do or not do, the issue of bullying can become static or background noise. Unfortunately, students can turn off and tune out when they hear incessant rules and warnings repeated at them. Any incident of an adult bullying a student and getting away with it only increases both their disrespect and cynicism for bullying prevention in general.

8. **Lessen students' sense of ownership and commitment to the school.**

    The more the adults in the school try to tightly control student behavior, the less ownership and responsibility students need to take for what happens in the school. Bullying becomes a problem that the adults need to solve. If students refrain from bullying, that is all the school requires of them. The more in control the adults appear, the less likely that students will feel needed or believe they are expected to do anything more than follow the rules.

9. **Make reporting bullying an act of betrayal to the peer group.**

    When students are tightly controlled and perceive the adults as not respecting them, they tend to view their reporting of bullying as betraying their peer group. When penalties and consequences for bullying are severe, students are also more likely to view the consequence given to a peer who bullies, as worse than what is happening to the student who is bullied. The more adults create an "us against them" or "students as the problem" atmosphere in the school, the more students will choose to overlook it rather than *join with adult authority.*

The messages that the current frame of bullying prevention sends to students are comparable to my earlier examples of the fences in the baseball training camp: they create the very behavior that they are trying to control. Schools may want students to be responsible and caring bystanders, but this desire doesn't overcome the influence and impact of the *messages* that students receive in daily experiences and interactions in the school.

THE NOTS OF BYSTANDER BEHAVIOR

There is now a shift in emphasis in bullying prevention that is a positive development, but unfortunately has little impact on student behavior. Since research demonstrates quite consistently that students/peers have more direct influence in stopping bullying than adults, students are now being urged to stand up to bullying.

As the previous section describes, the current frame of bullying prevention in schools makes this new directive a very difficult one for students to follow. Social psychology research reveals the complexities surrounding the act of helping and how easy it is to look the other way and walk by people who appear seriously hurt.

Even if schools could radically change their current frame of bullying prevention and work with students rather than try to control them, responsible and helping behaviors would not automatically appear in students. For students to feel empowered to help, schools must understand why it is a challenge and then intentionally educate students to develop the knowledge, skills, and attitudes necessary to do what they want to do—help others and make a positive difference in the world.

Students who are told to *stand up to bullying* could reply to schools with the following comments:

- We already don't bully and we follow the rules and now you want more from us.
- All your laws, rules, consequences, programs, and procedures are not working, so now you want us to solve your problems—problems that you helped to create.
- Sure, standing up to bullying sounds great, but it isn't so simple. Do you know how hard that is in our social world?
- You are out of touch with our world so how can you tell us to do this when you are not around.

- Even though you tell us to stand up to bullying, you still devote almost no time to helping us successfully know how to do that.
- What if we stand up to bullying and we end up getting bullied ourselves, or get accused of breaking some other rule, can you guarantee us that we won't get in trouble?
- Before you ask us to stand up to bullying can you help to answer these two simple questions: Is it worth it? Can I do it?
- It is quite a lot to ask us to follow the rules and do what we are told most of time and then expect us to shift gears and act confidently and assertively when we witness bullying situations.

In addition to the problems it creates by how it views and treats students, the current frame of bullying prevention also impedes effective bullying prevention by *what it doesn't do or the little if any time that is devoted to* empowering students to be responsible and caring toward others.

When students witness an act of bullying, they are not objective observers who can be expected to accurately report what happened to those in authority. Although the bullying is not directed toward them, they personally experience a wide range of different emotions that occur simultaneously. Before they have time to realize what has just happened, both in their environment and inside their hearts and minds, the incident is over and there is usually something else for them to do. The reality of a typical bullying situation is unlike the dramatic scenarios they see in the media or as part of an anti-bullying campaign. In many ways, these dramatic depictions too often mislead and confuse students because there is a great disparity between what they are told is bullying and what they actually experience.

As a result, after witnessing an act of bullying they are left confused, uncertain, and often with a vague unvoiced sense of unease. Given the rapid pace of school and the little if any time provided for reflection and discussion, many students unfortunately learn to buffer and desensitize themselves from these unpleasant and unarticulated emotions. They get better at doing so over time—they need to in order to survive.

Asking students to be empowered and responsible bystanders is tantamount to telling them to be a good readers or safe drivers without giving them instructions, guidance, and opportunities to practice. It is difficult for anyone, adults included, to help others in need. It is also very easy to look the other way or walk by even when others are in obvious physical need of help.

Social psychology has researched the reasons why people help or don't help others. Since helping requires people to change their predictable and routine behaviors, there are many more reasons NOT to help than to help. These are the internal, but unvoiced statements that bystanders make to themselves to justify their inaction and hesitation to help. As if there were actual knots, these internal reasons can restrain people from doing what they know is right, and under better circumstances, what they know they should do (Dillon, 2014).

EXTERNAL NOTS: VIEWING THE SITUATION

Most students want to help others, but many "NOTS" (thoughts and feelings that impede their acting) can surface in their mind when they witness bullying:

Not wrong. Students may not view the words and actions as bullying; therefore, they don't see it as wrong. Since teasing, joking, and fooling around occur in rapid succession, some bullying behaviors can blend with non-bullying actions and make them easy to overlook, ignore, or accept as normal behavior.

Not harmful. Students could hear hurtful words or witness harmful acts, but if the recipient of those words and actions does not appear hurt or bothered, bystanders could easily conclude that no harm was done. When adolescents have a need to appear cool and unperturbed, this response only makes an accurate interpretation that much harder for the observer.

Not like me. The more different the student who is bullied appears to the bystander, the easier it is for the bystander to refrain from helping. As previously noted, this reluctance to help people perceived as different reflects the robust research findings traced to infant behavior demonstrating heightened concern about those who appear different. When schools stigmatize students who fail to conform in some way, then that difference is highlighted and judged negatively by others. This is probably the most powerful "NOT" in preventing bystanders from helping.

Not my "tribe" or group. This is an extension of "not like me." Even if a bystander liked a particular individual, they still might be reluctant to help that student in order to avoid being associated with that student's social group.

Not worthy of help. Students might think that certain students who are bullied deserve the treatment they receive. They might think that they brought that treatment on themselves. Bystanders might often accurately think that such students are not well liked or approved of by staff.

Not my job. Students might think that the bullying should stop, but that it is someone else's job to stop it. Ironically, since bullying is treated like other discipline issues, it is natural that bystanders assume that it is the staff's problem to solve, not theirs. This notion is often reinforced by messages from staff that tell students to mind their own business. The more that adults assert power and control to solve problems; the more that their actions tell students that those who are not in authority are powerless to do anything about problems.

Not against the rules. Many students can bully others in subtle and fleeting ways through looks, gestures, and even smiles. Students can be reluctant to report this type of bullying since they know that the student who bullied can easily deny it and assert that such behavior was misinterpreted and not against the rules.

Not sure of backup or adult support. Since students know that ultimately staff and the school have the real responsibility for addressing bullying, they will be reluctant to initiate reporting it in any way if they doubt that staff will support them or back them up. Without this support they know that they will only be making themselves vulnerable to bullying or social disapproval.

Not worth the risk. Students who witness bullying and intervene or report it have much more to lose than they have to gain. Since most schools are risk adverse environments, bystanders quickly estimate the degree of personal risk involved and decide to play it safe. In their judgment, their intervening or reporting would not do any good, but they also risk getting in trouble for not minding their own business.

INTERNAL NOTS: DOUBTS AND FEELINGS

These "NOTS" are the doubts and emotions that can both confuse and restrain students from helping others.

Not my word. What adults might term bullying, students often call *drama*. Students need to disassociate interaction in their social world, which often includes fooling around, teasing, and kidding, from the black and white, rule-oriented world imposed on them by adults. Since most adults appear to be unconcerned about the social world that is so important to them, students respond by distancing themselves from adults by ignoring the word *bullying*. In their mind, adults are overly concerned about things they know little about. Even if students are concerned about bullying and the hurt inflicted on students, adults with their heavy-handed controls are viewed as incapable of stopping it. By narrowing the meaning of the word *bullying*, adults rob students of the language they need to differentiate how they interact with each other and distinguish between joking, and kidding, and hurting.

Not my decision; others are right. When a student sees other students not helping they infer that the group is making the right decision about what to do. If no one is helping then the situation is not one that requires help, or the person in need is not worth helping. This is called pluralistic ignorance or the "tendency to mistake another's calm demeanor as a sign that no emergency is actually taking place" (Keltner & Marsh, 2010a).

Not confident in skills and abilities. Some students might want to help a student who is bullied, but doubt their ability to be effective in intervening.

Not my school. Very often the difference between taking a risk and playing it safe is the degree of connection between the bystander and the school. If bystanders have a strong sense of ownership and connection to the school, they are more likely to view bullying as something that shouldn't happen in their school. When the connection and ownership is weak, bystanders are much less likely to stick their necks out and more likely to play it safe.

Not me and not my friends. Since bullying is now considered a crime, some students think that only really bad people bully others. Since a bystander might know and like the student who is bullying, that bystander diminishes the severity of the act because the person doing it is a good person.

Not wanting to be told what to do or think. As they mature, students want to be viewed as independent and capable. When they are told to do something by those in authority, they often resist not because they disagree with the message, but they resent the implication that they are unable to act based on their own judgment.

Not even thinking; not a choice. Sometimes bystanders are so conditioned to avoid getting into trouble that any situation that presents any degree of risk triggers a fearful response. This fearful response usually results in freezing or doing nothing. Students in this state don't even see that they have a choice; they are not even thinking, but rather just reacting in a self-protective manner.

Not sure what exactly to say or do. Bystanders usually have a very short period of time to decide what to do when confronted with a bullying situation. By the time they decide, that situation has passed so that the decision to do nothing was already made for them.

Not do any good—probably make it worse. Bystanders can easily view many of the school disciplinary practices as only making the situation worse, even for the student who is bullied. If they report a popular student bullying an unpopular one and that popular student gets in serious trouble, they know that the backlash could be much worse for the student who was bullied—possibly even worse than the original act of bullying.

Not what a good student would do. Very often the concept of being "good" is so closely equated with following the rules and deferring to an adult authority figure that students can be reluctant to do anything that is not clearly defined by the rules and the adults.

UNTYING THE NOTS

There is no reason why students cannot develop in their daily experience of school what they need to become empowered bystanders and responsible citizens. When all students are considered valuable members of a learning community, every member of that community learns the importance of caring for each member. Untying the NOTS that keep students from helping others means

- giving students the knowledge that they have great influence in shaping their school's culture and climate;
- helping them develop the skills to responsibly intervene and report bullying; and
- fostering in them the confidence to act assertively and to consistently demonstrate leadership.

Reframing bullying prevention is reframing how people think about themselves and how they perceive their role and responsibilities toward their community. Reframing bullying prevention requires a lot more than telling students what they shouldn't do; it is about providing a supportive positive environment that affirms them and allows them to discover and articulate the shared values that can guide them in making moral decisions in real-life situations, not just ones covered by simple rules or supervised by adults.

The next chapter presents research showing how the process of reframing positively impacts organizations, individuals, and our understanding of human motivation. Reframing bullying prevention is about untying the NOTS that prevent schools from becoming strong communities.

SUMMARY

- Students are not the problem, but are the solution to the problem of bullying prevention; however, they don't typically receive this message.
- Many of the messages that the school environment sends to students convey a mistrust of them and a doubt about their ability to act responsibly.

- In reality, the fear of losing control is the driving force for the existence of those controls and not the fact that students are incapable of being trusted.
- Research confirms that humans have innate tendencies toward right and wrong, so these tendencies are not something that have to be taught, but rather something that should be nurtured.
- Research also confirms that this moral sense is tempered by an initial distrust of those who appear different.
- Schools, instead of assuming that students need to be controlled, should develop more time and energy to help students understand and appreciate the differences among people.
- The tighter controls and sterner consequences are ineffective at stopping bullying, yet those in positions of authority have difficulty in seeing this and accepting it.
- The consequence of tighter controls is to limit the potential effectiveness that the great majority of students have to prevent and reduce bullying.
- The focus on controlling student behavior also prevents schools from devoting the time and effort needed to give students the knowledge, skills, and attitudes they need to be empowered bystanders.
- Shifting the emphasis from telling students not to bully, but instead to stand up to bullying is a step in the right direction, but then fails to give students the tools they need in order to be effective.
- Students are like all people because the act of helping is not simple. There are many legitimate reasons for *not* helping.
- Adults need to empathize with the difficulty required for students to become empowered bystanders and devote the time and energy to helping them understand what is going on inside of them and outside of them when they confront a bullying situation.

5

The Promise of Reframing

"Change the way you look at things and the things you look at change."

—Wayne Dyer, *The Power of Intention*

MY EPIPHANY

I was fortunate to work in a school where we learned that students didn't need to be controlled in order to learn. For us as educators, it was also a process of unlearning what school was supposed to be, in other words, we had to *change our frame*. As a principal, I knew we were heading in the right direction, but I wasn't able to articulate exactly what was happening. My epiphany occurred one day in a first-grade classroom when I saw what it was we were doing for the students.

It was in a classroom that was a wonderful place for anyone to be! The teacher truly enjoyed the children she taught and valued what she learned from them. She loved her "job," as she often told me. I happened to walk in at a time when the students were doing research on insects. (Note that it wasn't "science" or "reading" or "writing"—it was all of those things wrapped up together; to the students it was learning.)

Here is what I saw and heard:

- Students looking at and talking to each other as they worked.
- Some students reading, some writing, some drawing, some talking and asking questions.
- Students shifting between actions whenever they decided to change.
- Piles of books about insects on tables, on shelves, in baskets. Students were selecting books as needed.
- I heard some laughter, some questions, and some stories about insects.
- Every student was engaged and not distracted by the principal poking around.
- They welcomed me and told me what they were learning; why they were learning it; and what they thought about what they were doing.

Here is what I didn't see or hear:

- I didn't see the teacher right away. She was at a table in the corner of the room and was moving from table to table.
- I didn't hear the teacher having to correct or keep students on task.
- I didn't hear any talking that didn't relate in some way to insects for any significant length of time.
- I didn't see any behavior charts or stickers.

This was typical of what was happening in most of our classrooms. What was different was that I was finally able to put into words what was happening in our school: *the students had no reason to misbehave and therefore didn't need to be controlled.* Instead they had the following:

- a caring environment where each student was accepted and belonged no matter what they did
- a teacher who enjoyed each student and every student knew that
- a choice within limits of what they wanted to learn
- a choice in how they demonstrated their learning
- a purpose for learning: they were making a book to share with their parents at an upcoming classroom sharing event

I realized that what I had learned in all my years as a principal was this simple truth: if you meet students' basic needs then you take away their reasons for misbehaving. Students want and need to learn, so when educators create the conditions for learning, control is no longer a relevant issue.

Conversely, when students are given little or no choice about what they are learning, and are expected to learn it in a standardized way, and in an arbitrary length of time, and are evaluated based on how well they learn it in relation to their peers, then they need to be controlled. So, when schools are truly about learning and the experience of learning matches the learning that students experience outside of schools, students have no need to either misbehave or require external motivation to learn.

My core assumptions about students were confirmed; they want to learn, they want to get along, they want to belong, and they want meaningful, engaging, and challenging work. They want to be able to make mistakes without being judged as failing or being stigmatized if they make mistakes.

This doesn't mean that there were never problems; there were many of them in that classroom and all the classrooms in our school. Problems, however, were natural occurrences in these environments; they were an integral part of the learning process. Teachers didn't wish them away in favor of having everything running smoothly. They were accepted as part of the learning process, the human process of getting along and learning together. When given the time and the right conditions, students became more skilled in negotiating how to meet their needs when others are involved. The teacher and her students were living together and learning together in an environment designed to support that process.

That classroom didn't need *fences*; it didn't need to keep people separated and controlled. The teacher didn't need to operate out of fear, rather out of respect and care. The teacher didn't have to *control* the students. Her role was to facilitate, coach, and influence the students. She was like an architect who designs the learning environment in a way that creates the conditions necessary for the students to accept ownership and responsibility for their learning.

In that type of environment, the conditions for optimal learning and the conditions needed to prevent and reduce bullying were one and the same.

The conditions that lead to bullying were also removed (the game board was changed):

- There were no designated students who were the winners or the losers in that system. No one was perceived as deserving of mistreatment.
- There was no need for students to seek control outside of the classroom when they had outlets for it in the classroom.
- Diversity was valued and contributed to the richness of the environment.
- Communicating socially was connected to learning.
- Problems and mistakes were things you talked about and learned from.
- Communicating and negotiating with respect for each other and with attention to the common good replaced power and control of one group over another.

REFRAMING: REASONS FOR OPTIMISM

One of the biggest problems with school change is that it is hard to imagine schools being anything other than what they currently are and have always been. So many educators have spent so many years struggling to control students or trying to motivate them to learn that when they hear stories about the first grade classroom I described, they attribute it to the children being different from the children they teach.

I empathize with them because it is very difficult to accept the possibility that you might actually have spent all those years being "wrong" about everything you believed was true about school. Also, hearing about new and different ways that can work in the classroom does place a lot of responsibility on the teacher for making the changes rather than the students. It is a much safer feeling to believe that someone else needs to change and not yourself.

It would be nice to think that schools could read all the theory about reframing and then come to a rational decision to reframe teaching and learning. It doesn't happen like that, nor can it happen that way. Reframing is a process not a solution to a problem; it is a human process not a technical one. It involves people interacting, listening, respecting, and learning from each other over time.

I realized after writing the first four chapters of this book that change—especially change in schools—might appear to be too difficult, almost impossible. However, I found that the opposite is true that there is great reason for hope. Although changing a frame is difficult, there are many compelling reasons to believe that many people are waiting and willing to change. They just need to know and be able to understand the end product of the change; they can't change until they know what the change looks like and sounds like.

Here are some of those compelling reasons why I am very hopeful that schools are on the edge of great positive changes:

- **The current school frame with its embedded beliefs, values, and assumptions was not one that educators chose—they inherited it.**

Educators inherited their mental frame of school and all its assumptions about students and the need to control to educate. Ironically, this aspect of how they do their job is probably the one that gives them the most trouble. I strongly believe that almost every teacher would like to teach like that first-grade teacher in my school rather than like the teacher in Chapter 3 who reprimanded the girl who chuckled. When given a choice, almost every teacher would readily embrace and accept the opportunity to work with students and support them instead of engaging in an ongoing power struggle.

- **If teachers didn't feel controlled, they would be less likely to control their students.**

School leadership can have a tremendous influence on teacher behavior. If school leaders work with teachers and refrain from asserting their power and authority as a primary way of managing staff, educators will have a greater openness to exploring alternative approaches that rely less on controlling and more on influencing and supporting.

- **Most people have a universal preference for valuing and respecting individuals.**

No one likes to be controlled and manipulated. This basic human desire for autonomy remains a reference point for discussing the traditional view of learning compared to the experience of learning outside of school.

- **Reframing not only would decrease bullying, it would increase creativity and achievement.**

When schools rely on rules and consequences as a way to control students, fear is an unspoken emotion, no matter how subtle, it is always present. In this type of environment, students are more concerned about themselves and not their peers. This lack of empathy is linked to a lack of creativity and the inability to think expansively from different perspectives.

- **This frame reflects the challenges and nature of the 21st century workplace.**

When schools nurture creativity and empathy, learning increases. Students embrace learning for its intrinsic enjoyment rather than see it as a means to an end. The more that learning is embraced and driven by passion and curiosity, the better prepared students will be for the jobs that await in the 21st century world. If schools stay mired in the power and control framework, the less they will reflect a workplace of cutting-edge companies and opportunities.

- **This change encourages commonly shared goals for students.**

Parents want their children to become adults who can think for themselves and approach problems and challenges with confidence. They want their children to be individuals who think and care about others rather than simply following the rules. The qualities and characteristics they would like to see in their children do not align with the traditional experiences of school that emphasize conformity and compliance.

- **The problem of bullying plus the need to keep students safe can be a more compelling reason for school change than just raising test scores.**

John Kotter (2008) who studied and researched the change process in business lists a "sense of urgency" as essential in any change initiative. The basic moral purpose that lies behind an educator's career choice (the desire to improve the lives of children) can be tapped as motivation for reframing bullying prevention and change in the schools. Ultimately, people are motivated to work for change when there is a strong, compelling reason for keeping students safe and able to learn. As more and more schools and educators reframe education and build community in schools, they will discover that they have achieved more than just keeping students safe, they will also find that learning (even test scores) will increase as well.

- **Begin with small steps in the right direction and it will be enough to keep moving forward.**

As schools move toward replacing power and control with greater student engagement and active participation, even small steps in the process "feel" better for everyone involved. Progress becomes inevitable. Once members of the school community see that change is possible, they will be able to make a choice for the type of school they want rather than assuming that schools can only be framed in one way.

- **Many schools have already reframed and are showing positive results.**

Even though there are many laws and policies that seem to reinforce schools' tendencies to tighten controls on students, many schools have moved in a different direction and are producing very positive outcomes.

- **As the "needle stays stuck" on reducing rates of bullying and academic progress, schools will eventually start looking inward and realize that** *staying with the frame* **is not working on many levels.**

Schools may get better at controlling students, but that doesn't translate to improving learning or to stopping bullying. Students may be more cooperative in completing assignments, but the depth of their learning will not increase when they are doing it to please others rather than from a desire to learn. Bullying can continue to appear to be under control and not be a problem, but students will still be hurt and excluded. At some point, the real problem of *schools resistance to change* will come into clearer focus.

- **The research documenting the immediate positive and lasting impact of changing how people think about themselves and the world (reframing) will get harder to ignore.**

Social psychology research has demonstrated how people change and what prevents them for changing. In many situations, a simple phrase injected into a conversation with another person can dramatically change how that person thinks, talks, and acts. In business, companies who fail to change face going out of business, yet this research is only just beginning to affect the institutions of education that typically rely on behavioral approaches to inform policy and practice. More and more universities are taking their research findings out into the world and are starting to work with schools. There are schools that have studied the research and are putting it into practice with impressive results.

REFRAMING IN ACTION: THREE AREAS TO EXPLORE

I have chosen three areas of research to provide a clear explanation and specific examples for how reframing works to create positive changes in people and organizations:

- Organizational Reframing
- Individual Reframing: Mind-sets
- Theoretical Reframing: Self-Determination Theory

ORGANIZATIONAL REFRAMING: THE RESEARCH OF AMY EDMONDSON

When leaders empower rather than control; when they ask the right questions rather than provide the right answers; when they focus on flexibility rather than adherence, they move to a higher form of execution. (Edmondson, 2012, p. 8)

The factory model adopted by schools is also no longer suitable for businesses that want to survive and prosper in today's world. Even though the type of work done today is very different from assembly line work, many companies also have found it difficult to change how their employees are viewed and managed. Businesses who resisted change have failed to prosper or even survive. Many companies have had no choice, but to rethink how they were organized and functioned on a daily basis, especially the companies that require creativity and innovation to succeed. Although schools are very different from businesses, they can benefit from seeing how some organizations have transformed all aspects of their operations in the world.

KEY ASPECTS OF EDMONDSON'S RESEARCH

In her outstanding and valuable book *Teaming: How Organizations Learn, Innovate and Compete in the Knowledge Economy*, Amy Edmondson explains the reasons why organizations need to change and the challenges they face. She describes how organizations can reframe their very mission and conception of how people should do their jobs. She also presents empirical research demonstrating how organizations have successfully made the shift from a traditional top-down command and control structure to one characterized by collaboration, shared leadership, problem solving, and innovation. There two key interrelated issues she highlights in studying organizations: the frame governing how people think, talk, and act, and the role that fear plays in that environment.

PROBLEMS WITH THE TAYLOR MODEL (FACTORY FRAME)

Edmondson's description of the lingering effects of the factory frame on businesses echoes the very same conditions that currently define what most people think of as school conditions.

> Despite the rhetoric to the contrary, many of us still expect ourselves and others to get things right the first time. We view failures as unacceptable. We issue directives to those below and look for direction from supervisors above. We prefer going along with the majority opinion rather than risk conflict or job loss if we truly speak out. In many ways, the old mind-set is comfortable and reassuring. Job duties are fixed. Goals are clearly stated. Targets are objective and immutable. The industrial factory system took adults and treated them as children inside the factory walls. At work, they were required to ask permission for everything: to go to the bathroom, to punch in and out on a clock to verify hours worked, to eat only when permitted, and to do as they were told without asking questions. (Edmondson, 2012, p. 40)

If the factory model treated adults as children in order to stay efficient and productive, it is not surprising that the dominant parent/factory frame had such a tight and lasting hold on how schools typically manage *real* children. The problem with this approach was not that it didn't work, *but that it did work* as long as the criterion for success was efficiency involving work that didn't require thinking or any type of creativity. For managers who valued this type of efficiency, the costs of this approach were never visible and not fully understood. Sometimes *what doesn't happen* is either overlooked or thought to be irrelevant to the task at hand. For example, the most obvious hidden cost of this approach as it relates to bullying in our schools was that it only tightened the NOTS of bystander behavior described in the previous chapter; it silenced, limited, and restrained the people who have the greatest influence on stopping bullying in schools.

PREDOMINANCE OF FEAR AND ITS NEGATIVE EFFECTS

Fear is the quiet invisible yet ever present element behind the levers of control in all organizations shaped by the factory frame. If questioned on the spot in a school or work environment, most students or workers would not say that they were fearful. This lack of testimony does not mean that fear is not present; it is proof that fear is so integral and embedded in the experience or frame that it eludes recognition by the very people it touches and controls.

Edmondson is most concerned about the negative effects of fear on people feeling free and safe to speak up when in teams. Speaking up and voicing ideas, opinions, insights, and questions is an essential element in the process of teaming. It is how the team learns from its members. However, fear has a very tight hold on us; it is the default setting that we have as we face the world. It is easily triggered by the slightest suggestion (verbally or nonverbally) of disapproval by those in positions of authority. Fear creates self-protective responses that eliminate or severely limit any expansive thinking and questioning. It also inhibits people from trusting each other and working together.

EMPIRICAL RESEARCH ON REFRAMING

Edmondson's research is so important because it is done in real-life settings and not in a laboratory. She has studied how organizations either enhance the individual and collective learning of its members and hence succeed and prosper or suffer consequences. From her analysis of what worked or didn't work, she has extracted critical elements that organizations need to put into place if they want to thrive in an environment that requires flexibility, collective learning, innovation, and adaptability. Her research tells the story of how reframing can actually *work* in the world.

In one study, she observed four cardiac surgery teams that faced the challenge of learning a new and less invasive procedure to use with patients. Two of the teams succeeded in learning the new procedure and integrated it into their practice; two of the teams abandoned the effort all together. The critical difference between the teams that learned the procedure and the ones that abandoned it was "how the project was framed by each project leader" (Edmondson, 2012).

There were three dimensions evident in the reframing of the successful teams:

Leader's role: The leader intentionally framed himself or herself as an interdependent team member and not the expert. The leader became someone who shared power and authority with the team, instead of trying to control a team of people who had less expertise and less knowledge. The leader shifted the power structure from being above others to working with others.

Team's role: The change in the leader's role had a dramatic positive impact on the role of the team members. Members of the team viewed their contribution to the process as essential for its success. Rather than waiting to be told what to do or hesitating to share ideas, they assumed responsibility for speaking up, raising important questions, and providing constructive feedback to each other. Team members became empowered to share leadership and responsibility for the success of the project.

Project purpose: Without the hierarchical power structure, the team members didn't adopt a defensive self-protective approach. They didn't worry about being judged negatively for doing something wrong or saying something that would get them into trouble. The entire project was framed as an important and aspirational endeavor that required each person's commitment and best effort. The assumption was that all involved cared about improving service to patients. *The compelling purpose for the work became the source for the team's motivation and commitment to face the inevitable failures, setbacks, and uncertainty on the way to success.*

Edmondson summarized the leadership role in framing a project for success:

> Leaders must frame their role in the project to invite others to participate fully. They need to ... ask for help, listen, and acknowledge their own limitations. (Edmondson, 2012, p. 96)

The leaders of the teams that successfully adopted the new procedure created the conditions for optimal learning. Since the procedure was complex and all members of the team had to learn it, the communication among the team members needed to be free-flowing and honest. The best learning takes place almost at the moment a problem or an issue arises. Team members need to communicate on the fly and be able to process what is happening as it happens.

When the leader verbalized that he or she was challenged by the task and also had a lot to learn, the team members became less concerned about making a mistake or admitting a problem. When the leader emphasized that the input and questions from each member of the team were essential for the ultimate success of the project, the team members felt affirmed and inspired to meet the *noble* goal of serving patients. This approach to viewing their work is much different from one where the goals are either to please the person in charge or avoid criticism or reprimand. Consequently, when all the members of a team see and understand this greater purpose and their role in achieving it, their commitment and determination allows them to persist and encourage each other when they face adversity, uncertainty, or doubt.

When the team members feel safe to make and admit mistakes, express feelings, notice problems, share feedback, and speak up when necessary, they are also creating social norms of collaboration that increase the commitment of all team members. Edmondson (2012) described the combined conditions of psychological safety and high accountability as creating an environment for optimal learning.

Removing the fear that drives both the need for control and the means for controlling is a bottom-line condition for any organization that wants to switch from what Edmondson calls an *execution frame* to a *learning frame*. The organizations that succeed today are the ones that are able to continue to learn in a constantly changing environment. The desire and the commitment for continuous learning by organizations or any group of people was the difference between success and failure, as demonstrated with the cardiac teams. Since schools are supposed to be about learning, it is hard to ignore any research that reveals the fundamental conditions necessary for schools to achieve their basic mission—learning.

THE NEED FOR PSYCHOLOGICAL SAFETY

> In psychologically safe environments, people are willing to offer ideas, questions and concerns. They are even willing to fail, and when they do, they learn. The need for psychological safety is based on the premise that no one can perform perfectly in every situation when knowledge and best practices are in flux; . . . people intuitively understand that their workplace is psychologically safe or unsafe. (Edmondson, 2012, pp. 125–126)

Students need to feel safe in order to learn. There are few if any educators who would disagree with that statement, but when the words and concepts are more closely examined, it is no longer a simple, straightforward declaration. When *safety* is defined as the conditions to allow free expression, to take risks without fear of judgment or condemnation, or to question those in authority, then it is apparent that schools are not designed for this type of safety. When *learning* requires embracing uncertainty, listening to diverse voices, struggling through adversity with mistakes and accepting problems as opportunities, it might be difficult to find that type of learning in many schools. Ironically, most schools are concerned about threats from outside, when the real danger to learning is coming from within and is hidden in its very structure.

Although the use of language is a crucial element of framing, reframing is more than just saying things differently. It requires that those in positions of power and authority rethink how they want to use that power and authority and rethink their role and the role of the people they lead. Edmondson comments on this practical aspect of the leadership's role in creating psychologically safe environments.

> The most important influence on psychological safety is the nearest manager, supervisor, or boss. Those authority figures, in subtle or not so subtle ways, shape the tone of interactions in a team or a group. Therefore, they must be engaged as the primary drivers in establishing a more open work environment. They must take practical steps to make the workplace psychologically safe. Psychological safety is a shared sense developed through shared experiences. (p. 137)

In bullying prevention, safety doesn't come from controlling what students say and do to each other, it comes from working with them to create a psychologically safe environment for all members of the school community. Schools cannot truly be psychologically safe for students unless they change how they view and use power. The belief that schools must control students to educate them is incompatible with the concept of psychological safety and the concept of empowering students.

Psychological safety cannot come from getting students to follow slogans or rules or from inspiration assemblies; it requires a change in how those in leadership positions treat others. Edmondson lists a specific set of behaviors that can cultivate psychological safety (p.139):

- Be accessible and approachable
- Acknowledge the limits of current knowledge
- Be willing to display fallibility
- Invite participation
- Highlight failures as learning opportunities

- Use direct language
- Set boundaries
- Hold people accountable for transgressions

Many people might think that giving up control over others is tantamount to adopting a laissez-faire attitude or creating an "anything goes" type of environment. On the contrary, a psychologically safe environment does require clarity for what is acceptable behavior and what is not. High standards are an inherent aspect of such an environment because working hard and striving for excellence becomes a social norm instead of a directive from above. In a psychologically safe environment, the members of the group hold each other accountable. When there is an aspirational compelling purpose for the work that people do, then any lack of effort or commitment on the part of an individual draws attention; those individuals are then supported in making the necessary adjustments to their work and commitment. This approach is totally different from condemning or punishing students who don't do what they are told.

IMPLICATIONS OF EDMONDSON'S WORK ON REFRAMING BULLYING PREVENTION

Empirical research demonstrating the importance of reframing and the positive results obtained by conversion will not be sufficient to change the hearts and minds of those responsible for reframing schools and enforcing bullying prevention. However, what it can do is provide an important reference point for people to study if and when they show an interest in creating the type of change needed to make progress in reducing and preventing bullying and in how schools operate. Seeing and hearing the stories of how reframing actually works can reveal the real hope of positive change for many who have worked in organizations or environments where change has not been viewed as possible. Edmondson's research also provides a strong and practical theory that can help people see new possibilities and concepts that they have been unable to see due to their current frame. Her work gives a *sneak preview* of what is possible along with a tangible set of directions for getting started and moving in the right direction.

INDIVIDUAL REFRAMING: MIND-SETS/ NONCOGNITIVE FACTORS OF LEARNING

When a student feels a sense of belonging in a classroom community, believes that effort will increase ability and competence, believes that success is possible and within his or her control and

> sees school work as interesting or relevant to his or her life, the student is more likely to persist at academic tasks despite setbacks and to exhibit the kinds of academic behaviors that lead to learning and school success. (Farrington et al., 2012, p. 10)

Academic mind-sets are "the psycho-social attitudes or beliefs one has about oneself in relation to academic work" and these attitudes and beliefs are often what compel students to engage in learning—or not (Dweck, Walton, & Cohen, 2011). These same mind-sets are also related to how students view and interact with each other and the entire school community. These mind-sets are also the key factors determining whether or not students bully others, are bullied, or intervene or report bullying when they witness it. To a very large extent, how students come to view themselves and their peers is determined by how adults view and treat them. So, the mental frame that governs how adults view school ends up projecting a role and identity on the students. Mental frames that govern organizations create the mind-sets that govern what people think, say, and do within those organizations. It is as if a script is written and given to students to play, except the students confuse their roles with their true identities.

THE CHALLENGE OF INDIVIDUAL REFRAMING

> People have core narratives about relationships that are rooted in their early interactions with primary caregivers. We could solve a lot of problems if we could get people to redirect their interpretations in healthier directions. (Wilson, 2011, p. 8)

Social psychology research has demonstrated the positive and lasting outcomes that happen when people reframe how they view themselves, others, and their role in the world. These results can be startling, especially to educators who have experienced prolonged frustration in their role of trying to control uncooperative students. Most of the strategies that they employed in trying to control students are based on behavioral approaches using positive and negative reinforcements. For these interventions to be successful, educators must diligently monitor students and make sure that the reinforcements are provided in just the right way and at the right time. When these interventions and programs don't achieve the desired changes in student behavior, it is interpreted as a lack of program fidelity on the part of the educators. These programs and interventions represent a chain reaction of control: teacher behaviors must be controlled in order to control student behaviors. What doesn't *change* is the identity of the teachers and students identified as people who have to be controlled to change.

Significantly, the research that demonstrates the positive results of helping people change their mind-sets can also be threatening to many educators for various reasons.

- It implicates them as having a role in creating and maintaining the mind-sets that impede learning for students.
- It indicates that what they thought was so true and unchangeable about students is now subject to change.
- It implies that they are the people who have to change and have a responsibility to change.
- It changes their basic notions of education and what it means to be an educator.
- It reveals barriers in the educational system that they will encounter if they want to change how they teach.
- It results in a response that it can be safer to complain than it is to change.

"THEY'RE NOT MAGIC"

So dramatic are some of the results of the research on changing mind-sets or cognitive reframing that David Yeager and Gregory Walton published a paper titled *Social-Psychological Intervention in Education: They're Not Magic (2011)* in order to explain how the underlying principles of social psychology had such a dramatic and lasting positive impact.

> Recent randomized experiments have found that seemingly "small" social-psychological interventions in education—that is, brief exercises that target student's thoughts, feelings, and beliefs in and about school—can lead to large gains in student achievement and sharply reduce achievement gaps even months and years later. (Yeager & Walton, 2011, p. 267)

Here are some of the results they are referencing:

- First-year college students were given information that lead them to attribute their academic setbacks to typical problems that all students experience rather than to something being different or wrong about themselves. This resulted in a significant increase in their GPAs that lasted four years compared to students in the control group (Wilson & Linville, 1982, 1985).
- Teaching middle school students that intelligence is malleable, can grow with effort and by working through adversity through eight weeks of instruction in how their brain works resulted in significantly higher grades for the school year as compared to students

who were just taught study skills (Blackwell, Trzesniewski, & Dweck, 2007).
- Asking minority students with academic problems to write about personal values that matter to them at the start of the school year resulted in significantly higher GPAs than similar students who wrote about values in general, not their own (Cohen, Garcia, Apfel, & Master, 2006).
- Minority students who worried about belonging as a college student were asked to write down what they learned as freshmen. This served as a method to help incoming students learn from their experiences and significantly increased their motivation and achievement over the remaining years of college as compared with students who were just exposed to information regarding adjusting to college (Walton & Cohen, 2007, 2011).

Yeager and Walton persuasively argue that what these interventions did was to remove psychological barriers that depressed and constrained the students' abilities. "Even a seemingly small intervention, but one that removes a critical barrier to learning can produce substantial effects on academic outcomes" (Yeager & Walton, 2011). The identities (who they tell themselves they are) that students assume as a result of their school experience can add unseen stress, limit what they view as possible for themselves, and lower their confidence when confronting challenges and adversity.

The authors conclude that when students change how they view themselves, they react more positively to the instructional program and the supports that are available to them. They state that social psychological interventions "can unleash the potential of students and of the educational environments in which they learn."

Just as a chain reaction occurs with the command and control structure of schools, a similar one can occur once educators and students are freed from the conflict that continually arises when the primary goal of those with more power is to try to control those with less power. Schools will become better places when the "control to educate" is not their primary mind-set.

IMPORTANT CAVEAT

If these interventions are so relatively brief and effective, why can't they just be used with students in schools? The problem with these interventions is that their success is very dependent on how they are presented to students and how students interpret what is happening to them. For example, if students felt that they were being told about how their brain worked because they were failing and viewed the intervention as a remedial service being delivered to them, the mind-set that they were not smart would be stronger than the content they received about how their brain worked. Interventions designed to increase a sense of belonging in school will be undermined if teachers and school staff do not know their names when interacting on a daily basis. Interventions that help students believe that their efforts lead to success with also be undermined when arbitrary timelines for mastering skills and concepts define success and failure, for example, passing a course in 10 months will typically be viewed as success while taking an extra six weeks to pass it (going to summer school) will be viewed as a second-rate success, if not failure.

> Instead of, or in addition to, relying on intervention programs to change student mind-sets, another strategy involves changing institutional structures and practices so that everyday educational experiences lead students to conclude they belong in school, that they can succeed in their academic work, that their performance will improve with effort and their academic work has value.... [i]mproving classroom contexts would seem likely to have a larger and broader impact on student achievement and achievement gaps than one time interventions that only can address a limited sample of students. (Farrington et al., 2012, p. 36)

Instead of analyzing all the reasons why students have problems in school (family issues, lack of motivation, and so on.), the research on mind-sets focuses on the type of thinking that successful students have about themselves as learners. When students don't succeed in school, instead of viewing them as deficient (in need of being fixed), the approach to helping them is to discover practical ways to change their mind-sets toward how they approach their learning—change their identities as learners. Successful learners answer "yes" to four key statements related to mind-sets. These same four statements can be applied to students who are empowered bystanders; those people who answer, "Yes" to these statements are more likely to help peers in need.

FOUR KEY MIND-SETS: APPLICATION TO BULLYING PREVENTION

I belong to this academic community.

Making that statement and believing it, is predicated on each member of the school community believing it to be true about every member. The term "community" is incompatible with exclusion or conditional membership. If all students are viewed as members of a community, no one member can become "the other," or be someone who doesn't belong or fit (e.g., Joey who kicked the wall in Chapter 3). Community requires that members know and respect commonalities and differences. Some students might not like a particular student, but community requires a responsibility that transcends "liking" as the criteria for helping and supporting. The example I use with students is to think of teammates on a baseball team: you might not like who is playing right field, but you want that person to do well and will help that person do well for the sake of the team. Members of a community are all on the same team. At the very least, a sense of community where each member belongs will make it very difficult for any student to be selected as a target for bullying based on the belief that he or she will have no defenders or allies.

My ability and competence grow with my effort.

When all students have this mind-set, it changes the perception that there are some students who are smart, some in the middle, and some not smart. Students who take longer to learn something do not have to feel like they are failing, so they will be less likely to detach or withdraw from participating in school. Their persistence and positive attitude will also make them less likely to be stigmatized or lead them to think that something is wrong with them. Students who feel that their efforts will lead to success have less need to feel good about themselves by exerting control or using those with less social status.

I can succeed at this.

When all students have this mind-set, they have more confidence in trying new activities and taking learning risks. This mind-set can also lead students to intervene when they see another student being mistreated. Without worrying about getting into trouble or thinking that their only responsibility is to follow the rules, students can take risks to help others. When more students act this way, helping becomes more of the social norm and a high moral standard is set for everyone.

This work has value and meaning for me.

Any work done in an atmosphere of community where individuals feel connected in working toward common goals takes on added value. The process of learning in a community motivates students to try new things and discover the value of topics and activities that they otherwise might not try. Ironically, individual motivation and achievement increases the more that people feel connected and supported. Research on happiness also consistently reveals that people derive greater satisfaction from giving than receiving, so the act of helping others has great value to all who help. Motivation for helping others can also provide the impetus for people to develop the skills and knowledge to get better at helping.

IMPLICATION OF INDIVIDUAL REFRAMING (MIND-SETS) ON REFRAMING BULLYING PREVENTION

Since bullying is not simply a rule infraction, but rather a result of how students view themselves and their peers, changing their mind-sets should be an integral part of any attempt to reduce and prevent bullying in schools. Reframing bullying prevention is essentially the same reframing (changing mind-sets) that, as the research shows, results in higher levels of achievement and better learning. As students feel that they belong to their social group, they are less vulnerable to being bullied and suffer less if they are bullied. As students feel that they have autonomy and choice in their learning, they are less likely to resort to manipulating others to impress an audience. As bystanders take greater ownership for their learning and their school community, they are empowered to help those students who might be targets of bullying.

The power or "magic" of changing mind-sets really shouldn't be so surprising when it is viewed as a lifting of barriers or restraints that were placed on capable and motivated students who were waiting for someone to tell them that they are better than they thought they were. When more and more of these barriers (false identities that were unintentionally placed on students) are lifted, students can view one another as valuable to their common and individual efforts. Removing these barriers, giving students their true identities, helps them feel safer and more motivated to learn together. Bullying in this type of social context loses it meaning and purpose, and becomes itself a target for disapproval and rejection—*it can then just fade out of the picture.*

THEORETICAL REFRAMING: SELF-DETERMINATION THEORY (SDT)

> "There is nothing as practical as a good theory."
>
> —Kurt Lewin, *Field Theory in Social Science: Selected Theoretical Papers*

Given the number of demands imposed on educators today, I hesitate to even use the word "theory." Unfortunately, many educators who are under great pressure to "change" schools are immediately turned off by anything other than a clear set of procedures, directions, and action plans that will lead to the desired changes that will improve schools. In today's pressured environment, educators can merely become *deliverers of* content given to them from those in a higher authority. This is an unfortunate and unproductive way of affecting positive change in schools. If substantial change is to occur in schools, educators must be viewed as thoughtful and reflective professionals who can learn as they educate. Substantial change will not occur if educators are going through the motions of implementing policies and programs that they don't understand nor believe have value. Instead, when educators can understand what they are doing and why they are doing it, they can develop the professional wisdom that comes from experience, reflection, and meaningful collaboration with colleagues. Understanding "why and how" becomes part of the shared knowledge that promotes the growth and learning of individuals and organizations. Theory becomes an essential reference point for practice and a guide for when educators hit roadblocks or perplexing problems.

Self-determination theory developed by Edward Deci and Richard Ryan provides an alternative theory for reframing how to view student motivation and how the environment affects it. It is theory that has developed and elaborated through analyzing and interpreting the results of empirical research testing its basic tenets and assumptions. If the current frame of school operates on the assumption that students need to be controlled and are motivated to do certain things or not do certain things based on obtaining rewards or avoiding negative consequences, reframing requires a different way of understanding student motivation; self-determination theory provides that alternative. It is based on the key assumption that children are born to learn and do not need to be controlled or manipulated to learn.

What is also helpful about the theory is that it recommends a *clear set of behaviors that contrast with the traditional ways of interacting with students.* Educators don't have to be experts in the SDT theory to start changing how they interact with students; they do however need to understand enough of it to get started. When students are treated differently, they act differently and then staff understand the theory even more.

SDT: ENOUGH TO UNDERSTAND AND BEGIN

I do not attempt to fully summarize self-determination theory in detail for the purposes of application to reframing bullying prevention procedures. I do review some the most relevant concepts pertinent to bullying prevention and focus on the recommended teacher behaviors that can create the conditions that prevent and reduce bullying and that promote more positive and prosocial treatment of all members of the school community. Self-determination theory is also very consistent and complementary to the reframing approach advocated by Edmondson and to the theory of mindsets developed by Dweck, Yeager, and Walton.

There is an excellent summary of the theory (Deci & Ryan, 2000) in the American Psychologist journal. There is also a less technical explanation of the theory in the book *Why We Do What We Do* by Edward Deci with Richard Flaste (1996). (There is also a TEDX talk by Ed Deci that can be found on YouTube at http://www.youtube.com/watch?v=VGrcetsOE61, which provides an excellent and succinct description of what his theory means in action.)

ORIGINS OF SELF-DETERMINATION THEORY (SDT)

Ed Deci and Richard Flaste (1996) described the origin of their work and how SDT has been an attempt to answer some basic questions about why people do what they do

> For young children, learning is a primary occupation; it is what they do naturally and with considerable intensity when they are not preoccupied with satisfying their hunger or dealing with their parents' demands. But, one of the most troubling problems we face in this culture is that as children grow older they suffer a profound loss. In schools, for example, they display so little of the natural curiosity and excitement about learning that was patently evident in those very same children when they were three or four years old. What has happened? Why is that so many of today's students are unmotivated, when it could not be more clear that they were born with a natural desire to learn? (p. 19)

Self-determination theory rests on the basic assumption that all people are naturally motivated and have an authentic self; in other words that they don't have to be shaped or formed into a person by schedules of positive and negative reinforcement. This authentic self manifests itself when individuals are drawn by curiosity and interest to different experiences in their world. In this way, people are different in what they might be interested in or drawn to, but they are the same in that they have this basic or intrinsic motivation to explore the world for its own sake and enjoyment.

Therefore, self-determination theory embraces the assumption that people are different and unique. This way of understanding and interpreting the social world avoids the stigmatization of being different that can often justify the mistreatment of any individual. Any reframing of bullying prevention must be based on acceptance of the differences among people along with the recognition that all people have some basic needs in common.

BASIC NEEDS: THE RIGHT CONDITIONS FOR SELF-MOTIVATION

> The proper question is not "how can people motivate others?" but rather, "how can people create conditions within which others will motivate themselves?" (Deci & Flaste, 1996, p.10)

Self-determination theory articulates the environmental conditions that either promote intrinsic motivation or thwart it. The conditions that promote intrinsic motivation, those that allow the authentic self to naturally pursue interests are the ones that meet an individual's three basic needs:

Autonomy: to be autonomous means to act in accordance with oneself; the feeling that one is acting freely to meet one's needs, achieve one's goals, or pursue one's interests. To be self-governing or to being charge of one's actions.

Competence: "refers to feeling effective in one's ongoing interactions with the social environment and experiencing opportunities to exercise and express one's capacities" (Deci & Ryan, 2002, p. 7).

Relatedness: to feel connected to others, to be cared for, accepted, and valued by others. Feeling a secure sense of belonging to a community that is not contingent on performing a certain way or conforming to an arbitrary standard.

When people's basic needs are being met, they are intrinsically motivated to learn and grow. When these needs are not being met, people often demonstrate what appears to be a lack of motivation to learn.

CONTROLLED MOTIVATION AND ITS CONSEQUENCES

Controlled motivation is when someone (usually an authority figure) tries to get anyone to do something that they would not do willingly or freely. Usually controlled motivation takes the form of rewards or negative consequences and threats. Controlled motivation can also occur when a person in authority gives approval and extends positive regard for performing a certain way and then withholds those feelings if the person fails to perform that way. When people experience controlled motivation, they feel anxious, tense, and worried about how their actions will be judged or evaluated. Controlled motivation produces two basic choices for individuals: to comply or to defy. Very often individuals who complied because of consistent and tightly enforced external controls, often at a later point in time start to rebel and defy the authority that imposed those controls.

Research also shows that people whose motivation is controlled by external means tend to take the shortest path to completion. Research demonstrated that when people are given extrinsic motivation to do something that they might otherwise be intrinsically motivated to do, they might do what is expected, but they will value that activity less and become less likely to do it in the future unless another extrinsic reward is offered. In essence, the act itself is a means to an end—the person ends up doing it solely to meet the external demands of the person who has the rewards or consequences. If someone does not choose an action freely, the actual enjoyment or experience of that action is greatly diminished.

AUTONOMOUS MOTIVATION AND ITS CONSEQUENCES

Autonomous motivation is when a person chooses to do something freely and with volition. It is an activity that the person endorses and finds interesting and intriguing. This freely chosen activity can be difficult, but since it is chosen the person can find satisfaction in overcoming the adversity experienced in the process of facing that challenge. A person can also be autonomously motivated to engage in an activity because of a deeply held value or belief. Hundreds and hundreds of research studies (Deci & Flaste, 1996) demonstrate that autonomous motivation leads to greater creativity, improved problem solving, positive emotions, deeper levels of learning, and greater reported physical and emotional well-being.

AUTONOMY SUPPORT

Critics of self-determination theory often equate intrinsic motivation with a lack of structure and a laissez-faire approach to letting students just do what they want to do. Deci and Flaste (1996) address this criticism:

> By taking a general stance against reliance on rewards, demands, threats, surveillance competition and critical evaluations as avenues for motivating people's behavior, I am not by any means advocating permissiveness. The use of goals, structures, and limit setting is often important in schools, organizations and cultures even if people cannot be expected to like them.... [T]he really important question, then, is how can we avoid being permissive, without creating gridlock? How can standards and limits setting co-exist? How can standards and limits be used so that the person in the one-down position can live within limits and still retain a feeling of self-initiation, and thus not lose intrinsic motivation. (p. 43)

The approach to resolve this dilemma is called autonomy support. Autonomy support is characterized by the following:

- Taking the person's perspective as a starting point
- Offering choice whenever possible
- Offering opportunities to explore and reflect on the situation
- Allowing self initiation
- Providing a rationale, value and/or compelling reason

When a person feels that the person in authority is not trying to control or manipulate him or her, there is a greater openness to considering what that person has to offer. Providing the basic need of relatedness and belonging through trusting relationships provides the emotional support for the person to try activities that might otherwise be avoided or refused.

Deci and Flaste (1996) sum up the advantages of using autonomy support this way:

> By setting limits in an autonomy supportive way—in other words, by aligning yourself with the person being limited, recognizing that he or she is a proactive subject rather than an object to be manipulated or controlled—it is possible to encourage responsibility without undermining authenticity. (p. 43)

When people in authority act in autonomously supportive ways, the person receiving the support is more likely to discover and enjoy the benefits of the activity and is more likely to internalize the rationale and value of the activity. Those people receiving autonomous support learn on a deeper level and develop a greater sense of competence and confidence (Deci & Flaste, 1996).

TEACHING STYLES

As fear is a way of controlling students, the fear of losing control is an unspoken motivation for how many educators interact with students. If educators are ultimately going to change, they need a set of *replacement behaviors* for their default, or controlling styles of interaction with students. Without one, educators will continue to cling to what they are used to doing, even if they might believe in theory that students can be trusted and don't need to be controlled all the time.

The following two stories illustrate that the shift from controlling motivation to autonomous motivation doesn't have to be as dramatic as many educators might initially think:

> I observed a first grade student who was having some behavioral problems in the classroom. He brought out his snack of potato chips earlier than the schedule indicated and the teacher directed him to put them away. He initially ignored the teacher and continued to eat them. As the teacher repeatedly directed him to follow the instruction, I could feel the tension mount in this power struggle between what the teacher wanted and what the student wanted. The teacher sharpened her tone of voice and physically moved toward the student. The student, probably realizing that he would not "win" this battle, reluctantly put them away.

During lunchtime, the teacher and I discussed this student and his needs. I suggested that his interest and obvious strength in drawing could be used as a building block for turning his behavior around. Later that day, the same problem arose and the chips came out again during a lesson. This time, the teacher must have noticed a drawing the student made lying on his desk. Instead of just directing him to put the chips away, the teacher rephrased her statement: "Joey, your chips are greasy and I wouldn't want them to ruin your drawing, would you find a place to put them?" It was as if the student heard magic words; he immediately got up, walked over to his cubby and put the chips into his backpack, far away from his desk and the temptation to take them out again.

Although this change in wording might seem insignificant, what really happened was that the teacher shifted from controlling motivation to autonomous motivation: the student willingly put the chips away. Why? The teacher simply explained how it was in his own best interests to put the chips away as she simultaneously affirmed the value of his drawing. She gave a reason that the student accepted as reasonable and helpful. He no longer felt he was being controlled and on the losing end of a power struggle.

◆ ◆ ◆

It was the end of the school day in another first grade class, and I was talking to the teacher, as the students were getting ready to go home. The students had several housekeeping tasks to perform, which the teacher observed without having to say too much because the students all knew the routine. She noticed that one student had forgotten to put up her chair and turn it over on her desk. This was just an oversight, not a refusal. The teacher just calmly said, "Amanda, remember Mr. Green." The student then picked up her chair and put in on the desk. I wondered about who this Mr. Green was and how he figured in this gentle reminder to the student.

After the students left for the day, the teacher explained that Mr. Green was the school custodian. At the start of the school year, she invited him into the classroom to meet with her class. He explained what his job was and it entailed cleaning and straightening each classroom in the school. The students also had an opportunity to ask him questions about his job and who he was as a person. He asked them to help him do his job and part of that was putting their chairs on their desks at the end of the day. The students were eager and happy to help him, so every day the act of putting their chairs on their desks was not following the teacher's direction, it was helping a nice man do his job.

The teacher explained that she did a lot of these activities with the students during the first six weeks of the school year. She viewed these introductory lessons as an investment and not as a time drain, which many teachers might.

(Continued)

> (Continued)
>
> When the students understood the reasons why they were expected to do things in the course of the day, they did them willingly without power struggles and without feeling controlled.
>
> It was in March when I had the conversation with this teacher and it was very clear to me that her investment was paying dividends in many ways in the classroom. It was also very evident that this teacher enjoyed her job and looked less tired and stressed because she wasn't trying to control a group of twenty-four students all day. I also asked her what her colleagues thought since many of them still taught using the typical controlling frame. She replied that some of them thought that she had lucked out by getting a good group of cooperative students. She assured me that her students were similar to the rest of the student body in the school. The teacher might not have been able to call what she did autonomous motivation, but she was proving that it worked.

In both stories, the students involved were not intrinsically motivated to do what the teacher wanted them to do, but they ended up doing the expected activity. Unfortunately, the fact that they did what they were expected to do, might be all that matters for many educators, but what the students learned from the experience has a impact on how the students view themselves and their subsequent actions. When students feel that they are acting for a purpose beyond merely doing what they are told by someone who has more power, they internalize the value of the positive

Autonomy-Supportive Instructional Behavior

Behavior	Description
Listening	Educator spends time listening to students during instruction.
Probing for what students want or need	Educators incorporate student interest into lessons. Asks them to relate what they want or need. Offered choices when possible.
Creating independent work time	Students are given time to work on their own or with peers; offered choices for how to do work
Encouraging student voice	Students are given frequent opportunities to state their thoughts and opinions about what they are learning and how they are learning; they have input in the learning process. Time allotted for students to think and reflect.
Adjusting seating arrangements	Environment designed to facilitate student to student interaction and greater access to learning resources.

Chapter 5 The Promise of Reframing

Behavior	Description
Providing rationales	The purpose for learning is addressed and time provided for discussing it. Connections are made to student experiences and possible benefits in life.
Praising as informational feedback	Students are given positive comments on their work that also supports them in doing their work.
Offering encouragements	Checking in with students to demonstrate support and offer assistance as well as affirming and acknowledging their efforts.
Being responsive	Actively seeking student questions, comments. Being attuned to levels of student engagement and able to make adjustments to support it.
Supporting perspective when taking statements	Demonstrating an empathetic understanding of how students respond to challenges and expectations. Explicitly stating and recognizing that the work might be hard. Sharing similar experiences.

Controlling Instructional Behavior

Behavior	Description
Uttering directives and commands	Voicing commands and directives with little explanation or reasons provided. Lack of "please" and "thank you" in teacher statements.
Uttering *should, got to, ought to*	Voicing statements without allowing choices or opportunities for student input.
Telling the right way	Providing instruction emphasizing student production of the right answer rather than emphasizing the process of thinking and gaining understanding.
Showing the right way	Making it clear that there is only one way to do a task, providing little or no student choice.
Contingent approval and positive regard	Conveying to students that teacher approval and positive regard is dependent on meeting expectations and following directions.
Controlling learning materials	Students have limited access and freedom to use learning materials.
Controlling questions	Questions designed to put students on the spot with possible embarrassment in front of peers.
Use of sarcasm	Using position of power to "play" with student emotions and social standing.

(Continued)

(Continued)

Behavior	Description
Comparing students	Using competition to motivate students to perform better.
Tight deadlines	When time limits are emphasized with little flexibility or no room for extenuating circumstances. Allowing no student input for determining the time parameters.
Surveillance	Viewing all students with mistrust, suspecting them of being one step away from exceeding a limit.
Pressured evaluations	Using evaluations as a means to make students do what is expected.
Criteria for success externally determined	Criteria for success either is not discussed or is arbitrarily imposed by the teacher. Students think that "success" is pleasing teacher or complying with teacher demands.

Source: Adapted from Reeve, Ryan, Deci, & Jang (2007)

action. They are, therefore, more likely to act positively in all situations, including bullying situations, when rules, consequences, and adult authorities are not present.

IMPLICATIONS OF SDT FOR REFRAMING BULLYING PREVENTION

When individuals don't bully in order to avoid a punishment, they continue to think more about themselves and less about others. The satisfaction that can come from helping is diminished because the actual experience loses value for individuals; they don't attribute their actions to their own sense of generosity, courage, or caring, but rather to keeping themselves safe and following the rules.

When students are provided autonomous support, they are more likely to internalize the reasons and the values for both not bullying and for helping others when they witness bullying.

When students have internalized moral values, they learn to use them as the basis for making decisions. As they develop this moral conscience, they become more responsible and make better decisions when they confront ambiguous situations, including bullying.

Students whose autonomy is supported develop a greater confidence in their skills. They are more likely to actively advocate for their own needs. Therefore, these students are also less likely to appear helpless and less likely to be viewed as targets of bullying. If they are bullied, they are less likely to feel that they deserve it and more likely to seek help from peers and trusted adults.

In classrooms that are designed to support student interaction rather than compliance with teacher expectations, there are more opportunities for students to discover commonalities with peers and to value their diversity. This should increase the likelihood of bystanders defending and supporting their more vulnerable peers.

SUMMARY

- The assumption that students need to be controlled to be educated can be questioned. Looking deeper at why students misbehave can reveal how the learning environment might not be meeting student needs.
- Although the dominant parent/factory frame seems to define school for most educators, there is reason for optimism that schools can develop a more inclusive and flexible frame based on cooperation and engagement and not merely compliance and control.
- Since it is almost impossible to ask educators to change what they think, say, and do without offering viable reasonable and clear alternatives, an important element of the change process should be exploring the theory, practice, and empirical evidence of reframing in different contexts.
- Three areas of theory, research, and practice that have implications for reframing bullying prevention are (1) organizational reframing (Edmondson's work); (2) individual reframing (Dweck, Walton, & Cohen's work); and (3) theoretical reframing (Deci & Ryan's self-determination theory).
- In all three of these areas, significant positive results have been obtained when individuals reframe how they view themselves, others, and their roles and responsibilities. When individuals feel respected and are given opportunities to think, interact, and become active participants in their own learning and in collective endeavors, their behaviors change further demonstrating that they don't need to be controlled. When individuals are empowered to take ownership and responsibility, they usually do!
- Reframing depends on those in authority being willing and able to view those they lead in a more positive light. They must intentionally share their power with those they lead rather than automatically attempt to control or manipulate them.

6

Reframing Bullying Prevention

Building Community Spirit in Our Schools

"We cannot solve our problems with the same thinking we used when we created them."

—Albert Einstein

The most dramatic example of reframing I ever heard happened during the lunch break of a workshop I was conducting. Two teachers were sitting at the same table with me talking about some of their students. One teacher commenting on a student said, "How can I possibly be expected to get him to pass the final exam when he is absent one or two days every week?" In reply, the other teacher, who also taught that student, said, "Given what he has to deal with in his family and home life, it is amazing that he comes to school three to four times a week."

Those two contrasting statements about the student

- reveal much more about the teachers than about the student;
- are neither right nor wrong, but can become *true* depending on which teacher has the most influence on the student;
- contrast how a teacher's fear or hope can determine what lies ahead for the student;

- reveal how the fear of repercussions if the student failed a course made one teacher view the situation from her own perspective;
- reveal how the hope of what was possible for the student led the other teacher to view the experience of school through the eyes of the student;
- show how one teacher saw the student as a problem interfering with her success, while the other teacher saw the circumstances preventing the student from achieving his success; and finally
- reveal the fragility of a student's success that it is so dependent on how a teacher views and treats that student; and reveal the almost frightening level of responsibility that teachers' hold.

The same student could either be a deadbeat or a hero depending on one's perspective. The questions I asked myself were "If this were my child, which teacher would I want teaching him? Which teacher would have the most success with the student?" The answer was a no brainer—the teacher that saw him as a hero. That would be the *role and script* for that student to follow that would lead to success.

To understand how to reframe bullying prevention, let's imagine two scenarios for addressing the problem of the student who was frequently absent from school.

Scenario One: Student is absent from school one to two days per week.

- The student is viewed as unmotivated and at risk of failing.
- The school must change his behavior in order to have him pass his tests and hopefully graduate.
- The primary goal is to decrease his absenteeism.
- To motivate him to attend, he could receive incentives to come to school and consequences for not attending.
- He has to attend a special program to teach him the benefits of staying in school. Perhaps as part of that program, he could hear students who have dropped out of school and the difficulties they have in finding employment.
- An attendance officer, or school resource officer could periodically check with him to make sure he is attending school.
- He might have to attend remedial programs designed to help him make up the work he has missed.

Scenario Two: Student attends school three to four times a week despite a difficult home environment.

- Student is not viewed as unmotivated. The educators who work with him see him as capable and wanting to learn, but they realize that he faces difficult circumstances preventing him from coming to school.

- One of his teachers meets with him to explore the differences between the days when he can come to school and the days he is absent. The teacher shares that she also has trouble getting up in the morning and shares her suggestions to help with the issue.
- When they review the differences, it seems that he oversleeps on the days that his mother has to leave for work extra early.
- The teacher and the student review options or changes that he can make on the days that his mother leaves early.
- They also explore issues at school and discover that he doesn't feel accepted by some of his peers. They talk about things that he can do to connect with them.
- The student develops a plan to increase his attendance and his teacher checks in with him daily to see how his plan is working and to offer encouragement and help.
- His other teachers are informed that he is having some difficulty forming positive relationships with peers. They design cooperative learning activities in the classroom where the students can discover commonalities and have opportunities to work together on academic projects and activities.
- After a few months of attending school regularly, he is asked if he could help a younger student who is also having problems attending school. He is told how his experience and what he learned could help this younger student.

Both of these scenarios are ways of helping the student, and they could both work if the goal was solely to get him to come to school. However, the second scenario has a goal that goes beyond the outcome of increased attendance—a goal to change how the student views himself and to make him an active participant in making the changes that he eventually wants to see in himself. This shift in his identity has benefits that transcend school attendance; he is learning how to take control of his life. This student emerges from the experience changed, yet it is significant that he never felt like he was being changed by someone with more power over him. Instead, he owned his own change. In this process, the school environment changed to address some of the circumstances that were preventing him from attending school.

Ironically, both teachers wanted the same thing, for him to come to school more often, and both teachers worked hard to help him succeed. But, having the right goals and working hard to achieve them are not enough for students to succeed. In this example, how the problem and the teachers' view of the problem (their frame) to a very large extent determines whether the best intentions and the hard work devoted to addressing the problem will ultimately succeed.

If the goal for helping this student is to control him, to get him to stop a negative behavior (to stop him from frequently being absent), frustration rather than success is the more likely outcome for both the student and the teacher. If the goal is to build on his strengths, empower him, help him learn how to meet his goals, then both the student and the teacher learn what they need to make success a reality.

Scenario #2 is a microcosm of how bullying prevention can be reframed by focusing on some essential elements of the change process.

- Positive assumptions were made about the student; he wanted to learn, but something got in the way.
- The positive goal of coming to school replaced the negative attempt to stop his absences.
- The school looked at the problem through the eyes of the student and expressed empathy for the student.
- Positive assumptions led to adults *not* trying to control his behavior, but rather to coach and empower him to make specific changes that he wanted to make.
- The teacher and the student worked together to discover commonly held goals and to develop plans and strategies to meet those goals.
- The school was willing to change in order to meet the needs of the student rather than just trying to make the student fit the status quo.
- The student was asked to help another student, which served to cement the student's positive identity as being someone who cared for and helped others in need.
- The school's actions and the student's actions were consistent with certain basic principles and the values of respect, caring, and cooperation.

Reframing leads to positive change: it determines the path you take to get to where you want to go. The time invested in viewing the problem and the task that lies ahead in a different way, is not just preferable, it is essential for success. Charging ahead with a mandate, a plan, a set of procedures, and a program to solve a problem may feel familiar and comfortable, require less time and may gain approval from many, but it will *fail to move the needle*, or produce positive results. When the solutions to problems stay "stuck" in the frame that contributed to their existence, it is foolish to think that real progress is possible.

To a very large extent, bullying is a result of the identities that students receive and assume through their experiences of school: how they are viewed and treated by teachers and educators. Therefore, reframing bullying prevention is dependent on how educators view and treat students, specifically the messages that they receive from educators about who they are. These messages determine how students view themselves, and in turn, their *identities* determine what they say and do.

Realizing that schools and education can be reframed is important because it gives educators options that they didn't know they had. They can choose what they want education to be (the experience of school for students):

- Education as a process for telling students who they are based on whether or not they fit the existing structure of school; or
- Education as a process of helping students discover who they are and what they can become.

The words used to describe the student in the story (hero or deadbeat) set the course and determined the outcome of his story right from the start; similarly, choosing the words to describe the goals and outcomes for bullying prevention is a crucial first step in making the needed changes. Reframing can start by changing the words used when thinking and speaking about what schools should really want for students.

REFRAMING REQUIRES RE-WORDING

Taken literally, bullying prevention is about making a negative behavior not happen in the first place. That term is now so loaded with meaning and has so many connotations that when it is uttered by anyone, so many different and often conflicting thoughts and feelings are triggered in the minds of those who hear those words.

- For students who don't bully, it is another dictum coming from adults who might not trust them.
- For students who are bullied, it could be another sign of the futility of adult efforts to protect them.
- For students who witness bullying, it tells them that they are already meeting their responsibility (following the rules), but offers little or nothing to empower them to act on behalf of their peers.
- For parents, it can increase their anger and frustration that even with the "law" on their side, schools still seem stymied to do anything to protect their children.

The term *bullying prevention* cannot be eliminated completely. All members of the school community do need to have an accurate and complete understanding of the problem, but unless those in leadership positions put the term in a different context and associate it with something more positive, bullying prevention will become more and more of a *turn-off* to students and staff. Although they don't verbalize it, many students might think the following when they hear about *bullying prevention*: "Okay, we are not supposed to bully, we are supposed to stand up to it, so what, now what!" Just as in the two scenarios with the student missing school, a very different question has to be asked before a plan can be put into place to address the issue.

> *Do we want to stop a negative behavior, bullying, or do we want to promote and strengthen the positive behaviors that will ultimately create the conditions where bullying becomes incompatible with the cultural and social norms of the school?*

Reframing bullying prevention is about creating the right conditions for all members of the school community to treat each other with care and respect. That is a simple and positive goal, but one that will require significant changes in how schools educate students, and it is a very different goal from the goal of just stopping bullying.

REFRAMING IS BASED ON POSITIVE IDENTITIES, EMOTIONS, AND ACTIONS

The importance of approaching problems in a positive, not negative, way is not just a *feel good* concept. Barbara Frederickson (2009) has researched how positive emotions are more likely to lead to positive actions:

> Unlike negative emotions which narrow people's ideas about possible actions, positive emotions do the opposite: They broaden people's ideas about possible actions, opening our awareness to a wider range of thoughts and actions than is typical. . . . Positivity opens us. The first core truth about positive emotions is that they open our hearts and our minds, making us more receptive and more creative. (p. 21)

Frederickson points out that it was previously thought that only negative emotions triggered actions; for example, that part of survival is the human need to escape or attack (flight or fight). Positive emotions were considered associated with contentment and a lack of action. Her research showed that although negative emotions function well for immediate safety, positive emotions also led to action, but over longer periods of time.

Positive emotions create broadened mind-sets. She states, "Such expansive awareness served to build our human ancestors' resources, spurring on their development of reserves, better equipping our ancestors to handle later threats to survival" (p. 22). Similar to the "thinking fast, thinking slow" concepts developed by Kahneman (2011), positive emotions seem to help people slow down, consider more information, and gain a broader, deeper, and more accurate understanding of the world. This is the type of thinking, perceiving, and responding that can lead to a more creative and adaptive response to bullying and the complex ways that people often interact. Fear or negative emotions only tend to make people fall back on self-protective and narrower responses to problems.

The following statement by Frederickson is not just an endorsement for a positive approach to any problem like bullying, it's a description of what *schools should be about*: "By opening our hearts and minds, positive emotions allow us to discover and build new skills, new ties, new knowledge, and new ways of being. Positivity broadens and builds. It transforms people and helps them become their best" (2009, pp. 24–25).

Students who have the most influence in preventing and reducing the amount of bullying in a school environment need to develop the positive skills, knowledge, and attitudes to have the courage, the competence, and the resources to help those in need. In the process of helping, they *become their best*. Students will not develop that capacity by chance. They need a school environment intentionally designed to help them acquire the knowledge, skills, and attitudes and to teach them how to use these fundamentals in their daily interactions. Students learn the reasons for respecting and caring for others when they experience receiving respect and care from the adults in their lives.

Typically anti-bullying campaigns have taken a different approach: they appeal to negative emotions by showcasing tragic situations involving students who have been bullied. Some depictions also show that students who bully are mean and nasty people. The thinking behind such approaches is that if students just knew how *bad and horrible* bullying really was then they would not bully and even might develop the courage to intervene or report it. (This makes commonsense to many, but as we have discussed, *commonsense* is too often the product of our mental frame and bears no relation to reality.)

There are several problems with this type of *scared straight, negative* approach:

- Most bullying situations are ambiguous and the students who bully are not "bad" people, in fact they are usually better liked than the students who are bullied.
- Most people do not think of themselves as capable of doing bad things; there are always reasons to justify any behavior. (Think of the teacher who publicly embarrassed the student. In the teacher's mind, she was doing it for the student's own good.)
- The research shows that the negative approach *doesn't work*.

The negative message is interpreted by students as being for someone else, or is dismissed as just another attempt by those in authority to control students. These types of messages also lose their credibility since they don't match the reality of what students experience in their lives. In addition, the urgency of stopping bullying does not exist for most students the way the way that it does for many adults. Reframing bullying prevention requires educators to see the problem through the eyes of the students and to understand how bullying really happens in the students' social world.

The Heath brothers in their book *Switch* (2010) summarize the differences between a positive and a negative approach:

> If you need quick and specific action, then negative emotions might help. But, most of the time when change is needed, it's not a stone in the shoe situation. The quest to reduce greenhouse gases is not a stone-in-the-shoe situation. These situations require creativity and flexibility and ingenuity. To solve bigger, more ambiguous problems, we need to encourage open minds, creativity and hope. (pp. 121–123)

Projecting and communicating a positive message to students is crucial in order to create the conditions for students to act in a positive, helpful, and caring way toward their peers. Students want and need to think of themselves in a positive light, to think of themselves as helpers; therefore, reminding them frequently *not to do something negative* contradicts the positive image they have of themselves. Heath and Heath (2010) describe how this phenomenon works: "Because identities are central to the way people make decisions, and any change effort that violates someone's identity is likely doomed to failure" (p. 154). The message, "don't bully others," though well intentioned can backfire because when students *don't bully* they are confirming adults' perception that they are people who *would bully* if they weren't told not to; the underlying assumption is that they are people who don't bully because it is against the rules and they fear the consequences of breaking the rules.

Students need the opposite from adults and adults need to keep their fears of students *not acting responsibly* in check. Educators need to give students a different message about themselves: *students are people who do more than not bully*; they are people who act in caring and responsible ways. Even if students don't outwardly show an indication of being caring and responsible, they rely on adults to tell them that they are caring and responsible. Students need adults to envisage a positive identity for them so that they can grow into that identity. Heath and Heath (2010) describe it this way:

> It shows us that people are receptive to developing new identities, that identities "grow" from small beginnings. Once you start seeing yourself as a "concerned citizen" you'll want to keep acting like one. That's tremendously good news for someone leading a change effort. (p. 161)

However, school leaders cannot address the "negative" approach by proclaiming "now let's be positive when we talk about bullying prevention" and simply expect others to do so. Positive words must be matched by a different set of actions, especially from those who are in positions of authority. This shift to a positive approach really means changing the cultural norms of school. Although this cultural shift might seem abstract and theoretical, norms can be changed the same way they were formed in the first place—get enough people to start to say and do things differently. Those in positions of authority must believe that those they lead *don't need to be controlled* to do good things, but rather that those they lead are capable of assuming responsibility and sharing leadership for making schools better places for learning.

In practical terms, school leaders and educators need to invite, welcome, and join with those they lead rather than direct them or tell them what to do and say. They need to listen, reflect, rephrase, and discuss with those they lead rather than only prescribe procedures for them to follow. Educators need to believe that students are in a sense just waiting to be invited to make their school a better place and to become involved in a noble endeavor.

Effective leaders start this reframing process by working with those they lead in learning new words to use and redefining goals and directions to take. They share power rather than wield it and this sharing and working together creates an environment that allows positive hopeful emotions to replace negative ones driven by fear.

REFRAMING IS *RECLAIMING* AN ORIGINAL FRAME/PURPOSE

How can bullying prevention change from stopping a negative to creating a positive goal and direction for all members of the school community? It cannot be transformed from *stopping a negative* into promoting and supporting a set of positive actions unless the basic dominant parent/factory frame loosens its hold on how schools operate and function on a daily basis. Schools need a frame that can be a strong foundation for reframing bullying prevention, but they don't need to invent a new frame. They can reclaim a frame that predates the factory/dominant parent frame, is tied to the roots of our democratic traditions, and was part of the school's original purpose.

Thomas Jefferson offered this original frame and purpose of schools that can be reclaimed. He envisioned schools as places to educate citizens who can make wise and informed decisions individually and collectively to sustain the type of democracy envisioned in the Declaration of Independence and the Constitution. Linda McNeill (1988) stated it this way: "The Jeffersonian ideal behind our educational purposes affirms the right of every citizen to be informed, to have knowledge that will help control one's own destiny and prevent the rise of oppressive forms of government" (p. 4).

John Dewey reiterated how education is an integral part of perpetuating our democratic society:

> We have taken democracy for granted; we have thought and acted as if our forefathers had founded it once and for all. We have forgotten that it has to be enacted anew in every generation, in every year and day, in the living relationships of person to person in all social forms and institutions. Forgetting this we have been negligent in creating a school that should be the constant nurse of democracy. (Dewey, 1940, pp. 357–358)

Schools are for empowering students to become citizens, not for controlling them to become efficient workers.

REFRAMING IS HAVING A DIFFERENT VISION OF SCHOOLS

If schools are not factories, what type of places are they? (Unfortunately, this is a question that is seldom if ever asked of educators.)

Here is a description of school offered by Thomas Sergiovanni (1996):

> Schools should be treated as special cases because they serve as transitional places for children. They stand between the protected, subjective environment of the family, and the objective, exposed environment of the outside world. Relationships between educators and students are characterized as being in loco parentis. As this role is played out, teachers and administrators are brought together into a collective practice that resembles a shared stewardship. Schools are responsible for more than developing basic competence in students and passing on the culture of their society. They are responsible for teaching habits of the mind and of the heart. Everything that happens in the schoolhouse has moral overtones that are virtually unmatched by other institutions in our society. (p. xii)

This description is consistent with the original purpose of Jefferson and reiterated by Dewey. It is very different from a factory frame where students are treated more like employees rather than people who need the habits of mind and heart for responsible citizenship.

This description of schools dramatically contrasts with the dominant father frame described by Lakoff (2004) that is so strongly linked to the factory frame that has governed how schools have functioned for so long. Just as Sergiovanni mentions the parenting role that schools play in developing students as citizens, Lakoff (2004) also provides a very different (nurturing) parenting frame that is more consistent with the democratic/community frame:

- Both parents are equally responsible for raising children.
- The assumption is that children are born good and can learn to become better.
- The world can be a better place with enough resources to support everyone.
- The parents' job is to raise, support, and nurture children to be full human beings who will be responsible caring people themselves.
- There is no one right way to do that, but raising children does require parents to be empathetic and responsible.
- Raising children is a learning process for both the child and the parents.

This description of schools that reflects the democratic/nurturing parent frame is probably the one that most teachers envisioned when they chose their profession; this was the type of place where they wanted to teach.

If given a choice, teachers probably would not choose the factory frame. Many educators have left education because they found that working in the factory frame was a profoundly different job than what they truly wanted to do with their lives as educators.

Reframing schools and bullying prevention should strike a chord within most educators by helping them to reclaim their own original purpose for their career choice. Just as students are waiting to be invited to assume a different more positive identity, many educators are also probably waiting for a different version of schools to appear to allow them to realize their original purpose in becoming an educator. Given a choice, most teachers would embrace a school that matches Sergiovanni's description. Reframing bullying prevention goes to the heart of protecting and caring for children, and it holds the potential for not just changing bullying prevention, but for how educators can do their jobs.

Reframing bullying prevention also allows educators to view the current assumption that students need to be controlled in order to be educated as only an assumption not a reality. This issue of power and control so central to how schools operate can be reframed by schools to emphasize sharing and working with others in keeping with democratic principles.

When any person is bullied or oppressed, everyone suffers. A democracy requires all (and not just a few) citizens to participate freely in exercising their rights and responsibilities in order to ensure that all citizen voices are heard for the common good. If schools embraced and accepted this democratic frame, there would be no diminishment of individual achievement. When everyone is invested in the success of all, individuals flourish as part of the process of safeguarding that all flourish.

In this context, reframing bullying prevention moves far beyond stopping a negative behavior, being a rule infraction, or deemed a crime to providing all students with the opportunity to control their own destiny while continuing the democratic tradition of promoting the common good. Thus, reframing bullying prevention transforms it from being another item on a school's list of things to do to being a central element in the vision of how a school educates students.

REFRAMING INVOLVES MORAL VALUES AND STANDARDS

Many educators shy away from Sergiovanni's mention of moral overtones when it comes to education. They assert that it is the parents' responsibility to promote moral behavior in their children and that part of the problem that they face as teachers when trying to teach many uncooperative students is the fact that parents have not been doing their job. From this perspective, on top of the challenge of teaching content matter, schools now have to take on the added burden of instilling moral behavior in students. This issue presents an *immovable obstacle* preventing them from teaching the way they want to teach; one that also generates anger, frustration, and pushback, especially toward bullying prevention programs. Given the factory/dominant frame that shapes the culture of most schools, this reluctance to assume this added responsibility is completely understandable. (Remember in the factory/dominant parent frame, morality is pretty simple—students should just do what they are told to do.) Any attempt, therefore, to force or impose a program or curriculum on a teacher is doomed to failure. Although resistance might not be overt, teachers simply can go through the motions of implementing any new policy or practice imposed on them, especially when they don't believe it is their job to implement it in the first place.

Any attempt to reframe bullying prevention must start by recognizing the source of this resistance to programs, mandates, or anything added to the list of responsibilities handed to an educator. This is why reframing bullying prevention is intertwined with reframing how educators view schools, students, and their roles and responsibilities. However, until school staff has assimilated the process of reframing, here are several significant practical points to emphasize (in an empathetic way) if teachers shy away from any hint of moral overtones in schools.

- Acknowledge that their job is harder and more challenging than in the past.
- Remind them that since parents might sometimes fail to do their job, it becomes even more important than ever that schools accept this responsibility because where else can this instruction happen. This is not fair, but it is the situation right now.

- Emphasize that students are already learning positive moral behavior by the adult models in the school. They are already teaching by example and for many students they are the best role models available to them.
- Remember that as students get older, they need to break away from just doing what their parents tell them to do. This is part of the human development that prepares them for adult life.
- Confirm that students often do things that conflict with what even the most responsible parent teaches them at home. The peer world is a very different arena for learning how to behave, and schools are the places where they to put into practice what they are taught or not taught at home.
- Acknowledge that many of the instructional methods they traditionally used and that they inherited, do not provide the tools they need to integrate the social component of learning with the academic.
- Offer the possibility that trying out some different *tools for how they instruct* just might help them efficiently integrate the social and academic.

This recognition and acknowledgement of the challenges that educators face when they view education through the factory frame, and use tools designed to deliver content knowledge to passive compliant students can at least soften some of their resistance and opposition to accepting the moral component of their responsibilities. Understanding their point of view and not forcing them to change is the best (and probably the only way) to open educators' minds to trying out some new ways of teaching.

If a teacher starts to integrate the social and the academic and to involve students in the learning process, they are already on the way to discovering that reframing their view of students, their jobs, and their role in bullying prevention is better for everyone, including themselves. Actions can precede beliefs, especially if they create different conditions and behaviors in students. When educators get greater student ownership and engagement, teaching itself becomes less and less about managing and controlling and more and more about facilitating learning.

Reframing bullying prevention is about reframing the act of bullying from the view that it is a simple rule infraction to understanding it as part of a larger continuum of moral behavior. This means that students cannot simply be told not to bully, but need to be taught what it means to treat others in a responsible and caring way. It means assuming that students face difficult moral choices about how they should interact and treat others. As they develop a clearer understanding of what those moral choices entail and the skills to act on choices, they become more responsible in situations not covered by rules and more responsible when adults are not present.

Reframing bullying prevention *does* mean that schools accept the responsibility for building on the moral education that students receive from their parents by helping them learn how those values can guide them with their peers in school.

Reframing bullying prevention means accepting students as works in progress on the path to developing a moral conscience, and as a result, they should not be judged and evaluated according to the same standards as adults. Merely condemning them and punishing only serves to alienate students and close their minds to adult support and guidance, thereby, impeding their moral development.

REFRAMING OF MORAL STANDARDS BENEFITS ALL STANDARDS

In the 1960s, President Kennedy raised the bar for what it meant to be an American: he reframed what it meant to be a citizen. He viewed citizenship as a noble adventure, a valued journey for the common good of our country and the world. When he set a goal for landing a man on the moon, in a sense, the entire country was going there too; it was a shared goal that automatically joined people together. When he established the President's Council for Physical Fitness, he sent a signal that getting into physical shape was part of being a strong and vigorous citizen. He created the Peace Corps to extend the idea of citizenship beyond our borders into the rest of the world. His message and inspiration brought out the best in people and connected them in meaningful ways. He created a new positive identity for all to develop, nurture, and assume as their own.

Students want to be inspired to do something noble and meaningful for their school community. They would prefer this message to one that just tells them not to do something negative. This invitation to responsible citizenship and commitment to community raises the bar for moral standards. Inspiring people to meet high moral standards can provide the energy that is often lacking for meeting academic standards.

With all the emphasis on academic standards, somehow the student voice seems to be missing from the discussion. If students asked for the reasons why academic standards are being raised, the best answer usually given to them is that it will help our country compete in the global marketplace. This is important, but students need a different reason, a reason with more meaning and purpose, one that has more heart and soul. Schools have a great opportunity to integrate moral and academic standards so that individual achievement can be wedded to developing the knowledge, skills, and attitudes needed to serve others, build stronger communities, and contribute to the common good. Helping students reach these moral and academic standards provides greater purpose and meaning to educators. By helping students become responsible citizens and caring members of the community, education becomes less about raising test scores and more about redefining and energizing the role of educator.

Reframing bullying prevention should be changing expectations for students and for educators; it should be inviting, inspiring, and challenging them to do great things. It can start with students and educators working together to make school a better place for learning for all students. It should add energy and spirit to what we do in schools.

Accepting the presidential nomination in 1960, here are President Kennedy's own words about his call to a different type of citizenship:

> I believe the times demand invention, innovation, imagination, decision. I am asking each of you to be new pioneers of that New Frontier. My call is to the young in heart regardless of age—to the stout in spirit regardless of party—to all who respond to the Scriptural call: "Be strong and of a good courage; be not afraid, neither be thou dismayed." (Kennedy, 1960)

This is the best description I can offer for how to reframe bullying prevention and educating our students. There are can be no deadbeats on this mission. Reframing bullying prevention is a call for all to be leaders and heroes.

A NEW MISSION: BUILDING COMMUNITY SPIRIT IN OUR SCHOOLS

Reframing bullying prevention into a positive and uplifting message can be accomplished by rephrasing it as **BUILDING COMMUNITY SPIRIT**. Each of these words are important and work together to convey what needs to happen in schools.

BUILDING

Schools are not starting from scratch. As discussed earlier, there are structural problems with how schools function that inadvertently contribute to the problem of bullying. This cannot negate the fact that schools are filled with incredible people who are very caring and competent and do great things with and for students. The changes that need to occur in schools to reframe bullying prevention can be built on the positive efforts and activities that have already started. School leaders who are committed to start the reframing process must first realize and recognize the positive experiences that students are having in schools. They must seek out stories of success: where caring and devoted teachers supported vulnerable students or inspired students to be responsible in the face of bullying.

In reality, schools can be filled with many contradicting words and actions. Some staff might inadvertently bully students while other staff are exceedingly kind, respectful to students, and accept them as people regardless of what they might have done. Reframing is the process of taking the positive examples and having them become the norm and standard for all to follow. Being critical, finding fault, or just citing problems only decreases people's openness and receptivity to new ideas and ways of acting. Every school has foundational pieces already in place that reflect the values necessary to reframe schools and bullying prevention.

Every school therefore has the foundation and the inner capacity to reframe bullying prevention and how they educate students.

COMMUNITY

This is the central concept of reframing schools and bullying prevention. Schools that are strong communities are places where bullying is incompatible with how people treat each other. This doesn't mean that bullying doesn't happen in strong communities, but it does mean that when someone is mistreated that act stands out in contrast to how people are typically treated.

The school where I was principal was a strong community. I recall times when a substitute teacher who was new to our school would occasionally yell at students who misbehaved. Typically, a teaching assistant, another teacher, or even a student would make it a point to calmly inform me about it. I am sure that if our school had teachers or a staff person who regularly yelled at children who misbehaved then I would have received no such reports. This is why bullying might occur in a strong community, but that it wouldn't persist. Bullying cannot be camouflaged in a strong community—it doesn't blend in, it calls attention to itself, and the members of the community say in effect, we don't act like that around here. A strong community takes ownership for continuing to be a strong community.

Two television shows capture what a community is in simpler terms. I once conducted a workshop with high school staff and I asked them to complete this sentence stem:

*Anytown High School is a place where_* (fill in the blank) _. I expected several phrases or descriptions to emerge, but one small group working on the assignment finished quickly and jokingly with this: "Anytown High School is a place where *everybody knows your name*" and used the theme song from the show *Cheers*. I thought that it was probably as good a way as any to describe a community: A place where you belong, where you can be your true self, and where you get to know everyone by name. A place where people want to go.

The other show that captures community (a reason why the show endures to this day on the air) is the *The Andy Griffith Show* featuring the town of Mayberry. Mayberry was full of quirky characters that got into all sorts of trouble, but it was a town where everyone had a place and everyone had something to contribute. Barney Fife, the deputy, did foolish things and had an inflated sense of ego, but he was accepted for who he was; when he made a mistake, he was always allowed to learn from it while saving face. Andy, the authority figure did not carry a gun, he led with wisdom, understanding, and kindness and, as a result, people listened to him and followed his advice when he was asked for it or the few times when he offered it on his own.

I have a simple definition of community and how it differs from a group: *a community is a group of people where each person cares about what happens to every person.* This doesn't mean that every person is liked, but it does mean that everyone is respected. It means that each person has value, has something to contribute and that everyone benefits when each person succeeds. Part of building community is having each member of the community think about and have the opportunity to discuss what they think the difference is between a group and a community.

Sergiovanni (1996) offered this definition of community:

Communities are collections of individuals who are bonded together by natural will and who are together bound to a set of shared ideas and ideals. This bonding is tight enough to transform them from a collection of "I's" into a collective "we." As a "we," members are part of a tightly knit web of meaningful relationships. This "we" usually shares a common place and over time comes to share common sentiments and traditions that are sustaining. (p. 48)

After reflection on the concept of community and the importance of establishing a sense of "we" in schools, I came to the following realization that bullying does not wound or hurt students (Dillon, 2013d). Bullying is the salt poured into a student's preexisting wound, which causes that wound to hurt even more. The preexisting wound is from existing in a group of people and not feeling a part of that group, or worse yet, feeling inferior or rejected by that group. As a result of that isolation and rejection, the wound is exposed and vulnerable to hurtful words and actions directed to the student. The wound is exacerbated by being used by someone to impress others. The wound is aggravated from seeing and feeling no one is helping you or protecting you from this mistreatment. The wound is intensified by feeling that you have nowhere to go after you have been mistreated, and by feeling defenseless against repeated hurtful acts.

Bullying is a byproduct of when a group of people are together for an extended period of time and *they do not* become a community. Schools should be places, communities, where no person is wounded in the first place—that is the best way to address the problem of bullying.

When people feel connected, when they feel that there are others around them who care about what happens to them, then hurtful words and actions become like grains of salt that bounce off skin that is whole and unbroken. Hurtful words that are said in a community setting don't ring true, and don't penetrate the heart and skin of the person receiving them. The insensitive words are seen more as a reflection of the person who utters them rather than a statement of fact about the person who is the target. Hurtful words and acts that occur within a community environment are nullified by the many positive and helpful words and actions preceding them. In effect, the members of a community say to any person who attempts to bully: "when you try to bully one of us you are bullying all of us, so don't bother because it won't have any effect." Hurtful words can damage certain individual "MEs" that exist in a group, but they cannot hurt the "WEs" that live together in a community.

An essential goal of any school should be to become a strong community, which is the simple and most effective way to reduce and prevent bullying. Reach for that positive goal, make that the focus of your energy and the negative problem of bullying falls to the wayside and loses its meaning in the process. This is what reframing bullying prevention is all about.

SPIRIT

Any reframing of bullying prevention needs to be a *familiar surprise*; the path to reframing has to be new and different enough to get people's attention, but similar enough to ideas or concepts that most people already know and understand. School spirit is a familiar phrase and every school tries on some level to tap into it whenever there is a special event or new initiative. Some schools have more spirit than others, yet every school probably desires more of it. Spirit is something you can't see or physically grasp, but you can feel it or notice the absence of it. If a school wants a new set of words to reframe bullying prevention then using ties to school and community spirit can be a non-controversial familiar way to start talking about this important issue (bullying).

The word *spirit* also captures the sense of positive energy that is so crucial to any change initiative. The reframing of bullying prevention means that schools shift their approach from communicating another policy, set of procedures, programs, or curricula onto students and staff and instead try to *move* its members toward positive actions and goals fueled by a desire to make their school a better place. Reframing bullying prevention should be a process of changing hearts and minds in order to step out of a previous frame that promoted self-protective responses and suppressed aspirations to help and support others.

Schools should be spirited places because learning is a fulfilling experience, especially when it is shared with others. This shouldn't be a far-fetched notion or one that is foreign to people's experiences. Typically, when people recount and describe positive learning experiences in their lives, they tell of situations where they felt connected and supported, when their learning had a sense of movement and progress that they could see and feel. Positive learning at its roots is dependent on people having a very human experience and influencing each other. People helping others and learning and growing in the process can be a dynamic process that becomes intrinsically motivating for all involved.

Frederickson (2009) describes what can happen once a few individuals step out of a negative frame and begin to help others:

> Beyond the dance of positivity between you and the person you helped, those who witness your good deed may well feel inspired, their hearts uplifted and elevated. This hue of positivity also makes people want to do good themselves. They're not passive bystanders. Their hearts are moved. When those onlookers act on those feelings, they too add more goodness to the social world. . . . As this cycle continues, you and others are inspired to act on your good feelings further and repeatedly, turning them into additional good deeds. In this way, positivity can change whole communities. It can create more compassion and harmony where we need it most. (p. 70)

Reframing bullying prevention can be a process of untying the NOTS of bystander behavior and turning them into *building community* spirit that empowers students and staff to make their school communities into places where bullying or any mistreatment or act of disrespect becomes incompatible with the values and social norms of the school.

SIX TENETS OF REFRAMING BULLYING PREVENTION AS *BUILDING COMMUNITY SPIRIT*

There are six tenets that can guide and direct any school's efforts for reframing bullying prevention. These are guides, signposts, points of reference for a students and staff to use as they face the complex and challenging task of becoming a strong community where bullying violates their social norms of acceptable behavior. The tenets (listed below) are also a way for a school during this ongoing process to check in with itself to make certain that it is working as a community.

- S-Student-centered
- P-Principle-based
- I-Integrated practice
- R-Relationships central
- I-Influence guides
- T-Ties strengthened

STUDENT-CENTERED

Being student-centered means that students are viewed as the solution to the problem of bullying, not the source of the problem. It means that students are not the people who need to be changed or controlled in order to stop bullying. Instead students should be recognized and acknowledged as having the greatest influence on each other in promoting positive behavior and reducing and preventing bullying. First and foremost, adults must accept their own responsibility to reflect on their own words and actions to assess how they treat others and if necessary change their words and actions to meet the highest standards of respect and care.

Being student-centered means that educators must shift from directly controlling students to empowering them with the knowledge, skills, and attitudes necessary for them to positively influence each other.

A student-centered approach includes

- **making positive assumptions about students**. Students are assumed to be people who want to do well in school and want to learn. They are assumed to want to get along with and help others. All students and not just a few students are viewed as capable of being leaders. Adults recognize that students form their identities from how they are viewed and treated by those in authority. These identities determine to very large extent what they say and do in school.
- **looking at the school environment and problems through the eyes of the students**. Educators should try to see and understand the world as students do. They need to look for the reasons why students act the way they do in relation to how their needs are being met in the school environment.
- **intentionally giving students the knowledge, skills, and attitudes to exercise their influence on each other in a positive way.** Educators must also recognize that bullying is not a simple rule infraction, but is an unacceptable behavior that arises as students are learning the complex skill of navigating the social world and what it means to be a responsible moral human being. Bullying is part of the larger issue that all communities must face in determining how its members should treat each other. Adults have an essential role to play in facilitating the process of determining those social norms; recognizing the role that developmental issues play in what students say and do. Educators need to help students understand what is going on inside themselves and their social world. Time can be devoted to helping students talk about and reflect on their experiences. As students learn about themselves and why they are concerned about how their peers

perceive them, they will be able to make better choices in their social world.
- **involving students as much as possible in the process of planning and goal setting for the school.** When students are given an opportunity to be a part of the *change process* in their school by offering their ideas, thoughts, and opinions about the school, they learn a lot in the process about themselves, others, and the school. This also helps to create their identity as problem solvers not problem creators.

PRINCIPLE-BASED

The following are definitions taken from *The New Oxford American Dictionary*:

- Value: one's judgment of what is important in life.
- Principle: fundamental truth or proposition that serves as a foundation for a system of behavior or for a chain of reasoning.

Although rules have a place and a role to play in bullying prevention, they need to be viewed as connected to and derived from the school's core mission, values, and guiding principles for how people should treat one another. When rules and consequences are emphasized, the unspoken assumption is that people cannot be trusted to act in positive ways and therefore need to be controlled by those who established the rules and consequences.

Rules can tell students what they can't do, but reframing bullying requires more than clarifying limits. It should mean discovering the shared values and articulating the principles that can provide the foundation for everyone (not just students) to acquire the knowledge, skills, and attitudes needed for creating a strong community. Values and principles are needed to guide moral behavior in situations not covered by rules or externally controlled by those in power.

Moral authority, therefore, does not just reside with those in leadership positions, but comes from the development of shared agreements among the members of the community to act consistently with their values and principles. Sergiovanni (1996) described the school leaders' role in a community as "Principals and other administrators remain important, but are differently important. They have special responsibilities to behave as head followers of the communities' ideas, values and shared commitments" (p. 58).

The time invested in developing and articulating a set of values and principles for the school helps everyone see the reasons why responsible and respectful behavior is essential and beneficial to each individual.

This type of investment in understanding the principles behind positive and responsible behavior increases each member's sense of ownership and pride in their school. When all members of the school community (administrators, teachers, staff, parents, and students) are unified in their efforts to act in accordance with commonly held values and principles, then the school itself becomes "whole" instead of being divided into a collection of groups each with a different and competing level of power and authority. The process itself of shifting from a rule-based to principle-based approach is one that educates and unites all members of the school community.

I recommend that each school develop a process for including everyone's voice in articulating and accepting a set of meaningful values, beliefs, and principles that can shape and guide the culture and climate of the school. In my book *No Place for Bullying*, I proposed six principles for schools to consider for guiding their bullying prevention efforts:

1. Reflect on your own use of power in relationships.
2. Treat students the way you want them to treat each other.
3. Help all students to become valued in the eyes of their peers.
4. Take action when bullying is observed or reported by a student.
5. Accept the person, but don't accept the person's mistreatment of others.
6. There is never an excuse or justification for disrespecting any person.

Source: Dillon, 2012 adapted from Morrison and Marachi (2011)

These principles or any set of principles derive the most benefit when all members of the school community discuss how each element translates into actual words and actions that can be observed on a daily basis in the school environment.

I do not recommend that schools simply adopt these six principles and place them on a poster on the walls. The process of development is more important than the finished product or even which principle is accepted by a school. Also, a onetime adoption of a set of values or principles cannot sustain a true shift in emphasis from a rule-based to a principle-based school culture. Schools must be committed to periodically revisit their set of values and principles. They must also use them as a practical guide for solving problems and making decisions. When schools address problems using principles and values rather than relying on formulas of rules and consequences, problems become opportunities to explore issues more deeply. This problem-solving process, because it is principle-based, usually produces creative solutions that benefit the school beyond the original problem it addressed.

INTEGRATED PRACTICE

In education words matter a lot, but are drowned out by practices that contradict their meaning. For example, teachers might say that what they value most is hearing how students think in response to their questions. However, their actual practice sends a different message to students when they state their question in the form of "who can tell me," then wait for a few hands to go up, and select one student who supplies them with the correct answer. This typical question and answer format that happens day in and day out in schools conveys this message: "I am the teacher, I know the answer and I want to see who can give me the answer quickly if you want to gain my approval and praise." Students are really taught that those students who think faster and can raise their hand in the most visible and eager way and show how much they know to the person in charge are rewarded.

Compare this traditional practice with a simple rephrasing: "No hands please. Take a few seconds and think about the following question: (Insert question and then *wait five to ten seconds*). Turn to the person next to you and share your thoughts. Then be prepared to share your thinking with the whole class." This alternative practice is designed to get students to think and talk to each other. It also tells the students that their teacher values reflection and sharing and that learning is a social process where every person's idea is important to class. This is the type of practice that promotes autonomy in students. It also allows students to see how each student has something valuable to contribute to the learning process. Although this would not be considered a bullying prevention strategy, an educator who designs the classroom with these type of instructional practices is promoting the values and the skills that students need to be empowered bystanders and to care about their peers.

Reframing bullying prevention means that schools must intentionally choose and promote the instructional practices that are consistent with their positive assumptions about students as learners and community members. Instructional practice must convey to students that learning as a community benefits each individual student and the whole school.

Bullying prevention or social emotional learning programs might have excellent content, but if they are delivered through the traditional dominant parent/factory frame of teacher-centered instruction, then in the perception of the students they hope to change, their positive messages are rendered meaningless at best or hypocritical at worst.

RELATIONSHIPS CENTRAL

People, students included, generally resist being changed by others without their own volition. This resistance to feeling controlled or manipulated, unfortunately, can prevent students from accepting changes that they might in different circumstances benefit from and embrace. Students need adult guidance and support as they mature and grow into responsible adulthood. Educators lose a precious opportunity if they let the nature of their relationships push students away from them and block their receptivity to the wisdom that adults can offer them.

Therefore, reframing bullying prevention is dependent on changing the nature of the relationships between the members of the school community: power should be shared rather than used to change or control those with less power. Sharing power doesn't mean that adults forfeit their inherent leadership. It is quite the opposite: they use their power to facilitate, structure, and gradually release responsibility when they judge that students are prepared to accept it. Educators act on the assumption that students want to do well and do care about others. They may have to modify the environment, create better conditions, and clarify limits as to what is possible, but they do so in a way that makes it clear to students that they are helping and not just controlling. (Educators can depend on this certainty: students know the difference between those who truly support them and those who pretend to. Students can see right through adults whose ultimate goal is just to get them to comply and to follow the expectations of the school.)

When relationships are based on respect, transparency, and trust, people tend to discover the *changes* that are needed for themselves and for the common good of the community. Trusting relationships are the foundation for all positive growth and learning. Michael Fullan (2001) summed it up this way: "The single factor common to successful change is that relationships improve. If relationships improve, things get better" (p. 5).

Relationships create identities; identities change if the quality and nature of a relationship changes. In my work in schools, I encounter very hard working and dedicated teachers who are demoralized because they feel that there is little if anything than they can do to change a challenging student who does not respond to their directions or instruction. When they encounter these difficult students and have tried "everything" they know, they begin to look for answers outside of school and often blame the student's home environment, which seems even more impossible to change. They are demoralized (as anyone would be) when they encounter a problem that is central to their job and feel unable to influence any change at all. When teachers think that students *can't change*, those same students then act in ways that provide the evidence confirming that belief and nothing changes!

Ironically, these teachers don't realize that they have tremendous influence on these "unchangeable" students who are in reality looking and wanting to change and succeed in school. The most troubled student with many difficult problems presents a great opportunity for educators. When these students are accepted as people and treated with respect regardless of what they might have done, all students learn an important lesson central to reframing bullying prevention: there is never any justification for treating any person in a harsh or demeaning way. When educator-to-student relationships "follow" the golden rule—*treat others as you would want to be treated*—students are taught that there are no exceptions to respecting others. This is a foundational element of reframing bullying prevention and it starts at the top: the relationship between those with power and those without power.

The dominant parent/factory frame that governs how educators do their jobs makes it very difficult for them to put aside the pressures placed on them to control students, for example the pressure to improve test scores. Consequently, students are very sensitive to how adults feel about them and even the slightest hint of disapproval on the part of their teachers tells them that they are the "problem." As these students grow older, it becomes harder for them to accept this identity since they have the possibility of establishing a different persona outside of the sphere of adult authority; they can be someone different in the eyes of their peers. This desire for establishing a self-definition apart from the adult world becomes a strong impetus for students to bully other students.

Unfortunately, unless adults change their relationships with students, then bullying becomes part of the developmental process of students separating from an adult world that they perceive as trying to control what they do and who they are. Similarly, students who don't bully, but witness it will tend to maintain a greater allegiance to their own social world. They refrain from reporting the bullying to adults because they feel the adults don't respect them as individuals who are capable of acting responsibly.

Conversely, when relationships with adults afford students the opportunity to explore and experiment with different identities within the school environment, students are less likely to bully others. When all students are treated as potential leaders and given respect, the students who witnessed the bullying become more likely to accept this identity and act with confidence to help their peers regardless of how they might feel about them.

Students want and need these types of relationships: relationships characterized by mentoring and coaching instead of directing, correcting, and controlling. Students want and need their teachers to stop seeing them as "problems to solve" and instead see them and treat them as people with strengths and abilities who have something to contribute to the world.

Students are more willing to accept reasonable limits and explanations from trustworthy adults for how to navigate the social world rather than from mistrusting ones. Adults become trustworthy when they listen to students, affirm, and trust them. Open lines of communication between adults and students can literally become lifelines providing students with the guidance and adult wisdom they need to ultimately become responsible and successful adults. (Adults who stay stuck in a frame that is always trying to control or manipulate them are not the type of people that students aspire to emulate, anyway.)

Reframing bullying prevention requires that educators gain their true authority with students from the nature and quality of their relationships with them. Those who have power and don't use it to control, but instead share it to help and serve others can have tremendous influence; their leadership promotes leadership in others. Educators *lead* through relationships where they act with integrity; listen without judging; act with respect toward everyone; admit mistakes; and show their own humanity. When educators act with integrity, they provide the right model for students to follow and imitate. These types of relationships create supportive and inclusive learning environments, ergo strong communities.

INFLUENCE GUIDES

It is unreasonable to ask anyone, especially educators, to relinquish "control" unless there is a readily available alternative concept for them to use. Most educators are too dedicated to their job to even contemplate turning over their classrooms or schools to what they perceive as "chaos," or leaving the students in charge, when they firmly believe that the students need to be controlled in order to learn. This fear of having no control can make educators cling more tightly to the traditional command and control structure of school operations.

The same educators who complain about students being unwilling and unmotivated to change also complain when a principal or administrator imposes some new format or policy on them and then uses the threat of consequences to get compliance.

The concept of *influence can offer a viable alternative* to the concept of control for even for the most skeptical educator. Influence offers the greater possibility of achieving a more deeply held common value for educators: the value that students will do what is right because it is right and not in order to get a reward or to avoid a consequence. Most educators want students to be altruistic rather than self-centered.

Controlling students using consequences and rewards can produce positive results, if the criteria for success are compliant behaviors, order, and efficiency. When compared to chaos (a significant number of students acting out of control), any stability can be welcomed and most educators would not be concerned about how it was achieved. The temptation for educators to embrace any means of gaining control is great especially when they have learned to pay more attention to the negative (what is not working) and have a great desire to return to the status quo or the familiar.

It is only when the discussion can look beyond temporary stability for the school and instead focus on greater goals for the students that a different approach can even be explored.

I have yet to meet an educator who wouldn't prefer to have a student learn to make good judgments, act responsibly, learn to care about others, and do so even when "no one was looking." Rather than trying to convince an educator that a less controlling way is better, a better strategy is to start the discussion with this vision of what they really want students to be. Once this common ground is established then a productive discussion can take place on the best way to achieve that goal.

Using influence instead of control also requires more time and puts the responsibility on the educator to establish positive and trusting relationships with the students who are giving them the most trouble (and whom they might not even like). Ironically, many students who act out in a class of twenty to twenty-five students would respond very positively to a teacher who invited that student for lunch and a one-to-one experience. This option allows both the student and teacher to see each other in a different light and to learn to appreciate individual qualities that might not appear in the group context. Many educators however resist this alternative approach because they are afraid that it is rewarding the student's behavior and might cause all the rest of the students to act out in order to get the same treatment. In the factory/dominant parent frame, fairness is treating every person exactly the same with no exceptions made for individual differences or needs. Relationships cannot be a one-size-fits-all. Because each person has a different set of strengths and needs, each meaningful relationship between people has to be different. True and lasting influence can only result from honest and trusting individualized relationships among people.

Educators don't have to be friends with students in order to influence them, but they must have empathy and accept them as people even when they may not approve of their behavior. The students must know that their teacher makes this separation of person from behavior. When students feel that their teacher truly wants what is best for them and they are not viewed as problems getting in the way of the class running smoothly, they will start to internalize the values and reasons offered by the teacher who affirms them and supports them.

This internalization of reasons and values forms the basis for their decision making in situations where the external controls of the teacher or the school are not present. It certainly might take more time and effort to establish these trusting relationships, but they are worth the investment because they are the only way to reach the goal of having the desired change become ingrained as a habit and part of the culture.

I once had teacher whom I supervised say to me, "I ask myself, how would Jim handle this?" That was the best feedback I ever received regarding the influence I had as a leader.

TIES STRENGTHENED

Teachers are professionally trained to instruct a group of individuals. They learn to collect and analyze data to manage and improve individual student learning. It is as if the purpose of school was to train individuals to work in cubicles where they perform solitary tasks. However, the world of work is no longer designed for people to work in isolation from each other.

In the world outside of school, people tend to get jobs, keep their jobs, and advance in their careers by how well they interact with other people. Those who communicate well with others learn more because they receive more information from different points of view. Most companies, organizations, and sporting teams know that the whole is greater than the sum of its parts: a "We" culture learns more and is more productive than a "Me" culture.

Reframing bullying prevention requires educators to invest time in strengthening the connections among individuals. The knowledge and skills needed to build community is not automatically in most teachers' repertoire, so schools must recognize that any hope they have of actually preventing and reducing bullying requires an investment in professional development. As previously discussed, the outcome of getting students to work together goes far beyond stopping a negative; it leads to higher levels of performance and satisfaction for both students and staff.

Susan Weinschenk lists seven drivers of motivation in her 2013 book, *How to Get People to Do Stuff*, and her number one strategy is this:

> **Get people to feel connected to others and they will work harder.** . . . [w]hen people feel they are working with others as a team to reach a goal, they are more motivated to achieve that goal, even without any extrinsic reward, than if working alone. They work harder and longer at the task, become more absorbed and perform better. (p. 10)

Students who might appear to be unmotivated to their teachers often become not just motivated, but animated when they feel a sense of belonging and connection to their peers.

The six tenets for reframing bullying prevention into Building Community Spirit in Schools are dynamically interconnected. Making them the foundation of the change process is not a quick fix for the problem of bullying. It can, however, replace patching together a collection of school improvement initiatives with a coordinated, integrated effort to improve relationships and educational practices toward a core mission of empowering all students as learners and citizens.

Comparison of current frame of bullying prevention and "Building Community Spirit in Schools"

Current Frame of Bullying Prevention (Based on dominant parent/ factory frame) Hierarchical power structure	Reframed as "Building Community Spirit in Schools" (Based on community/ nurturing parent frame) Collaborative power structure
Based on behavioral theory and practice: primary reliance on external motivation with positive and negative reinforcements.	**Based on social psychology theory and practice: mind-set, self-determination theory with intrinsic motivation and autonomy support.**
Bullying is a rule infraction and in some cases a crime. Primary focus on stopping a negative behavior from occurring.	Bullying is a social behavior that is highly influenced by the environmental and social factors affecting how all individuals view themselves and others. Primary focus is on positive behaviors directed toward building strong communities.
Students are cause of the problem; they need to stop bullying.	Students are the solution to the problem. Adults need to model treating them with respect.
Students need to be controlled with rewards and consequences in order to comply with rules.	Students want to learn and help others, but need the right conditions in place to learn their responsibilities as citizens and community members.
Rules and regulations are the primary way to insure that bullying doesn't occur.	Shared values and guiding principles lead to positive words and actions that form social norms for how all members treat each other.
Educators need to enforce the rules and apply consequences for students who break the rules.	Educators' primary role is to help students learn the knowledge, skills, and attitudes needed for them to become empowered bystanders.
Schools need to implement programs, curricula, and other activities designed to stop bullying.	Schools need to make sure that educational practices view and treat students as active participants in their own learning and as responsible citizens.
Students are the primary people who need to follow the rules against bullying. Adults are justified in just expecting students to comply with rules and regulations.	Students need to be involved in the process of learning about the needs of the community and their responsibilities as community members.
Since rules are clear and consequences are predictable, there should be no reason why any student should bully. Problems shouldn't occur.	Students are "works in progress" and inevitably make mistakes in the process of learning responsible behaviors. Problems are opportunities for adults to teach students better ways of meeting their needs.

CLARIFICATION: IT'S NOT EITHER/OR

Reframing bullying prevention into building community spirit in schools does not mean that a school has to drop or eliminate bullying prevention policies, programs, and procedures. These elements of traditional bullying prevention can stay in place and can play an important role in creating a strong school community. They can set limits, provide important information, and support the educational practices emphasized in the reframing process.

Here is an analogy that can illustrate how the more familiar elements of bullying prevention can work with the six tenets of reframing:

Most people might attribute highway safety with people following the traffic rules and staying within the speed limits. Those are necessary, but not sufficient conditions for keeping the roads as safe as possible. People are most safe when there are greater and greater numbers of safe, responsible, and careful drivers on the road. However, if most people just followed the rules of the road while only thinking of their own needs and how to get to where they want to go, then they might stay within the rules of the road, but there would be more accidents than necessary.

Reframing bullying prevention means developing more and more responsible and caring people in the school community. Individuals can know what *not* to do and are more likely to refrain from those negative behaviors when they have developed habits of mind and heart essential for being a member of a strong school community. Reframing bullying prevention doesn't have to be an either/or choice but should provide many options and ways of making each school a better environment for learning. Schools can simultaneously use a prevention approach to bullying and a positive promotion approach to build community.

SUMMARY

- How educators talk about students reveals the frame that governs how they do their job: how they treat students and how students respond to that treatment.
- Educators have a choice to view problems with students from their own perspective or from the students' perspective. This difference in perspective determines the direction of all subsequent actions related to the students.
- Students can be viewed as problems to solve or viewed as the solutions to the problems. This reframing of how students are viewed serves as a reflection of how bullying prevention can be reframed.
- The term bullying prevention itself can be counterproductive because it is about stopping a negative behavior from happening. Effective bullying prevention requires an array of positive practices integrated into the culture of schools.

- Reframing bullying prevention requires tapping into positive emotions and identities that generate creative and adaptive strategies to transform the school climate.
- Reframing bullying prevention needs a different frame from the dominant parent / factory frame of schools. This more productive frame doesn't have to be invented. Schools can reclaim their original purpose to become a community where students learn how to be responsible citizens and maintain our democratic form of government.
- Reframing bullying prevention is about embracing the concept of schools as communities with the moral function of helping students form habits of heart and mind and establishing social norms of caring and respect.
- Reframing bullying prevention into Building Community Spirit in schools connotes the positive energy needed to transform schools into places where people care for and value all members of the community.
- The six tenets of reframing bullying prevention are as follows:

    o **Student-centered**: students are considered the solution to the problem of bullying and not the cause of it. Educators must view problems through the eyes of the students they serve.
    o **Principle-based**: members of the school community are guided by values and principles rather than just rules and procedures.
    o **Integrated practice**: bullying prevention cannot be a program or curriculum delivered to students. Educational practice must reflect the values and principles of a student-centered approach to teaching and learning.
    o **Relationships central**: the establishment of trusting and respectful relationships with students is the basis for all progress in bullying prevention and higher levels of learning.
    o **Influence guides:** instead of viewing students as people who need controlling, educators can shift to the concept of influencing students using positive relationships and common values and guiding principles.
    o **Ties strengthened**: time and energy need to be devoted to nurturing and strengthening the ties among all members of the school community.

- Reframing bullying prevention does not mean that policies, programs, and procedures related to bullying prevention need to be discarded. Reframing bullying prevention works with those elements and actually enhances their meaning and effectiveness in the school environment. Schools can have prevention and promotion approaches occurring simultaneously.

ACTIVITY FOR REFRAMING BULLYING PREVENTION INTO BUILDING COMMUNITY SPIRIT IN SCHOOLS

Premise for the Activity

Many staff might agree that schools need to "change," but don't know what that "change" requires. Even if they did have a clear vision of that "change," they might not know how to achieve it and might not feel confident in moving in that direction.

Most educators have become "who they are" by being successful in the factory/dominant parent frame, so it is not surprising that they have difficulty envisioning schools differently from their own experience of school.

The best way to start the change process for reframing is to tap into people's own experiences and allow them to reflect on their own learning. If their own experiences can be reconciled with the theory and research that provides the rationale for change, they will be more open to considering making changes in how they do their jobs.

This activity attempts to integrate the theory and research into practical first steps for changing educational practice. There are several phases of the activity that mirror the reframing process from theory to practice for the participants. This activity can also serve as a model for how to instruct students in the classroom.

Outcomes

- Connecting personal experience of positive learning to theory and practice
- Comparing and contrasting the "framing" of schools
- Aligning the mind-set research and self-determination theory with personal experience of positive learning
- Specifying instructional and teaching practices that facilitate growth mind-sets, student autonomy, and stronger community

Phase One: "Tapping into Your Own Data Set" (ten minutes)

Set up: Assign individuals to groups of no more than five people. Sit each group at a separate table.

Materials: Chart paper, sticky notes, and markers.

Rationale: Since there is emphasis placed on data informed practice, this part of the activity reframes data from being just a set of numbers into the personal data that people carry related to their own experiences as a learner. Participants tap into their own data set (i.e., personal story), hear other stories and then analyze that data to form some conclusions about the conditions necessary for positive learning experiences. (Make sure to share this rationale for the activity with the participants.)

Individual Task: Present this statement to the participants "Recall a very positive learning experience in your life. This can be one that happened in school or out of school. It can be recent or in the past, formal or informal, a group experience or individual experience."

Distribute a reflection guide or sheet for each person and provide at least ten minutes for participants to work individually and quietly.

GUIDING QUESTIONS FOR INDIVIDUAL REFLECTION

What is the positive learning experience?

Who was involved with this experience?

Where did it happen?

When did it happen? (Your age, stage of your life, over how long a period of time)

Why were you learning this?

How did you learn it?

What were your feelings prior to learning it?

What were your feelings while you were learning it?

What were your feelings right after you learned it?

Looking back on the experience, what feelings come to mind?

How did the person (people) involved in the learning experience treat you?

Describe the actual process of learning that you experienced.

How did you go from being a novice to gaining competence?

What did you learn about yourself from that experience?

How has that experience influenced your life?

List any memorable words or incidents that stand out in your recollection.

Group Sharing and Note-Taking: (five to ten minutes)

Each participant takes two to three minutes to share their experience using the guide to tell *the story*.

Those listening should take notes related to what they think made the experience positive.

Participants can ask brief clarifying questions following each story.

Individual Element Generation: (five to ten minutes)

After each participant has told his or her story. Have the group stand over a sheet of chart paper placed on their table.

Ask each participant to write down **one** element or factor that they think contributed to the positive learning that each person experienced. For example: "Choice of what was learned" would be written on a sticky note.

Make Sure There Is Only One Element Listed per Sticky Note

After they write one element per sticky note, they randomly stick the note on the chart paper without regard to what the other participants are writing down and placing on the paper.

There is no limit on the number of elements each participant can place down on the sheet of chart paper.

After each person has exhausted the number of elements that they can think of then they can stop and scan what the group has put down.

Group Vision: (ten to fifteen minutes)

Depending on the group, the activity leader can assign roles (facilitator, recorder, reporter, and timekeeper) or leave it to the group to organize how they do the task.

State that the group has the task of analyzing and illustrating all of the elements of positive learning into a visual representation. They can use the sticky notes themselves or remove the sticky notes and translate them into pictures, images, concepts or mind maps, as an example, but it should represent their collective vision of what constitutes a positive learning experience.

Each participant can briefly summarize the key elements that he or she put down on the sheet. The group can ask clarifying questions to make sure that each member understands each sticky note statement.

It is the group's task to arrange the sticky notes into categories. They should also articulate and label those categories on the chart paper.

When they are finished the sheet of chart paper with the group vision of the positive learning experience can be put up on the wall so that it is visible to all of the participants.

Large group sharing: Depending on the size of the whole group, the visual representation of each small group can be shared in different ways:

- The entire group can walk around the room to view each small group's visual representation. Individuals can be instructed to take notes on what they noticed.
- One person from each small group can be asked to briefly describe their visual representation to the whole group.
- One person from each group can be asked to stand by the visual representation to answer questions from the people from the other groups walking around and viewing the visions placed on the wall.

The activity leader can ask the whole group for comments and questions about the elements of the positive learning or the activity itself.

REFRAMING THE ENVIRONMENT

Rationale: This part of the activity presents contrasting visions of the work environment. It shows a factory and a modern day workplace. Not only are the two environments very different, participants have to specify how they are different and then connect them to their own experiences as learners.

Procedure

Show a video clip of a factory: a scene from *Modern Times*, a movie directed and starring Charlie Chaplin where he works on a conveyer belt, or a scene from *I Love Lucy*, a television show directed by William Asher and starring Lucille Ball where she is working on a conveyer belt wrapping chocolates (Asher, 1952).

Ask participants to write down their observations of the working conditions of the factory.

Allow time for them to share their observations with a partner.

The facilitator then asks each group to contribute one observation about the working environment and writes it down on a sheet of chart paper.

Repeat this procedure for a different work environment—for example at the computer animation studio of Pixar (Ryzik, 2011).

Show the video clip at http://www.youtube.com/watch?v=CXtsEhUwTmc-which is a six, minute tour of the Pixar studios.

Ask participants to write their observations about the Pixar work environment.

Allow time for them to share their observations with a partner.

The facilitator asks each pair to share their observations about this work environment and to write them down on a sheet of chart paper.

Put the two sheets of chart paper next to each other. Give participants thirty seconds to study both sheets. Open the discussion to the whole group to comment on how the two environments differ.

Ask the groups that created visual representations of positive learning environments to indicate where their visual representation best fits on a continuum of factory to Pixar.

ALIGNING THEORY WITH EXPERIENCE

Rationale: Good theories help us make sense of our world. The theory of mind-sets can help the participants gain a deeper understanding of why their learning experiences were positive.

Procedure

Show the video by Eduardo Briceño about mind-sets which can be found at http://www.youtube.com/watch?v=pN34FNbOKXc.

Ask the participants to take notes on the video (about 14 minutes). Ask them to be prepared to share two or three most important points (MIPs).

Ask them to share their MIPs with a partner.

The facilitator can then ask each pair to share one MIP and proceed until each pair has contributed one point. These are written down on a separate sheet of chart paper.

JIGSAW FOLLOW-UP

Rationale: The video is a good introduction to mind-set theory. The participants gain a deeper understanding by responding to the same ideas and concepts in print.

Procedure

Use the following resource:
Teaching Adolescents to Become Learners: The Role of Noncogntive Factors in Shaping School Performance: A Critical Literature Review (2012) by Camille Farrington, Melissa Roderick, Elaine Allensworth, Jenny Nagaoka, Tasha Seneca Keyes, David Johnson, and Nicole Beechum.

The participants should still be in their small groups.

Have every person read the introductory column on page 28 and page 73 of the section titled *Students Earn High Grades When They Show Perseverance and Strong Academic Behaviors.*

After each participant has read those pages, one person from each group is responsible for reading a section and reporting back to the group about what they read.

Person 1 reads section "I belong in this academic community."

Person 2 reads section "My ability and competence grow with my effort."

Person 3 reads section "I can succeed at this."

Person 4 reads section "This work has value for me."

After each person has reported back to their small group, the group can discuss their reaction to the readings.

Following their discussion, ask each group to look at their vision of positive learning that developed. Working as group, they should decide to place an appropriate number on the element of positive learning, for example, if an element for positive learning was "I felt supported by the other people in the class," then a number one (I belong in this academic community) is placed on this element. They should try to have each of the elements correspond to one of the four mind-set numbers.

SELF-DETERMINATION THEORY

Follow a procedure similar to the one for the mind-set theory and research using the following YouTube video featuring Daniel Pink, and produced by RSA animation: http://www.youtube.com/watch?v=u6XAPnuFjJc.

Use follow-up jigsaw activity reading on self-determination theory selecting from the articles cited in this book.

Have groups identify the elements on their positive learning visual representations sheet using A for autonomy, M for mastery, R for relatedness, and P for purpose or meaning.

Edmondson's Research Activity

Amy Edmondson's research identified two essential conditions necessary for positive growth and learning for any organization: psychological safety and accountability.

Psychological safety means that people feel safe to make mistakes and take risks. Accountability means that people are committed to continuous growth and learning.

She provided a matrix showing how the combinations of those two elements produced different types of environments.

	Low Accountability	High Accountability
High Psychological Safety	**Comfort Zone** Socializing Unchallenged Low work ethic Buddy-buddy relationships	**Learning Zone** Collaboration Risk taking Openness to new ideas Creativity Learning from mistakes Work can be playful and productive Commitment
Low Psychological Safety	**Apathy zone** Top-down management Resistance to change "It's not my job" attitude "It's just a job" attitude Nothing will change	**Anxiety Zone** Risk adverse Narrow focus on self Fear of consequences Doing "just enough" to please Rule focused Lack of confidence in self Compliance

Source: Adapted from Edmondson, 2012

Participants can work in small groups to "operationalize" psychological safety and accountability. They can create separate lists of words and/or actions that promote high levels of psychologically safe environments and high levels of accountability.

After they generate these lists, they can return to their original visual representation of positive learning experiences and label their elements as HPS for high psychological safety and HA for high accountability.

SELECTING SPECIFIC TEACHING / INSTRUCTIONAL LANGUAGE ACTIONS

Have each small group generate a T chart for specifying words and actions that an educator can use to promote a positive learning environment; an environment where students have more autonomy, better connections and community, and opportunities to develop competency and mastery.

Based on their own analysis of positive learning environments, mind-set theory, and research and self-determination theory and research, each team should select at least three ways they can speak differently to students and three things they can do differently with students to improve the conditions for learning in the classroom.

Have participants review the controlled motivation chart and the autonomy supportive chart and compare the list they generated with the instructional behaviors listed on these charts.

IMPACT ON BULLYING PREVENTION EFFORTS

Have small groups generate three ways that improving the learning environment and promoting a positive mind-set in students can positively impact bullying prevention efforts.

CONCLUSION

Provide time for staff to reflect on the activity itself.

Ask each individual to write down one thing that they are willing to try to change and/or add to the current repertoire of words and actions toward students.

FOLLOW-UP

The group can determine how to best measure how they are implementing their recommended changes in how they speak and act toward students. They can also determine ways to measure how students are responding to their changes.

At subsequent meetings, it is important to monitor how the staff is doing and to share stories of how students are responding to their changes in words and actions.

SECTION II

The Process of Reframing Bullying Prevention

Educators have inherited, not chosen, the current frame of bullying prevention, so helping them discover other ways to view the problem of bullying is a crucial step in the reframing process. Chapter 7 describes three overall guidelines that can set the parameters of the whole process of reframing. Then, Chapters 8–10 offer eight strategies for reframing bully prevention that are designed to guide educators to rethink and redesign the school and classroom environment. The strategies are offered along with a set of resources, activities, and recommendations. Taken collectively, they provide a common set of concepts and vocabulary to allow members of the school community to have meaningful and productive conversations about what type of school they want and need.

The aim of these strategies is to get people thinking and talking to each other in ways that they typically are not used to doing. To make these discussions the basis for concrete actions, these strategies are worded as *verbs*: they describe what a community should be "doing" or trying to achieve.

Effective change strategies reach beyond merely trying to rationally convince people to change. They are designed to inject a new and different element into their way of looking at the world, to gently disrupt typical ways of interpreting the world. These strategies should catch people slightly off guard, pique their curiosity, provoke reflection, and connect some dots that usually are not connected. These strategies also are grounded in the human element of their professional lives that is forgotten in the daily interactions and preoccupations that fill up a person's day.

A basic assumption that guides each strategy is that people need to *own* their change. The decision to change what one thinks, feels, says, or does is not a one-time occurrence and typically does not happen with a flash of insight followed by a dramatic transformation of the person who changes. Change is a dynamic process of people influencing each other over time.

Another basic assumption that guides each strategy is that positive change requires people to communicate on a deeper level than usual. When people enter into open honest discussions in the context of trusting relationships, they can explore more deeply held and often undiscovered values and beliefs. When these belief systems are not just uncovered, but are placed front and center in the discussion, people begin to collectively affirm values and beliefs different from the ones that are *concealed* in many school practices. This type of deeper discussion can form the foundation for aligning shared values with words and actions.

These strategies are designed to be direction setters, not complete travel plans. Each community must design its own journey for where it wants to go; there must be a collective decision about goals and tentative plans for achieving them. A community must also trust itself to communicate about how they are doing to make adjustments and course corrections.

I deliberately tried to be as concise as possible in labeling the strategies. Effective strategies do little good if no one can remember them. I tried to make them rhyme whenever possible as another way to help people remember them.

The strategies are divided into three categories:

"Heart" strategies (Chapter 8): These strategies are related to issues of moral purpose and the human element of education. They are designed to emphasize the basic idea that education is about people interacting and influencing other people. These strategies should help people discuss some basic questions, such as Why are we here? What are we really doing? Who are we in relation to each other?

"Who" strategies (Chapter 9): These strategies are related to the roles and identities that people assume in schools and how these affect what they say and do. These activities are designed to demonstrate how what one says or does with another person shapes that person's identity. Changing how we treat others has a profound impact on how a person acts and what a person subsequently feels, thinks, and says.

"Do" strategies (Chapter 10): These strategies are related to specific and intentional actions that can leverage significant change in any organization. These strategies provide a menu for those in leadership positions for shifting the direction of how people view themselves and others.

ORGANIZATION OF EACH STRATEGY

Each strategy section is organized in the following manner.

- Quotation
- Story/anecdote
- What it is
- How it works
- Resources
- Activities
- Recommendations

7

Guidelines for Reframing Bullying Prevention

"If you want truly to understand something, try to change it."

—Kurt Lewin

"So what? Now what?" These are the very valid questions to ask after reading the first section of this book. Educators who are convinced that bullying prevention should be reframed can be left wondering where to start and how to navigate the process of reframing. However, my response has to be consistent with the key concepts of reframing: if I offered a program that provided the "answers" to the process of reframing, I would be contradicting all that I know about the change process.

There are, however four responses that I can offer.

- Right now, schools have the knowledge and capability of reframing bullying prevention and building a stronger school community.
- However, being able to change is directly related to believing that it is possible to change and that students, staff, and parents can create environments that reflect the key tenets of what it means to be a strong community.
- Importantly, the process for reframing requires a different way of thinking about school change and subsequently a different way of interacting with others in the school community.

- Finally, the reframing is a process not a product. It requires that people listen to each other, are open to new ideas, and are willing to invest in the effort and accept the struggle that sometimes is required.

The rest of this section provides some guidance and direction for starting and navigating the reframing process. It offers information and resources that are not typically found in books about bullying prevention. There are activities for members of the school community to participate in that *show* rather than just *tell* many of key ideas and concepts essential to reframing. There are specific recommendations for schools to consider that can support the reframing process, not just for bullying prevention, but also for reframing the school environment.

I offer some useful concepts from social psychology filtered through the eyes of a long-term participant in schools who now has the time to read and reflect on this research. Although I am not the perfect messenger to convey these concepts, because I worked for thirty-five years in schools, I might have some credibility with educators whose jobs often prohibit them from doing this reading and reflection. They have my empathy and my admiration, so my work is designed to support their work.

THREE GUIDELINES FOR REFRAMING FOR BULLYING PREVENTION

These three guidelines offer the essential elements of successful change that typically are not present in most school change initiatives. (This is not a criticism, but an observation derived from many years working in schools.) These guidelines are primarily designed to make certain that well-intentioned educators who are seeking positive change don't act in a way that inadvertently complicates the problem or contradicts the main message of the change initiative. Hopefully, educators who use these guidelines in their thinking, strategy, and planning will find that they offer a viable alternative to traditional approaches that seem to yield little if any success in bullying prevention.

GUIDELINE 1: GIVE THE BENEFIT OF THE DOUBT: RECOGNIZE THE FUNDAMENTAL ATTRIBUTION ERROR

"Please don't understand me too quickly."

—Andre Gide

Full disclosure: I originally titled this guideline "Avoid the Fundamental Attribution Error (FAE)." I offered this recommendation at workshops for educators where I also admonished them about making this error. Looking back, I realize that I was the one making an error. It is impossible to avoid making the FAE; it is part of what it means to be human. It was presumptuous of me to declare that professionals should be able to avoid making the FAE; it was asking them to do the impossible. I was telling them to be free of preconceived notions; I was telling them not to draw conclusions or make sense of the world in a way that allows people to function on daily basis. I didn't realize how off base I was until I went back to where I first encountered this concept in Malcolm Gladwell's *The Tipping Point* (2002) and reread this passage:

> The mistake we make in thinking of character as something unified and all-encompassing is very similar to a kind of blind spot in the way we process information. Psychologists call this tendency the Fundamental Attribution Error (FAE), which is a pretty fancy way of saying that when it comes to interpreting other people's behavior, human beings invariably make the mistake of overestimating the importance of fundamental character traits and underestimating the importance of the situation and the context. It's a kind of shorthand. If we constantly had to qualify every assessment of those around us, how would we make sense of the world? How much harder would it be to make the thousands of decisions we are required to make about whether we like someone or love someone or trust someone or want to give someone advice? (pp. 161–162)

Recognizing the FAE makes a lot more sense than expecting people to avoid making it. Many people routinely recognize the FAE, however, it is called something different: "giving people the benefit of the doubt" or "cutting people some slack." We intuitively know the importance of recognizing the FAE because none of us ever wants someone to judge us based on observing us at our worst (e.g., when we might have been sick, tired, or haven't had our first cup of coffee). Since we don't want to be judged this way, we often suspend our judgment of others and wait for a better situation to arise or wait to catch the person on a different day. Making the FAE is probably one of the most common examples of *fast thinking* that we employ.

However, the FAE is recognized and applied more in the business world than in schools. Since businesses really have no controlling power over consumers, they recognize that they can't just demand that people buy their goods or services. Instead, they believe that people can be influenced without being forced to change. Few businesses sit on their hands and just hope that people change enough to favor them over another company; they know they must do something to survive and thrive. Wise companies analyze all of the circumstances and contexts that influence how people think and act and then use this knowledge based on empirical research to design strategies to influence people's behavior. (These strategies have been so effective for businesses that one of the premier researchers, Robert Cialdini wrote the book *Influence* (2001) in part to alert the general public to the levers of influence being used to manipulate consumer behaviors.)

The reason why schools don't readily accept the FAE is that they do have the power to get people to do things that they might not want to do. Students have to attend school and educators have a clear job description and position in the hierarchy where they can be told what to do. Why should any person in a position of power be concerned with what is going on inside the hearts and minds of those persons with less power? Why is it important to try to figure out circumstances or context when the school can already tell them what to do? When students fail to comply with a direction and comport themselves differently from the school's expectations, it is typically interpreted as a sign that something is wrong with the students and/or their families. It is seldom interpreted as a sign that the school hasn't figured out the best strategy to connect with those students. In the book *Influencer* (Patterson et al., 2008) the authors state that failing to recognize the FAE is a lost opportunity for change, "We assume that when people don't change, it's simply because they don't want to change. In making this simplistic assumption, we lose an enormous lever for change" (p. 112).

Although it can be liberating in a way to know that there are many levers available for change, it can also be threatening, especially for those who feel the responsibility for changing students. It can be threatening because they don't yet know that there are *levers* for change, and what those *levers* are. Even if they know what the levers of change are, the truth is that most educators don't have the skills or experience to use them effectively. So, instead of exploring the circumstances or factors influencing a person's behavior, educators tend to remain "stuck" in exerting power and control over those individuals who in their minds need "changing." In those situations, it becomes safer to put the blame on those who refuse to change or are uncooperative, and attribute this refusal and lack of cooperation to a deficiency in the students' character or because of a recognized disability.

When it came to students who had problems adjusting to school or cooperating with educators, in my years of experience in schools, we were successful when we recognized our natural tendency to make the FAE and

- acknowledged our feelings;
- put our feelings on hold;
- slowed the problem-solving process down; and
- explored a variety of options and variations in the circumstances surrounding the student and the problems he or she was having in the school environment.

We were unsuccessful when we failed to suspend our judgments and recognize our tendency to make the FAE. In those situations, we were less effective in finding ways to alter the circumstances in the environment based on taking the student's perspective; instead, there was usually an escalation of the power struggles with the student and subsequently with the student's parents.

WHY SCHOOLS TYPICALLY FAIL TO RECOGNIZE AND MAKE THE FAE WITH BULLYING

Sometimes bullying behavior is so abhorrent, causes such damage, and appears to be so difficult to address that educators easily make the fundamental attribution error as a way to figure out how students could violate a basic sense of decency. There is also a lot of pressure exerted on educators from legal mandates and the general public to stop bullying, so they don't feel they can afford to take the time to slow the process down and get a more accurate understanding of the social dynamics that drive most of the bullying that occurs in schools. As I stated earlier, the emotion at the heart of the need to keep students safe should spur all educators to action, but when those same emotions govern all actions needed to address the problem, then the problem usually just persists.

For example, the bullying on the bus incident recounted in Chapter 1 followed this pattern: the act was horrific; the students who did it were "bad"; their parents were at fault; and the only way they would learn not to do it again was for them to receive severe consequences. That pattern is played out over and over again in schools everywhere and the rate of bullying in schools stubbornly refuses to decrease.

The problem of bullying will continue to confound and frustrate even the most well-intentioned actions unless there is a recognition that FAE plays a key role in interpreting and understanding how bullying manifests itself in schools. It is the type of problem that requires *"slow thinking"* or a controlled response that leads to a more thorough analysis of how social, psychological, and developmental factors influence how students interact with one another. This way of approaching the problem may initially generate some uncertainty, but that is preferable to adopting approaches that provide comfort and familiarity, but are ineffective.

BULLYING: A PRODUCT OF CIRCUMSTANCES AND CONTEXT

Bullying is a problem that is ideally suited to examination using the concept of the FAE. The very act of bullying is highly dependent on all of the people involved and both the internal and external circumstances of a situation. Very seldom is an act of bullying a simple intentional act to hurt another person in isolation from the social context of the peer group. Bullying is usually done for an audience, or serves a social function to change an individual's status in the social group. Research consistently demonstrates that the most effective interventions to decrease individual acts of bullying are interventions that seek to change the social dynamics of the situation, specifically to change the audience response to bullying. This is precisely what the social psychological concept behind the FAE advocates: a shift from attributing causation to character issues and focus attention on the internal and external circumstances of the social context where the incidents occur. However, most policies and procedures make the FAE by relying on interventions focused on the perpetrators of bullying and try to change their behaviors through the use of external controls, such as rewards and consequences.

The current frame of school and bullying prevention profoundly affects *where* a school looks for solutions to problems. The FAE and other concepts from social psychology really don't fit the frame of dominant parent/factory frame. The FAE requires those in positions of power to explore the circumstances and influences (seen and unseen) that influence people to act in certain ways; it requires empathy and taking the perspective of another. The current factory/dominant parent frame, the command and control structure of schools, can easily dismiss any discussion of these circumstances as excuses for behavior as not holding people accountable for their actions. The bottom line or all that matters for this frame is what people do or don't do, and not what might have influenced their actions.

If people comply, the system (schools under the current frame) works as it should, and if people don't comply then the system can't work. People are there to fit the system; they are the ones who need to change. The people in authority use power to get the status quo restored. Anything else is superfluous to the discussion and distracts from the real issue of getting the system working as it should. In this type of system, problems are aberrations that shouldn't happen in the first place, so when they do, those with the power tend to respond emotionally, often with anger, and more likely than not attribute the problem to the person and his or her unwillingness to cooperate. The perpetrator who breaks the rule or law does so because of a character flaw or a problem with upbringing. Since a person's character and upbringing are not very amenable to change, those in power react emotionally to their own feeling of powerlessness and view the students who have problems as immovable objects. Therefore, the only recourse is to exert greater force or power in order to change people who need to be changed and who are hard to change.

AN EXAMPLE OF NOT RECOGNIZING THE FAE IN SCHOOLS

Here is a story from school that illustrates how not recognizing the FAE can lead to confusing and frustrating power struggles among well-meaning, dedicated professionals and young children who act with little awareness of how they are so easily influenced by what is going on inside and outside of them.

I was observing in a first grade classroom a student who was having behavioral problems. This student was clearly identified, even to his peers, as someone who caused trouble for the teacher. He was a student who was vulnerable to being bullied and someone who would consequently retaliate by bullying others. The teacher expressed both frustration and confusion regarding why this student did what he did. He disrupted her teaching so much that it was almost impossible for her to view the problems through the eyes of this student. She was stuck in seeing him as a problem that was impacting the rest of the class. She attributed it to his lack of respect for her, which had to be because of a failing in his upbringing. He became "an immovable" object who seemed impossible to change.

I happened to observe him during a lesson that allowed him to draw and to write about a schoolwide assembly that was very interesting to him. He did very well with this lesson and remained on task as well as any other student. When the lesson was over, he and the rest of the class were leaving to go to lunch, but I called him over to me, with his teacher sitting next to me, and asked him how he thought he did during the lesson. He lowered his head and said that he didn't do well because he made a mistake (he had to erase and respell some of the words he wrote). The teacher was surprised to hear that the student viewed his positive learning experience negatively and clarified for him that she didn't expect him not to make mistakes, but just to try his best. She sincerely believed what she said, but obviously this was not the message that he received from her. The student believed that success was not making mistakes; this was what he learned from his daily interactions in that classroom environment.

This real-life example points out some important issues for reframing bullying prevention and classroom interactions.

- The student made his quick, *fast thinking* interpretation of his teacher as someone who expected and wanted no mistakes in order to give him approval. He internalized this unspoken expectation and evaluated his performance by it.
- If his best was not good enough in his own eyes, how must he feel about lessons where he doesn't perform according to expectations?
- His behavior revealed how much he wanted to do well and his apprehension and fear of not doing well rather than a conscious decision not to cooperate or to show disrespect to the teacher.
- His uncooperative behavior was heavily influenced by what he *thought* about his teacher and himself.
- Simply reinforcing his positive behavior following the lesson would do little good if his own perception of his performance was negative; it could inadvertently create more confusion and anxiety on his part.
- Ironically, the behavior problems were influenced more by his desire to do well, please his teacher, and gain acceptance from his classmates

than from any desire to defy or disrespect his teacher. This desire to do well combined with a lack of confidence in being able to perform without making mistakes made him more anxious and uncertain, which caused his behavior to be more reactive, impulsive, and unpredictable.
- The "answer" to his problems could be found in examining those *circumstances* in the environment. When he was doing a task that involved a strength of his and a topic of interest, his behavior improved. It also improved when he was not threatened by the task: the fear of failing and displeasing the teacher was lessened.
- Failing to *recognize the tendency to make the FAE* can create the circumstances for future bullying. The student with problems can be stigmatized and identified as a possible target for mistreatment, which is justified in the minds of the students because he didn't comply and caused problems for the teacher and the class.

Trust, however, can be a positive product of recognizing the FAE in action. We suspend our initial judgments and conclusions about people until we see them in different situations and allow them to talk and act in ways that disprove our initial perception and judgment of them. For example, if the teacher in this story could have assumed that the student wanted to do well and invested some time in discovering how he felt about school and himself, then she could have avoided simply interpreting his behavior as a lack of respect for her and subsequently blaming his parents. When we realize that we need to give people a *greater sample size* of their words and actions before drawing conclusions about them, we avoid attributing all they do to their character or lack of it. Conversely, once we have made a positive or negative judgment about a person's character, we often ignore or discount words or behaviors that are inconsistent with our perception of that character. In sum, when we make the fundamental attribution error we are in essence saying, "My mind is made up so don't confuse me with the facts."

SOCIAL PSYCHOLOGICAL AND BEHAVIORAL APPROACHES

Traditionally schools addressed these behavioral problems by arranging for the right set of antecedent behaviors and consequential behaviors to occur in the right sequence at the appropriate times as a way to decrease some behaviors and increase others. So, in many ways there are similarities between behavioral approaches and social psychological approaches because they both consider environmental and contextual issues. The main difference is that the social psychological approach extends the circumstantial variables to what is going on in the mind and heart of people—something that can't be seen or directly observed. How people think of themselves involves factors that affect how they act, yet these factors are not ones we can observe, only infer. The social psychological approach adds a degree of *empathy* to analyzing environmental factors in order to figure out what is going on *inside* the people in problem situations. Using a social psychological perspective, the person or team intervening with the student who presents a problem looks at the world from the student's perspective and factors that perception into what needs to happen in the environment for the student.

The social psychological approach attributes a person's action to how a person thinks and feels about others, the world and his or her self rather than merely viewing behavior as a response to positive and negative reinforcements in the external environment. It is not easy to always correctly infer what is going on in a person's heart and mind, but the effort is worth it. For example, a student might feel like he or she is an outsider and not connected the other students in the class. This feeling of not belonging causes great anxiety that manifests itself in a variety of inappropriate behaviors. If educators change this situation and restore a sense of belonging to this student, the student changes his or her behavior for the better. Recognizing the FAE means that educators might just have to keeping looking and trying to find what the student needs and avoiding the understandable, but dangerous trap of attributing the problem to the person or just the observable aspects of the environment.

Going back to the story about the bus aide and the middle school boys, the FAE was not recognized by anyone in the media and therefore the problem was clearly attributable to the students as morally deficient kids raised by negligent parents. Since they were already so "bad," the only way they could learn or reverse their behavior was to suffer a severe consequence along with having to accept the condemnation of being bad kids. They needed to be punished for who they are rather than helping them to understand what they did and why they did it.

Students, therefore, are in a very vulnerable position because when adults fail to recognize their tendency for making the FAE and their tendency to draw definite negative conclusions about students, those students *believe* those conclusions about themselves and their characters. The FAE that adults make about them sadly can become their identity and often determines the subsequent reality that results when they act out that identity.

If adults are going to make the FAE about students' character, they should always make it a positive one and interpret any evidence to the contrary as being out of character for the student.

In sum, behavioral approaches focus on visible behaviors of the person and environmental factors around the person, while social psychological approaches focus on the thoughts, emotions and perceptions that people have about themselves and their world and interpret their words and actions as manifestations of those thoughts, emotions, and perceptions.

EMPIRICAL EVIDENCE OF THE FAE PHENOMENON

One of the best examples of how situational factors rather than innate characteristics influence outcomes or explain problems is the research on *stereotype threat*. This research is convincing proof of the benefits of including these often unseen or unobservable elements when evaluating a problem rather than assuming the problem lies within the person.

The best example of this research (Brown & Day, 2006) is one where the mere substitution of one word for another resulted in significant differences on an intelligence test. In this research, minority students were given a visual intelligence test. One group was told it was a *puzzle with no diagnostic purposes* behind it and the other group was told it *was an intelligence test*. The difference in scores was significant. The scores of the students taking the "test" were significantly lower than the ones doing a "puzzle" (*it was the exact same task*). This difference in scores represented the persistent gap in scores between minority students and nonminority students. In this situation, minority students' lower performance in the test was not because of any deficit in their ability. It was the unseen internal circumstance related to their identities as members of a minority and the stress that was therefore added to the testing situation. The "test" was a threat to them. Instead of performing as an individual, they accepted the added burden of having to prove or disprove the stereotypes existing in our culture. The "puzzle" presented no threat and they were able to separate their own performance from their minority group membership so that once this psychological burden was lifted, they performed as well as the nonminority students. Nonminority students, by the way, performed about the same regardless of whether it was called a test or a puzzle. There are many, many more research studies showing how this stereotype threat has a profound influence on how people perform in many situations.

RESEARCH ON BYSTANDER BEHAVIOR AND THE FAE

A colleague of mine who works at a high school told me about a situation where a high school student was walking out of his class and collapsed on the floor. The students who were walking behind him continued to leave the room, stepping over him, or around him. Finally, the teacher attended to the student on the floor, who turned out to be all right. This scene was recorded by a security camera. Staff were shocked and dismayed when the video showed that a significant number of students did nothing to help.

Chapter 7 Guidelines for Reframing Bullying Prevention   167

Initially, they wondered how students could so callous, indifferent, and uncaring when it was so obvious that a peer was in need.

My colleague decided to suspend judgment of these students and interviewed each of them individually. They each expressed their own concern for the student and their remorse for not helping. They all said that in retrospect that wanted to help and had remorse for not acting on their desire to help. The reasons they gave for why they didn't help varied from

- thought that the student might have been joking;
- weren't sure what to do;
- didn't know if they really could help;
- thought that the teacher would help instead and would know what to do; and
- it happened so fast that they were surprised by it, so they just continued on as usual.

These answers reflect the NOTS of bystander behavior described in Chapter 4. There was some constraining unseen psychological element that prevented these students from helping, when on some level they wanted to help. The thoughts and feelings they had were very much tied to the context of the event.

- For example, if a student collapsed on the playground when no adults were around, they might have acted differently.
- If they were given training in first aid or crisis management, they might have acted differently.
- If they had a different sense of their role and responsibilities as a student, they might have acted differently.

There are many, many research studies exploring the great variety of reasons why people very often don't help in situations when it appears to be so simple and clear-cut to those who are not in the situation where help is needed. When examining bystander behavior in bullying situations, there are even more situational and subtle factors that either constrain action or promote action on the part of people who typically are well-intentioned and of good character. Understanding the FAE is essential for ultimately untying the NOTS of bystander behavior in all members of the school community.

Another research study showed how just changing what students thought about what other students thought (an unobservable variable) decreased the rates of bullying in a school. In a 2011 study of middle school students by Perkins, Craig, and Perkins, the researchers hypothesized that given the prevalence of bullying incidents in the media and the increased awareness of it in the general public, that students thought the rates of bullying and the numbers of students who approved of bullying was much higher than in reality it really was.

They surveyed the students asking for their estimates of how much bullying was actually occurring in their school and also asking them about their own attitudes toward bullying. The researchers hypothesized correctly that there was a significant discrepancy between the students' estimation and approval of bullying and the actual attitudes toward bullying in the school. The intervention involved putting the actual statistical results on posters placed around the school. For example, there were posters that publicized statistics such as these:

- Most middle school students (9 out of 10) agree that students should always try to be friendly with students who are different from themselves.
- 95 percent of middle school students say students should NOT tease others in a mean way, call others hurtful names, or spread unkind stories about other students.
- 94 percent of middle school students believe students should NOT shove, kick, hit, trip, or hair pull another student.
- 9 out of 10 middle school students agree that students should NOT threaten to hit another student, even if they don't actually hit the other student.
- Most middle school students (3 out of 4) do *not* exclude someone from a group to make them feel bad.

The authors of the study summarized their results this way:

A pre-/post-intervention comparison of results revealed significant reductions overall in perceptions of peer bullying and pro bullying attitudes, while personal bullying and victimization of others were also reduced; support for reporting bullying to adults at school and in one's family increased. The extent of reductions across school sites was associated with the prevalence and extent of recall of seeing poster messages reporting actual peer norms drawn from the initial survey data. Rates of change in bullying measures were highest (from around 17 percent to 35 percent) for the school with the highest message recall by students after a one-and-a-half year intervention. Results suggest that a social norms intervention may be a promising strategy to help reduce bullying in secondary school populations. (Perkins, Craig, and Perkins, 2011, p. 703)

What is remarkable about this research was the degree of improvement in both rates of bullying and the reporting of bullying by simply correcting student's perception of what other students thought. (There were no bullying prevention programs implemented or assemblies containing emotional exhortations to the student not to bullying others.) Students were not rewarded for not bullying and/or for reporting bullying; they were simply told the facts. Once they realized that most students did not approve of bullying, they felt safe enough socially to act the way they really wanted to act. When this mistaken constraint, the fear of not being in the majority, was lifted they could show their positive character and become a more empowered bystander.

When research shows how a relatively inexpensive and minimally time-consuming intervention can produce significant positive results, why doesn't every school use this intervention? This research demonstrated how to untie one the biggest NOTS of bystander behavior. However, if schools, are stuck in a frame that doesn't acknowledge the concept of social psychological constraints preventing students from acting, then how could they embrace and use an intervention based on those concepts—even if it worked?

RECOMMENDATIONS FOR *RECOGNIZING THE FAE* GUIDELINE

Even though a more behavioral orientation relying on only observable words and actions has been the default and more compatible approach with the current frame of schools and bullying prevention, the empirical evidence of the utility of social psychological explanations and interventions is too strong to continue to ignore. This is especially true in light of the fact that the most recent statistics have indicated that behavioral approaches that might be effective with other behaviors are not sufficient for the problem of bullying.

To recognize the role that the FAE can play in bullying prevention, schools can do the following:

1. Make sure that all staff learn about the FAE research, especially as it relates to bullying and bystander behavior.

2. Let people express their initial opinions in the form of feelings in response to bullying or any problem, but make certain that these responses don't become facts or final conclusions.

3. Acknowledge the need that people might have to devote a short time to express frustration, anger, or search for someone to blame.

4. Allow time for that venting, but make sure that it is labeled as such, understood as venting, and kept separated from the decision-making process.

5. Do not let emotion (even if it is not recognized as emotion) trigger a wave of solutions that sound good, but only reflect quick judgments formed by a need for quick answers and explanations.

6. Realize that a negative behavior draws more attention and provokes stronger emotions, which distort and misrepresent the totality of a student's behavior that can lead to misjudgment and condemnation of a student who bullies.

7. As much as initial feelings might try to dictate judging a student negatively, always advocate for giving students the benefit of the doubt. Make the FAE in favor of the positive character of the student.

8. Search for explanations and explore the many possible reasons why students behave the way they do. Make sure that all involved in the process realize that change is more likely to emerge from exploring these variables rather than from trying to change someone's character.

9. Recognizing the tendency we all have to make the FAE can loosen the grip that fear has on the governing staff's response to student behavior and replace it with greater hope and trust among the members of the school community.

10. Highlight the fact that more options emerge from exploring the circumstances and the context of behavior than trying to directly change the student's behavior.

11. Create a process to follow that accounts for the tendency to make the FAEs, and construct a process which will avoid the likelihood of misguided decisions that result from making the FAE.

SUMMARY OF THE "GIVING THE BENEFIT OF THE DOUBT: *RECOGNIZE THE FAE*" GUIDELINE

The concept of the FAE appears to so central and pertinent to creating meaningful and effective strategies for addressing the problem of bullying (it should also apply to school discipline in general) that every member of the school community should have a familiarity with the concept and an understanding of its implications for addressing the problem of bullying in schools. Learning about the FAE and the empirical research supporting it should be an essential part of the reframing process. Understanding this one concept alone can also "open the doors" for many staff to rethink the roles that they have unconsciously assumed by working within the dominant parent/factory frame; a frame that has governed how schools operate.

GUIDELINE 2: PRACTICE CHANGE SQUARED: UNDERSTANDING CHANGE IS ESSENTIAL FOR CHANGING

Learning about the change process helps people to change (change squared). Since the fundamental attribution error discussed in the first guideline is a key element of change, learning about it and understanding it can help those who want to facilitate change. There are other important concepts and skills that can be used to facilitate positive change when all members of the school community learn about them and intentionally try to put them into practice. When all members of the school community learn more about change, the school will in essence learn to change itself.

Knowing about the change process and translating it into practice can make a significant difference in addressing real and perplexing school problems. Around the same time that I finished reading the book *The Wisdom of Crowds* (2004), by James Surowiecki, our staff at the school where I was principal had arrived at an impasse over an important issue, our annual fall open house.

We had experimented with replacing the traditional nighttime open house format with a daytime one. For two years, we tried a more student-parent participatory open house where the parents came to school during normal school hours. A great majority of parents approved of this approach even with the added inconvenience of having to arrange time off from their jobs. Although some staff initially were hesitant to try the daytime approach, after two years of doing so almost the entire staff preferred the daytime approach. However, there remained a persistent core group of parents who felt that it was too much of an imposition to ask them to take time off from work.

As the discussion of pros and cons of both the daytime and the traditional nighttime open houses evolved, it soon became clear that our staff were divided into daytime and nighttime advocates. The more group discussion we had, the stronger each opposing positions became. Our staff was stuck between the two positions and everyone's anxiety seemed to increase at the apparent unresolvable issue and the fear that one side would eventually lose to the other.

Feeling the eyes of the staff turning to me to make the final decision to declare one group the winner and the other the loser, I decided to reread Chapter 9 in *The Wisdom of Crowds*. The essential dilemma facing group decisions was how the issues of diversity and polarization could be successfully addressed to allow the group to tap into its great potential for producing quality decisions. The greater diversity in thought and opinion of the individual group members, the better the quality of the decision outcome. Even diverse groups can fall into "groupthink," where everyone eventually follows along with the opinions of a few and make a decision that turns out to be wrong and inadequate to the demands of the problem.

These types of poor decisions are created because the group does not draw on or benefit from its wider and more diverse range of perspectives and information that have the potential for higher quality decisions.

Surowiecki (2004) highlighted the key variables that can influence the quality of the decision making:

- those individuals with the most emotion, background information, and vested interests on an issue can have a profound influence on those individuals with less emotion, information, and interest;
- at the meeting, the speaking order of the people attending can also influence how the rest of the members of the group think; and
- people who spoke the most had a greater influence on the decision than those who spoke less.

So critical is the process of group decision making for all meaningful change initiatives that Kahneman (2011) came to this conclusion:

To derive the most useful information from multiple sources of evidence, you should always try to make these sources independent of each other. This procedure makes good use of the value of the diversity of knowledge and opinion in the group. The standard practice of open discussion gives too much weight to the opinions of those who speak early and assertively, causing others to line up behind them. (p. 85)

Knowing how to manage the change process in decision making is so important that on the last page of his book Kahneman comments,

At least in part by providing a distinctive vocabulary, organizations can also encourage a culture in which people watch out for each other as they approach minefields. This is much to be done to improve decision making. One example out of many is the remarkable absence of systematic training of the essential skill of conducting efficient meetings. (p. 418)

CHANGE PROCESS THEORY INTO PRACTICE

Based on what I read in *The Wisdom of Crowds*, I decided to try to structure our staff discussion with these points in mind. I also realized that some people would be afraid to speak up in a meeting if they felt others would challenge them in front of the group. I proposed some ground rules and procedures for the meeting and asked the group if they seemed fair. The group agreed that they were.

Here is what I did to facilitate the process.

- I made it clear that the purpose of the meeting was *not* to make a decision, but to gather information and to make certain that everyone's voice was heard.
- I asked the participants to reflect privately by jotting down their thoughts on paper prior to starting the discussion.
- I broke the large group into smaller groups with a designated recorder whose job was to listen to each person's thoughts on the issue and record them on chart paper.
- I set a ground rule that people could say what they thought without being challenged. After everyone shared without challenge, then the group could have an open-ended conversation on the topic.
- I indicated that our small decision-making group would study the collected input and thoughts of the whole group and then draft a proposal to be presented back to the whole group.

The tension that seemed to be in the room when the meeting started dissipated once the safe and equitable procedures were put into place. We collected a lot of good ideas that had never been voiced before. Some people spoke up who previously had been silent and their ideas were excellent. What the group discovered was that the goal of convenience for the parents coming at night and the goal of student participation in the daytime did not have to be as mutually exclusive as they originally appeared.

The small group decision-making team used the input from the large group meeting to draft a proposal that moved the starting time of the traditional nighttime open house from 7:00 p.m. to 6:00 p.m. and the plan was to have the students come in the evening with their parents, have activities for the students alone while the parents had time with the teacher, but also to have time when students, parents, and teachers could all be in the classroom together. We discovered a way to combine the best of both the daytime and the nighttime open houses. All the staff agreed to support this new proposal and it received overwhelming positive feedback from the parents as well.

TWO KEY OBSTACLES TO OVERCOME

This story of change at my school demonstrated how interjecting a little theory on the change process into group decision making can overcame these two big obstacles to change:

- **The preference for the "what" instead of the "how" when it comes to change in schools.** There is a tendency for school leaders to say to staff "here is the change" we are going to have and leave it at that. Effective change requires investing time in designing the process for change to make sure that everyone who is affected by the proposed change understands it and has some input into the process of changing.

In bullying prevention, many programs or trainings focus on teaching staff and students the facts, concepts, and procedures for stopping bullying. Knowing about bullying is not enough to actually effectuate changing how people interact with one another. Too often schools make the assumption that content knowledge on any topic can lead to changing a person's habits and patterns of interacting. A parallel assumption is having someone read about the history and rules of a sport and then expecting that person to be able to go out and play the sport successfully.

- **The general tendency for educators to avoid any direct conflict over contentious issues.** Educators for most of the day work independently with people (students) over whom they have a lot of control. When they have to work collaboratively, they often are afraid of conflicts that inevitably arise. They lack the skills for discussing differences constructively, consequently once they have a negative experience with conflict, they tend to avoid it altogether whenever it arises. This difficulty that many staff have for working through the problems and conflicts that arise in schools can be a significant obstacle for a staff moving forward together. People can easily retreat back to their classroom environment where they have control over their students behind closed doors. They may comply with implementing a program in their classrooms on bullying, but a commitment to understanding the issue and the accepting the responsibility for changing the cultural norms of the school is very often lacking or nonexistent.

IMPLICATIONS FOR BULLYING PREVENTION

Bullying prevention can become a convenient distraction from a larger more complex problem related to a school's resistance and immunity from positive change. Schools might readily (and often unconsciously) put a program or curriculum into place as a way to avoid confronting and discussing deeper more substantive problems in their culture and climate.

The simple decision to learn about and discuss the change process before imposing or even proposing a change initiative can make a significant difference in how a school approaches problems. It can be the difference between whether a school continuously improves or learns to cite the failure of change initiatives as more evidence for how the school can't change.

GUIDES FOR CHANGE

There are many valuable and well-written resources on how individuals and groups of people change. A small sample of them are quoted and cited in this book throughout each chapter. There are, however, three approaches to organizational change that emphasize how the right process can lead to the best results. They are deliberately content free. They don't promote any type of educational program or instructional approach, instead they provide the process for how individuals can communicate in way that leads to continuous growth and improvement.

Since social psychological research has demonstrated that even subtle emotions drive and distort thinking, following a process for collecting more information and for insuring that all points of view are included is a necessity for any meaningful change initiative or reframing. (Think how easy it is for anyone, or any group, to be convinced of being right while being totally off base.) Any school leader or leadership group who wants to establish a process for planning and making decisions should explore these or other well-established successful processes and practices for facilitating positive change.

1. Appreciative Inquiry

Appreciative inquiry, also called AI, is a process and system for changing by deliberately focusing on what is going right, or working in an organization. AI intentionally avoids having the typical discussions that analyze problems and propose solutions for fixing them. It is used primarily in business, but has been used in school districts. Cooperrider and Whitney (2005) provided this practice-oriented definition:

> Appreciative Inquiry is the cooperative, coevolutionary search for what is best in people, their organizations, and the world around them. It involves the systemic discovery of what gives life to an organization when it is most effective and most capable in economic, ecological, and human terms. AI involves the art and practice of asking unconditionally positive questions that strengthen a system's capacity to apprehend, anticipate, and heighten positive potential. AI assumes that every organization and community has many untapped and rich accounts of the positive. AI links the knowledge and energy of this core directly to an organization or a community's change agenda, and changes never thought possible are suddenly and democratically mobilized. (p. 8)

Appreciative Inquiry is a process for including all members of an organization in the process of changing. This process allows people to get to know each other better, to trust each other, and to value each individual's contribution to the improvement of the organization without expending time or energy focusing on what is wrong or needs fixing. In this process all individuals are affirmed, encouraged, and energized to move forward together.

2. Adaptive Schools

Adaptive Schools was developed by Robert Garmston and Bruce Wellman (1999) to help schools develop productive and practical sets of ideas and tools for communicating, collaborating, and decision making. It offers a training program with follow-up coaching for all members of the school community in developing productive norms for collaboration, procedures, and protocols for facilitating meetings and problem solving. It also offers skill development for listening more effectively, emphasizing paraphrasing and productive dialogue and deliberation. It provides a variety of meeting structures for allowing differences and assumptions to surface and be discussed in a positive and constructive way. The website www.thinkingcollaborative.com/seminars/adaptive-schools-seminars/ summarizes their work this way:

> It takes participants beyond the idea of professional learning communities to the actual implementation, describing specific ways to weave the collaborative fabric of a faculty, develop group member skills, and acquire the principles and understandings to engage in a continuous cycle of team and individual improvement. Adaptive Schools is the "how" of professional learning communities: how to behave in groups, how to lead them, and how to facilitate them for improved leading, teaching, and learning.

Schools looking to grow as a community need to recognize that communicating effectively cannot be taken as a given or achieved just by putting people into groups and expecting them to plan effectively and make decisions. The Adaptive Schools approach provides a set of tools and procedures that all individuals can use and benefit from as they work together to solve problems and to plan improvement in the learning environment for everyone.

3. Coaching

Reframing bullying prevention is about shifting the power structure of schools from *power over to power with:* coaching is a practical manifestation of that shift in action.

Elena Aguilar in *The Art of Coaching: Effective Strategies for School Transformation* (2013) provides a simple and straightforward definition of coaching.

> Coaching is a form of professional development that brings out the best in people, uncovers strengths and skills, builds effective teams, cultivates compassion and builds emotionally resilient educators. Coaching at its essence is the way that human beings and individuals have always learned best. (p. 6)

Coaching provides a clear alternative to the traditional approach of managing and evaluating an individual's performance as the primary method of changing someone. Coaching recognizes that all people are always learning and can always improve. It is based on a very positive assumption that people want to learn and to do their best. At its core, it contradicts the notion that people need to be controlled or motivated to learn. An effective coach provides a positive and trusting relationship with the person being coached as the foundation for continuous learning. As teachers experience being coached, they are more likely to have their teaching reflect the principles and assumptions of coaching.

There are many types of coaching (cognitive, leadership, instructional, content, life, etc.), but they share the basic assumptions mentioned in the definition by Aguilar. Each type of coaching is useful and can effectively serve different purposes; however, I found the work of Jim Knight (2011) to be very helpful in articulating how coaching facilitates positive change. He offers a clear and useful set of principles for translating the theory and research on how people change into educational practice. He identified five truths of helping that can be considered *the variables or circumstances* that can be changed as an alternative to attributing the problem to the resistant individual's personality, in other words, they are a useful resource for recognizing and avoiding the fundamental attribution error (FAE).

Knight's Five Truths of Helping (2011) are

1. people don't often know that they need help;
2. if people feel "one down" (i.e., feel that they have less power or are victims) they will resist help;
3. criticism is taken personally;
4. if someone does all the thinking for them, they will resist; and
5. people aren't motivated by other people's goals.

Effective coaches understand these truths, and therefore speak and act in ways that allow the person being coached to discover, embrace, and commit to the change that he or she *wants* to make. Coaching is a process of reframing "change" from being interpreted as "what you are doing right now is not good enough" into "what you are doing right now is the foundation for you to get even better." Coaching helps people to change without having them "lose face." Coaching helps people to change without feeling changed or manipulated.

Reframing bullying prevention is about helping all members of the school community interpret the goal of improving how people treat one another as a positive challenge for everyone to strive for rather than a condemnation of those who fail to be perfect all the time.

GUIDELINE THREE: "SAVING FACE": SELF-AFFIRMATION THEORY IN PRACTICE

> "When you come to a fork in a road, take it."
>
> —Yogi Berra

Educators can be a very challenging audience for anyone offering them professional development. As I discovered firsthand, it is extremely challenging to present to a group of educators who also have offered professional development to others. When standing before such a group, I made the respectful statement to them that "I was not an expert" and that they were the experts. My task, I explained, was to help them reflect on their knowledge and expertise and help them translate what they knew into practice. After the presentation, in response to that statement, the feedback from several people was fairly blunt and honest: why waste our time if you have nothing to offer us that we don't already know.

Deciding to take that feedback to heart, I spoke more authoritatively the next time I stood in front of the same group of people. I received some blunt and honest feedback again: who are you to presume to tell us that you know more than we do. Facing what appeared to be an impossible situation for what to do my next time in front of them, I was perplexed and stymied until I realized that my choices for what to say and how to say it were not to claim expertise or lack of expertise, but to understand the message that they were sending me. After much contemplation, I boiled the message down to the two attitudes that they were simultaneously conveying:

- Help me to get better at my job.
- Don't imply that *I need to get better* at my job.

As Yogi Berra's advice about the fork in the road indicates, my real choice wasn't to choose one or the other statements, but whether or not I could accept them both simultaneously. The acceptance of these two statements as filter for my comments would help me shape my message in a way that they could accept: I had to be creditable, transparent, genuine, but not profess to be better or more knowledgeable than they were; that is what "taking the fork in the road" meant. In fact, I discovered (as all school leaders do who ultimately want to connect with those they lead) that the "fork" was what social psychology has articulated as the self-affirmation theory:

> The theory of *self-affirmation* is a psychological theory that was first proposed by Claude Steele with the premise that people are motivated to maintain the integrity of the self. The ultimate goal of the self is to protect an image of its self-integrity, morality and adequacy.

> On the whole, integrity is defined as the sense that one is a good and appropriate person and the term "appropriate" refers to behavior that is fitting or suitable given the cultural norms and the salient demands on people within their culture. (Wikopedia, n.d.)

This theory is just another way of describing the five truths of helping proposed by Jim Knight. People want to change and want to be viewed as wanting to change and grow, but they don't want someone else determining for them what needs to change and how that change should happen. Self-affirmation theory also should remind all who are involved in education that the "self" cannot somehow be set aside so that the facts of the situation ("honest feedback") can bypass a person's feelings and go right to their rational brain. I have heard many school leaders wistfully state that the person receiving their feedback shouldn't take it personally. That type of thinking is the epitome of *wishful thinking* since learning is a human experience and the self, our personality and feelings, can never be objectively set aside in any interaction among people. Emotion is prominently in play whenever the person proposing a change holds more power over the people receiving the proposed change. Bottom line, people will resist, deflect, or redirect any piece of information that challenges their positive view of themselves.

Self-affirmation theory also explains why bullying prevention's emphasis on the negative and its portrayal of perpetrators as mean-spirited bullies, ends up counterproductive in achieving the goal of stopping bullying. Even the people most responsible for hurtful bullying will only defend or deny their actions the more they are accused, judged, and condemned by others. The only way these individuals can conceive of taking even the slightest responsibility for their acts is when, in some way, they are allowed to save face by being offered an explanation or interpretation of their actions as an aberration rather than a confirmation of their character or personality.

Self-affirmation theory also explains many educators' reactions to presentations and exhortations from school leaders to stop students from bullying. They often interpret such presentations as implying that they are presently not doing a good job in stopping bullying in schools. This implication is especially difficult for them to accept. How could people who chose a helping profession, whose purpose in life is to support children fail to adequately protect those children? This implication, no matter how slight, is very often perceived as not just a criticism, but as an accusation of them neglecting their basic responsibility as an educator. When a student from a school commits suicide, the general public points the finger and assigns blame to the educators in the school whom they then judge as callous and incompetent in protecting the lives of their students. It is almost impossible to expect educators to accept this level of responsibility that questions their identity as an educator and as a good person. This is why educators push back (overtly or covertly) on the imposition of policies, programs, and stricter controls placed on them from those above them. Compliance is a very weak substitute for commitment when it comes to a moral issue related to how people are treated. The reframing of bullying prevention from a negative to a positive (building a strong school community) can acknowledge the caring and moral purpose of educators and help them commit their energies to doing something positive rather than seeking to deflect or deny responsibility for a problem they truly feel that they have no control over.

RECOMMENDATIONS FOR *"SAVING FACE"*: *SELF-AFFIRMATION THEORY IN PRACTICE*

I translated *"Help me get better, but don't imply I need to get better"* into these statements about educators:

- Educators have a difficult job and do it well. Affirming and acknowledging their competence makes them more likely to accept any proposed change in practice.
- Educators want to do their jobs better and rightfully don't appreciate any implication that they don't.
- Educators don't want to be *fixed* or think they need fixing.
- Educators prefer to build on their successes rather than feel like they have to start from scratch.
- Educators care deeply about what they do, feel tremendous pressure for doing it well and have little patience for wasting time on anything they don't feel will them help do it. This care must also be affirmed.
- Educators need to trust that the person proposing a change wants to help them rather than control them.
- Educators want and need to have some choice and control over what it is they decide to change about their practice.
- Educators' sensitivity to criticism is heightened by implications that they are the reasons why schools are in trouble.
- If an idea for change has any value and educators think it will help them, they will embrace it enthusiastically. *It just needs to be presented in the right way.*

Taking the "fork" means crafting the message or presentation in such a way that both of these mind-sets (Help me get better, but don't imply I need to get better) are accepted and simultaneously addressed. It means putting the contents (new ideas or changes) in an *acceptable package* by removing any implied criticism and replacing it with acknowledgement and affirmation of the work they have already done.

In their haste to make change, it is easy for principals and administrators to forget about creating the right package for the change. The resistance that many administrators sense from educators is more the result of their poor packaging of the message than it is a staff's lack of openness or resistance to new ideas. Get the packaging right and the contents of the package are more likely to be accepted.

Here are some ways to create the right *package for change.*

- Give staff a legitimate explanation for the need for change and remove the expectation that the problem shouldn't have been there in the first place. Most staff are unaware of how bullying occurs under the radar of adult supervision (I term this as bullying that happens in a school's blind spot). Any failure to stop bullying is not because of any lack of caring or competence, but rather is a result of the fact that bullying is a complex and elusive problem. It is no one's fault that this problem was not better understood previously and that the staff were not given the training and resources to effectively address it.
- Indicate that there are more effective ways to address bullying that are different from the traditional ways used by schools to address other school problems. Again, it is no one's fault, especially not theirs, that it has taken a while to switch approaches. They could have not been expected to discover these approaches on their own. Now that a better way is known, the staff can move forward together in deciding how to best implement the new approach.
- Make sure that the staff knows that the principal, administrator, and the staff are all *in it together.* Many times, principals become middle managers and have to impose changes that were decided by the district office, school boards, or state policies. Adding anything new to learn to an already full plate is a form of adversity for staff. Adversity can split a team apart or bring it closer together. Expressing a need for help is not a sign of weakness; it is being honest, transparent, and shows respect for the staff.
- Don't pretend it is going to be easy or is "no big deal." Sometimes to a make a change more acceptable, a principal will downplay its impact. Although you want to avoid a "woe is me" mentality, the fact of acknowledging the difficulty and the impact of the change shows empathy and reinforces the *"we are in this together"* mind-set.
- Although they may be no choice in accepting the change, find ways of offering choices in the implementation of it. Involve staff in the decision-making process of how the change is going to manifest itself in the school. It increases their ownership of it and also provides a great source of feedback on how it is working.
- Use the group to change the group. Don't worry about gaining universal acceptance of the idea. It is not the principal's job to get everyone on board. If staff are involved in the decision-making process and have a say in how it is implemented, they have a greater impetus to get others on board.

- Baby steps are okay. Make it clear that change doesn't have to happen all at once. Staff can be involved in determining how the change can be broken into smaller steps. Be clear with staff that the goal is progress not perfection.
- Make sure that staff know that the change is a *work in progress.* Let them know that their feedback is needed to revise, tweak, modify the change in order to improve it. Make it clear that change is a process. It is about learning not performing.
- Plan a specific time to get together to check in and see how things are going. Many times a principal indicates that staff will have an opportunity to provide feedback, but then fails to provide a time for it. By setting a specific date and time to do so, staff know in advance their input is welcome.
- Use a *McDonald's for Lunch* strategy. My son told me about an article he read about the *McDonald's for Lunch* strategy: a group of people are trying to decide where to go to lunch and someone announces that they go to McDonald's. Since everyone in the group probably doesn't want to go there, it triggers a wave of suggestions that ultimately leads to a better choice. Sometimes to get started, a plan has to be put on the table; a principal can do that, but should announce the plan as a *McDonald's for Lunch* strategy. This tells the staff that it is safe to raise objections with it and to propose alternate ideas.
- Present the change to staff as a *familiar surprise*. Find a creative or unique way to introduce the change. This avoids the "here we go again" response that staff have to a change. Use video clips, photos, or stories to introduce the change, not to sell it to staff, but to get them to think differently about it. However, once it is presented make sure that staff understand how it is connected to established practices.
- Convey confidence and your belief that positive change is not just possible, but is inevitable when the school community works together.

By taking the fork in the road and crafting the right package for the change, you are sending this message to your staff: "You are competent, successful educators who want to get better. I have great faith and confidence that you will continue to do your job well, but here is something to think about and learn more about—it is your choice. We can do what we need to do to make our school an even better place."

SUMMARY

- Reframing bullying prevention is a process not a product. It is about changing the way the members of a school community treat each other. It is a process that requires that people work together and learn from each other as they attempt to improve the climate and culture of their school.

- School communities have the capability to make the changes needed to become stronger, more inclusive, and more caring.
- Progress in reframing requires that members of the school community rethink how they view education and student behavior. They have to explore resources and ideas that may be unfamiliar to them. Social psychological research is one valuable source of understanding human behavior and a source for developing interventions designed to address problems.
- Although there is no one formula for reframing bullying prevention and each school must approach the challenge differently; there can be certain guidelines for determining if a school is proceeding on the right track and making progress in the right direction.
- Three basic guidelines for reframing are

  1. "Giving the benefit of the doubt": Recognizing the Fundamental Attribution Error (FAE);
  2. "Change squared": Learning about change in order to change; and
  3. "Saving Face": Self-affirmation theory in practice.

- The Fundamental Attribution Error is the tendency to attribute problems to the person rather than the circumstances of the situation or the context where the problem occurs.
- It is very human to make the fundamental attribution error because it helps people make sense of the world in a time when they typically need quick and easy answers in order to understand reasons why something happened. Bullying triggers strong emotions; it is particularly suited for making the FAE because people need to figure out why people bully.
- Shifting from attributing the problem to people to examining the context of the problem provides more options for effectively addressing the problem.
- Rather than pretending to avoid it, the best that educators can do is to recognize their tendency to make the FAE, to develop a process for acknowledging their feelings, and to not allow those emotions to drive the solution to the problem.
- Since the concept of the FAE is so relevant to the act of bullying itself, all educators should be aware of it and apply it by directing their efforts to always explore, analyze the circumstances, and the context of the bullying.
- Learning about the nature of human change and the change process is an essential element for facilitating positive change in people and organizations.
- Since research in social psychology demonstrated how susceptible people are to self-deception, educators should focus on the *process* of how people communicate and make decisions.

- Three established processes for facilitating positive change are Appreciate Inquiry, Adaptive Schools, and Coaching.
- Those seeking to facilitate positive change need to consider the individuals' need to maintain a positive image of themselves, which in social psychology is termed self-affirmation theory.
- Reframing bullying prevention requires that the messages given to students and staff about bullying are crafted to affirm them and to direct them toward positive goals and actions.

ACTIVITY FOR CHAPTER 7: GUIDELINES FOR REFRAMING BULLYING PREVENTION

Purpose for activity

The three guidelines for reframing bullying prevention help educators break out of the typical ways of interpreting bullying and addressing it. They are designed to slow the automatic response to bullying and replace it with a more thoughtful and strategic response commensurate with the complexity of the problem. Although the guidelines don't provide "answers," there is a greater likelihood when they are followed that more effective approaches will be adopted. These guidelines can also help to insure that members of the school community commit to improving how all people are treated in the school.

This activity is designed for participants to reflect individually about their own experiences with change and to share those experiences with colleagues. Every person has a personal theory of change and this activity should give each person the opportunity to articulate it. Once participants have considered their own experience of facilitating change, they will be more open to entertaining possible alternative approaches.

Outcomes

- Reflect on and share experiences regarding successful change efforts.
- Integrate emotional and intellectual responses to situations relevant to bullying.
- Make connections between theory, research, and the experience of change.

ACTIVITIES

"Tapping" into personal theories of change

Present a worksheet to participants with a blank space for entering a response to this question: "How do you begin to get people or groups of people to change?"

Ask participants to turn to a partner and share their ideas.

Ask if they have had an opportunity to exchange personal theories and strategies for change, and then ask each pair to offer one idea to share with the whole group. Write each response on a sheet of chart paper.

Reacting to change scenarios

These are three brief video clips that illustrate the three guidelines of reframing bullying and the ten strategies for changing the minds and hearts of people touched by the problem of bullying.

Participants should be told that the content of these clips, plus their reactions to them, reflect the three guidelines and ten strategies for reframing bullying prevention. They can also compare and contrast what they see in the clips with their own theory of change.

Ask the participants to view the clips individually and immediately following the clips to write down their reactions in the chart provided. Once they have recorded their reflections, they can turn to a partner and share their reactions.

CLIP # 1: BOY ON THE PLAYGROUND

Show a short segment of a video featured on the TV program *20/20* with John Stossel (Goodman, 2002). The DVD can be purchased or it can be viewed on YouTube.

It shows a young boy walking on a playground holding a small toy. Another boy comes by and grabs it and throws it away. The boy goes to get the toy and is attacked by another student. No one comes to the aid of this boy.

Feelings on viewing	Thoughts on viewing

After each individual writes down feelings and thoughts, he or she can turn to a partner and share their responses.

CLIP #2: THE NATIONAL ANTHEM

Show the video clip of the National Anthem being played at the start of a NBA playoff game (Shapiro, 2003).

It shows a young girl who won a contest to sing the National Anthem at the start of the basketball game. She starts singing and after the third line forgets a word and freezes, unable to sing. The crowd lets out a nervous laugh and then Maurice Cheeks, the coach of one of the teams comes over to her, puts his hand on her shoulder, and starts whispering the words to her. Within seconds, the audience starts to sing along with her. Her face lights up and she sings with great confidence to the very end, while Maurice Cheeks stands next to her.

Feelings on viewing	Thoughts on viewing

Participants should follow the same procedure as after the first clip: write down their feelings and thoughts and then turn and share with a partner.

CLIP #3: TWO QUESTIONS THAT CAN CHANGE YOUR LIFE

Show the short two minute video called "Two Questions That Can Change Your Life" (Pink, 2010). It can be found on the websites danpink.com, vimeo.com or YouTube.

Chapter 7   Guidelines for Reframing Bullying Prevention   187

This video recounts the story of Clare Booth Luce visiting President Kennedy in the Oval office. She believed that Kennedy was trying to do too many things at once so she reminded him that a single sentence should be able to summarize a great man and his work and said that Kennedy needed to know what he wanted his sentence to be. The clip asks the viewers to ask themselves that question: "What is my sentence?" It also adds another sentence. "What can I do better tomorrow than I did today?"

Feelings on viewing	Thoughts on viewing

Participants should follow the same procedure as after the first clip: write down their thoughts and feelings and then turn to their partner to share.

EXTRACTING KEY ELEMENTS OF CHANGE

Participants need to again be reminded that these three clips taken together along with their reactions contain the key elements found in all successful change initiatives. Ask them to work either in pairs or groups of four to list what they believe are those elements.

Ask a spokesperson from each group to share the elements and state how the videos illustrated them.

Each small group or pair can create a visual representation of change using their observations and reactions to the three video clips. Each group can share their visual representation with the whole group.

Key points from videos

I found these videos serve as a kind of Rorschach test for participants where they project their own predispositions and ways of looking at the world into their responses. Each time I complete this activity, one of the participants offers a perspective and an interpretation that I have not heard before.

However, to guide the discussion there are some key points to stress about each video.

CLIP #1: PLAYGROUND

Most participants have a strong emotional reaction to the scene when the child's toy is being taken away, so this should be pointed out.

Many participants get angry with the students who bully the solitary boy and often speak disparagingly about them. This reveals the human tendency to make the fundamental attribution error (FAE).

This clip also can spur action since it does touch their emotions. This single act provides a visualization of the effect of bullying on a person and is often a more powerful motivation for change than viewing a bar graph of bullying statistics.

This clip also shows how bystanders proceed as if nothing is happening. This can illustrate how easily bullying can occur and how it often blends into the hectic flow of the school day.

CLIP #2: NATIONAL ANTHEM

This clip is a good illustration of how the identity that Maurice Cheeks has as a coach transferred to a non-basketball situation. He saw someone in need of help and support and coaches are people who provide it. He coached her by giving her just the right amount of support for her to regain her confidence.

This clip also shows how the crowd changed its behavior when one person stepped forwarded to help the singer. This is an example of how the missing element of leadership was the difference between the audience being supportive or indifferent.

This is an example of how culture can change within seconds illustrating that change is not just possible, but often is *waiting* for the slightest prompt to materialize. Participants can discuss why change happened so quickly and so dramatically and compare this situation to others where change sometimes seems impossible.

How did Maurice Cheeks help the girl and the audience "save face" in this situation?

Maurice Cheeks could be considered an empowered bystander who had the confidence to come forward and take a risk to help someone in need. He was not a singer, but stepped out of his comfort zone because he was thinking less about himself and how he looked and more about someone in need.

Participants can also take the perspective of the singer, the coach, and the crowd and articulate what each is thinking throughout the event. How did each perspective affect each element?

I often preface showing this clip by stating that it contains the ultimate solution to the problem of bullying. Participants in the activity can discuss how that statement is true or not true.

Consider asking participants to complete the following statement: "This video clip is a good analogy for _____," and then ask them to explain their comparison and then compare and contrast this clip to the first clip.

CLIP #3: TWO QUESTIONS THAT CHANGE YOUR LIFE

This clip illustrates the importance of positive and aspirational goals in the change process.

Suggest participants discuss the motivation that people need to change.

Often viewers reflect on what they want their sentence to be when they reflect on their careers. Here is an opportunity to personally share their motivations for their careers.

Ask participants to project what they believe Maurice Cheeks sentence would be.

Invite participants to explain how those two questions work together to produce change. What happens if someone only asks one of those questions?

SUMMARY

Two of the videos show how bullying can be reframed from stopping a negative behavior into promoting a positive sense of community. The third video shows the motivation that people need for the reframing: the positive energy and motivation that comes from the aspirational goal of helping others combined with very specific words and actions that can leverage change.

These three videos also contain the elements of change that are present in the eight different strategies offered in the next three chapters.

8

Heart Strategies for Reframing Bullying Prevention

1. Find the Human "Why"
2. Show Hope
3. Connect the "I's"

STRATEGY ONE: FIND THE HUMAN "WHY"

"Life's most persistent and urgent question is, 'What are you doing for others?'"

—Martin Luther King

I was demonstrating a lesson in a second grade classroom when three students decided to have some fun on their own. Each had a history of not being cooperative and were clearly a source of distress to their teacher and the entire school at times. I had the added support of the teacher in the room (that she typically didn't have), so I could proceed with the rest of the class while she tried to contain their behavior. When her calls for assistance did not produce additional staff to intervene and remove these students, they dove into their "fun" with each trying to outdo the other in "misbehaving."

It was as if they were creating their own school experience that was fun and exciting—even liberating. Although on some level they must have known that this behavior wasn't appropriate and would have to end at some point, they decided to enjoy the moment and remained oblivious to whatever was going to happen next. They were literally pulling posters from the walls, items off of shelves, all while moving around the classroom with abandon. Fortunately, I kept the rest of the class on task while these three were having their fun. When the lesson was over, I decided to provide some relief to the teacher and offered to take these students to the small conference room that I typically used during my time in the building.

After she agreed to let me take them, I had to improvise since I knew that they might not leave willingly with me. I casually said to them, acting like it was an afterthought and totally ignoring what they had been doing, "Hey guys, I have some movies to show, would you like to see them?" (I happen to collect videos for presentations and had my iPad loaded with many short clips that I thought might interest them, if even for a brief moment.)

To my surprise without any prompting, they all immediately accepted my invitation. I showed them some brief video clips that I thought had some humor and they sat and watched them. By chance, I decided to show the brief clip of Forest Gump walking onto the school bus and being shunned by the majority of the students who obviously did not want someone like him sitting next to them. These students watched the clip intently. Finally a little girl, Jenny, invited Forest to sit with her and she befriended him. That was all there was to the clip, it was less than two minutes long. As soon as it ended, since I had a brief moment of their attention, I asked, "What did you think of that?" Almost in unison, all three students replied, "I would be his friend, too." Knowing that this was my opening to get them involved in some task, I replied, "I agree. I also think that you would be a good friend and I think you could tell other kids how to be a good friend on the bus." They all smiled at me.

Since they liked this positive portrayal of being a friend, I followed up on my comment and asked them if they would like to help their school by making a poster telling kids how to be a good friend. They quickly agreed. Fortunately, I had chart paper and markers available in the room, so I gave them what they needed to help their school learn how to be a good friend on the bus. The three of them then worked intently on these posters: they sat in their chairs, calmly talked to me as they worked, and created detailed and colorful school bus drawings plus advice for how to be a good friend.

I thanked them and even though they weren't finished, I reminded them that they needed to return to the classroom. They accepted my direction and returned to the classroom in a much calmer and more cooperative state than when they left. (When I returned to the school a week later, they reminded me of their posters and asked to work on them.)

Although there can be many ways to analyze what was going on with the students, this situation reminded me of the power of finding a clear human purpose for doing any work. I don't think that these students had any idea of why they were in school; to them school was just a place that they had to go. Most of the work that they were given to do was just something some adult expected them to do. Probably in their minds, most schoolwork had no meaning or relevance to them, except at times when it only served to demonstrate that they were probably not very good at doing the work.

By chance, I happened to show a pretty dramatic scene that caught their attention and triggered an emotional response in them. Maybe they identified with Forest on some level, which was why it was important to them to act like Jenny and not like those who rejected Forest. Accidently, I somehow touched their hearts and supplied something that was missing from their daily experience of school: a human purpose for being there. This missing ingredient from their school experience settled their bodies into their seats and helped to focus and sustain their attention on work that they knew was important. I found a *human why* for their work.

Find the Human Why: What Does It Mean?

Finding the human why means that discovering the purpose of learning and social interaction is an essential condition for all positive change. When learning is grounded in the social world of the school, then students and staff find that their own individual learning is enhanced when they support the learning of each member of the community. *Finding the human why* means learning to value the process of learning together as a community; to accept the shared responsibility each person has for contributing to the common good of the school. The time invested in uncovering the WHY or purpose behind what people do is well worth the investment required to change what people say and do.

Walk into most schools and most students are busy doing the work that they are given to do. Because most students are cooperative and do what they are told, it can be easy to overlook the need to provide the *why* of school and learning. However, this fact should not be interpreted as a sign that meaning and purpose are not essential for learning. Students will learn on a deeper level and take greater ownership for learning when educators devote as much time and energy to finding and articulating the purpose and meaning of the learning as they do to the content of the learning.

Finding the Human Why: How Does It Work?

At the heart of reframing bullying prevention is the transformation of the problem of bullying from a rule infraction or a crime to a larger and deeper issue of how people should treat each other.

When each member of the school community discovers and subsequently values the importance of people working together, there will be more individuals who feel obligated to make certain that everyone is respected and included in the social world of the school. This adds a protective factor to those students who might not easily find friends or allies; consequently, when these students feel connected and supported, they are less and less vulnerable to those who choose to use them to improve their social position.

Students who might be tempted to bully other students to advance their social standing are deterred from those behaviors if they see that such attempts only produce peer disapproval.

When adults guide and support students in discovering the value and purpose of learning as a community, students feel respected as individuals who are assumed to be caring and responsible. Adults in a sense are only helping them do what they want to do.

Caring and helping others is something that all students can and should do. When students are given frequent opportunities to act in those ways and adults recognize those actions as essential elements of what it means to be a student, the stratification that occurs with an overemphasis on academic achievement is diminished. When students don't feel locked into a social group created by the structure of the school, there is less need to distance or disassociate from any class or group that is different from one's own.

When adults guide students in discovering the importance of caring and respecting others, and avoid imposing and forcing them to act in the way they want them to act, then students are more likely to seek out adult guidance, advice, and support when they face difficult moral situations.

Finding the Human Why becomes the basis not just for responsible action, but it is the source of all heroic action. Allowing students and staff to explore the concepts of leadership, sacrifice, and commitment to a cause greater than oneself, leads all members of the school community to see helping others, especially those students who might not be well liked, as opportunities to become the best people they can be. They also discover the joys and rewards of serving and supporting the common good.

When educators take the time to articulate the principles behind the rules and limits of individual behavior, students learn how these limits benefit everyone, including them. This investment of time for explanation and discussion helps students develop the moral reasoning that can guide their actions when they are confronted with situations that are not clearly governed by explicitly stated rules, which happens to be the majority of the bullying situations they encounter. *There is a big difference between doing something because "I told you so or else," and because "it will help you and your friends."*

Finding the Human Why is a way of restoring the concept of citizenship to the purpose and experience of education.

RESOURCES FOR EXPLORING AND SUPPORTING THE STRATEGY OF *FINDING THE HUMAN WHY*

Here are various books, chapters, articles, and research that can be used to learn more about this strategy, why it is so important, and how it supports positive change. I selected them to save busy educators the time needed to search for them; however, I urge all interested educators not to limit themselves, but to view the selections as a starting point for exploring these exciting and promising ideas and concepts.

Drive: The Surprising Truth About What Motivates Us **by Daniel Pink**

Chapter 6: "Purpose"
In this chapter, Pink discusses how finding purpose is now replacing the profit motive as a driving force and source of energy for businesses.

> We're designed to be active and engaged. And we know that the richest experiences in our lives aren't when we are clamoring for validation from others, but when we are listening to our own voice—doing something that matters, doing it well, and doing it in the service of a cause larger than ourselves. (p. 130)

Influencer: The Power to Change Anything **by Kerry Patterson, Joseph Grenny, David Maxfield, Ron McMillan, and Al Switzler**

Chapter 4: "Make the Undesirable Desirable"
In this chapter, the authors discuss how reframing "undesirable" tasks into moral choices is an effective strategy for influencing people's behavior. They give an excellent example of how this strategy worked in a program for rehabilitating people with a history of repeated criminal behavior.

> If we don't reconnect possible behavior to larger moral issues, we'll continue to allow the emotional demands of the moment to drive our actions, and in doing so, we'll make short-term myopic choices. (p. 98)

The Compassionate Instinct: The Science of Human Goodness **edited by Dachner Keltner, Jason Marsh, and Jeremy Adam Smith**

Part 1: "Wired to Be Inspired" by Jonathan Haidt
Jonathan Haidt discusses the feeling he calls "elevation." He describes it as a warm, uplifting feeling that people experience when they witness acts of kindness, courage, or compassion. He researched people's responses

to such acts and found that even as an observer these acts motivate individuals to help others and to become better people.

> Most people don't want to rape, steal and kill. What they really want is to live in a moral community where people treat each other well and live in a moral community where people can satisfy their needs for love, productive work, and a sense of belonging to groups of which they are proud. (p. 87)

Practical Wisdom: The Right Way to Do the Right Thing by Barry Schwartz and Kenneth Sharpe

This book discusses how an overreliance on rules, rewards and consequences, and the fear of being wrong, criticized, or even sued has lessened the opportunities that people have for developing what the authors term practical wisdom:

> Being a good friend, a good parent, a good colleague, or a good community member; being a good teacher, a good doctor, or a good lawyer—these are things we do for the sake of others and for the sake of ourselves. We can't do any of these things without practical wisdom. . . . Wisdom is not a mysterious gift of a handful of sages, but a capacity that we all have and need. (p. 287)

Chapter 5: "Thinking with Feeling: The Value of Empathy"

> The best route to raising empathetic, morally sensitive children is to be a parent who explains and gives kids opportunities to make decisions themselves. Empathy can be increased in school, but not by didactic education. Classrooms that emphasize community and foster concern for others increase empathy in children. (p. 72)

Start with Why: How Great Leaders Inspire Everyone to Take Action by Simon Sinek

Chapter 3: "The Golden Circle"
  Simon Sinek proposes that truly great organizations succeed because all of their employees have a very clear sense of purpose that governs how they operate on a daily basis. This sense of "why" helps an organization make better decisions and creates a culture where people are united by values and beliefs rather than profits.

> Very few people or companies can clearly articulate WHY they do WHAT they do. When I say WHY, I don't mean to make money—that's a result. By WHY I mean what is your purpose, cause or belief? WHY does your company exist? WHY do you get out of bed in the morning? And WHY should anyone care? (p. 39)

Research Article

"Boring but Important: A Self-Transcendent Purpose for Learning Fosters Academic Self-Regulation" by David Yeager, Marlone Henderson, Sidney D' Mello, David Paunesku, Gregory Walton, Brian Spitzer, Angela Duckworth

This recent article provides empirical research demonstrating the powerful effect of providing the purpose of helping others as a motivation to learn and persist at tasks initially viewed as boring and tedious.

This research involved seniors in an urban high school. They were presented with math problems that were perceived as boring and tedious (i.e., there was a very low motivation for working on them). Students who were told how learning the material would help them to help others persisted at the task, learned from it, and avoided distractions much more than a second group of students who were told that the reason for learning the problems was primarily for their benefit alone.

> This study was a contribution in part because it counteracts potential stereotypes that could exist about how to motivate low-income students attending urban public schools. Many of these students said that they wanted to contribute to the world beyond themselves, not just make money. And when they did, they were more likely to demonstrate self-control and make progress toward long-term goals. This suggests that telling these students to focus on how they can make more money if they go to college may not give them the motives they need to actually make it to college graduation. Instead, perhaps cultivating motives that transcend the here and now could provide them with the personal meaning that could help them sustain the self-regulation—which they will need to continue working even when the reason for a task is unclear and when tempting alternatives abound. (p. 22)

ACTIVITIES

Video Clip Discussion

Show a YouTube clip from the movie *Remember the Titans* directed by Boaz Yakin and starring Denzel Washington. Use this DVD to generate a discussion on the importance and value of moral purpose (i.e., the human why) as a way to motivate people to overcome obstacles and resolve conflicts.

In this clip, the coach is facing the challenge of getting his football team, composed of Black and White students, to play together. This was first time the school was integrated and there were many racial tensions between the students and even on the coaching staff. This scene shows the coach leading the team on a midnight run where they end up on the battlefield of Gettysburg. The coach intentionally brought them to that place to remind them of the sacrifices made there that allowed all people to be free. He wanted to connect playing football and playing together as a team to a higher moral purpose.

Text-based discussion

Martin Luther King Jr.: I Have a Dream: Writings and Speeches That Changed the World **edited by James M. Washington**

Although his letter from the Birmingham jail is now used frequently for social studies discussions using close reading and analysis, another of King's speeches, "The Drum Major Instinct," is more assessable for younger students and can be read in one sitting. This speech is particularly relevant for reframing bullying prevention because it acknowledges the desire that all people have for self-attention and personal gain, yet challenges the reader to channel this energy and desire into helping others.

ACTIVITY: THE PERFECT SCENARIO

Purpose: Help staff explore the "Why" of school

This activity is designed to help staff examine the underlying assumptions of school. By imagining school working the way it should according to its current frame, educators can reflect on what it would be like to get what they really want. Would that desired state be enough for them and/or their students?

Generate small group discussions using these guiding questions:

What if one day, teachers walked into their classrooms and all their students listened to their every word, followed every direction, handed in every assignment and passed every test?

- Would this be educational nirvana?
- Would this be the final destination of school reform?
- Is this ideal scenario the one that educators should strive to obtain?
- Is this really what educators want?
- More importantly, is it the best scenario for our students?
- What would they be learning?
- What would that experience prepare them for in a life beyond school?

It sounds farfetched to even imagine it, but if this is the goal, the Holy Grail of education, all educators should at least consider the possibility of achieving it and what that would ultimately mean.

Even if some educators embrace this vision, there should be others who believe that learning is more than just getting good grades, being responsible requires more than following the rules, and students should care about their peers. At least, this discussion should make the hidden frames more visible.

Recommendations for *Finding the Human Why* **in schools:**

- Have teachers devote time at the start of the school year to discuss the reason and purpose of coming to school and/or their particular subject area. This should include time to discuss how the knowledge and skills learned can benefit others.
- Provide opportunities for students to meet and interact with non-instructional school staff, for example, custodians, cafeteria workers, hall monitors, and bus drivers. When students see these individuals as people and not just as workers they are more likely to respect them, and in turn, more likely to view keeping the schools clean as not just following the rules, but as helping real people who have difficult jobs.
- Introduce service projects as a regular part of school life. Use these projects as opportunities for students who might not otherwise interact to get to know each other.
- Have students regularly view and discuss video clips of people helping people in real-life situations.
- Regularly ask students to share their stories of times when they were helped or when they helped and keep a record of these stories, even publish them regularly on a website or in print.
- Have a bulletin board devoted to displaying stories, photos, and news articles about people helping people.
- Ask students to help the school in any way they can. Don't just let the "top" students earn leadership opportunities, but regularly provide all students with these opportunities to help their school.
- Use the term *citizen* on a regular basis when referring to students. Relate the idea of citizenship to service for the common good.

STRATEGY TWO: SHOW HOPE

> "Everything that is done in the world is done by hope."
>
> —Martin Luther

As a coach of teachers, I knew that before I could coach them, I first needed to show them that it was possible for students to respond differently to a set of directions than their typical response. I needed to "put up or shut up." It's easy to offer advice or guidance about what someone should do differently, but if I never experienced the challenge presented by some of their students—although they might never say it to me—those teachers would be justified in thinking "who is he to tell me what to do." For me to have any credibility with these teachers, I needed to show that some of the ideas that I offered could actually work with their students. When teachers encounter difficulty every day, work their hardest and feel like they are not getting anywhere, it is only human nature to think that the problem lies somewhere else and not with what they said or did, or didn't say or do.

Since I knew I wasn't a miracle worker and it wasn't reasonable to expect to transform student behavior shaped by habits over the years, I needed to pick a specific classroom problem and illustrate a different way to approach it and then hopefully obtain different results. One particular teacher was still having difficulty even by the middle of the school year in getting the students to line up to go to a physical education class. After the class finally made it out of the room, I asked if I could try something different with them the next time they needed to leave the room. The teacher readily agreed, so I had my chance to *show what was possible (to hope).*

I announced to them that I needed their help. I explained that I went to other schools and tried to help teachers help their students, and that I thought that they could tell me what students needed to do to line up and get ready to leave the room. I asked them to think about it and share their ideas with a partner. After giving them an opportunity to think about the problem, I asked them for their advice and wrote down all of their answers on paper for them to see. I asked them to look them over and after they did, I deliberately hesitated and said, "I wonder if you could follow all these ideas in lining up and I wonder how long it would take to do it. Do you think you could try it?" They all enthusiastically said they wanted to. I pretended to be uncertain about whether it was possible, but this only prompted them to express their desire to show me. When I finally "gave in" and let them show me, I pulled out my iPhone to time them and said, "Ok, show me how to line up when I say, Go!" They lined up perfectly in less than fifteen seconds with no pushing, shoving, and without a sound. They stood there waiting for me to tell them how much time it took. When I told them fifteen seconds, their faces lit up and I thanked them and told them that I would tell the students in the other schools that I saw a class do it the right way in fifteen seconds.

The teacher thanked me and said she was impressed with how well her students responded. I just reiterated that all I did was put the lining up in a different context and put them in charge of it rather than have it be another direction from a teacher. I was able to "reframe" lining up so that it was not a command from a teacher, but a challenge they could meet that could help other students. I knew that my coaching would be viewed in a very different light since I showed that it was possible to get a different outcome: *I showed hope.*

Show Hope: What Does It Mean?

As much as a theory can sound good or make sense, and as much as data can reveal some truth of a situation, people usually still need *to see it to believe it* before they try anything new. People assume that their own perception defines reality despite knowing that our individual perception is very limited. Trying to pretend or convince anyone to try something or take a risk trying anything new is a fruitless endeavor unless on some level that person believes that the change proposed is possible and/or can do any good.

This is why it so difficult for educators to change anything in school; in most cases their experience has been that change initiatives imposed from above don't work so why would anything ever change. The *show hope strategy* means finding situations that tangibly demonstrate that change can happen and can be worth it. This is especially true for bystanders who need to "see" that any risk they take to help others can actually work.

Show Hope: How Does It Work?

Schools are very predictable, routine based, and stable places. Predictability and stability provide a foundation for learning, however too often this same predictability creates the illusion that nothing can really change. When students and staff are shown examples of people effecting any type of change, the "door" to change (that wasn't even considered before) is opened a crack: people need to see that change is possible.

There are two key questions that students and staff ask themselves when they confront any situation calling for them to change what they are used to doing: Is it worth it? Can I do it? When their attention is called to any event that affirmatively answers either of those questions, they find it easier to change.

The **Show Hope** strategy just like the **Find the Human Why** strategy are designed to first touch the heart in order to change the mind. These approaches are designed to create experiences where some emotion, excitement, passion is interjected into the mundane, "going through the motions" nature of school. Any experience that significantly differs from the normal routine of school has the potential for at least considering that "something" different is possible.

Show Hope can begin to override the hold that the *negative* has on people's attention and perception. Rick Hanson (2013) summarized brain research by saying that people have Velcro for the negative situations and Teflon for the positive ones. Unless there are intentional steps taken to put positive, hopeful words and actions before people, then hopeful events are easily overlooked and forgotten. When people see that other people can speak and act differently and effect positive changes in the environment, then they believe that change is possible and that they might be able to speak and act differently as well.

The *show hope* strategy doesn't have to work for everyone. If it can touch even one or two people and get them to start thinking differently, then the changed behavior of those few can prompt others to follow their positive lead. Educators using this strategy must believe that there are some students and staff who are just waiting for the slightest sign that their words and actions can make a difference.

Show hope doesn't mean showing miracles or dramatic changes in people or environments. A better strategy is to concentrate on how small and simple words or actions can have a positive influence on what other people say or do. Many times simple yet effective actions are overlooked, therefore highlighting those actions can show that little things can make a big difference.

The simple acknowledgment of the positive words and actions that are already occurring and are helping others and the school, can help staff and students see that they already possess the capability for effecting positive change. Staff and students can learn the value of acknowledging the positive words and actions of others.

Sometimes just stopping the negative messages about NOT BULLYING and replacing them with more positive and hopeful messages, sends an affirming message to students and staff about who they are and what they can do. Many of them want those in leadership positions to afford them this type of respect, and often respond eagerly to invitations to help and contribute to making school a better place.

Show hope is a strategy that also signals a shift in power and a change in attitude in those in positions of authority to those that they lead: from "you need to" to "we need you." Hope is *not* a guarantee for change; it requires those in power to let go of their need to control and replace it with an honest admission that true change comes from people choosing to act in more positive and caring ways.

Seeing other people who are perceived as peers take risks to help others can provide the inspiration that each individual needs to take the same type of risk. Consequently, anyone observing those altruistic acts then thinks, "If he or she can do it, so can I."

RESOURCES FOR EXPLORING AND SUPPORTING THE STRATEGY OF *SHOW HOPE*

The Progress Principle: Using Small Wins to Ignite Joy, Engagement, and Creativity at Work **by Teresa Amabile and Steven Kramer**

Chapter 5: "The Progress Principle: The Power of Meaningful Accomplishment"

This is a powerful book about what people need in order to be productive and feel fulfilled in their work. Using empirical research based on actual journals that employees kept that described how they felt about their jobs on a day-to-day basis, the book provides concrete examples of what happens when people feel that their work is meaningful and that they are making things better for themselves, their colleagues, and their organization.

> The secret (for a company like Google's success) is creating the conditions for great inner work life—the conditions that foster positive emotions, strong internal motivation, and favorable perceptions of colleagues and the work itself. . . . It starts with giving people something meaningful to accomplish. . . . It requires giving clear goals, autonomy, help and resources—what people need to make real progress in their daily work. And it depends upon showing respect for ideas and the people who create them. (pp. 1–2)

Switch: How to Change Things When Change Is Hard by Dan Heath and Chip Heath

Chapter 6: "Shrink the Change"

In this excellent book, the authors offer simple and effective ways for promoting and facilitating effective change in personal habits, people in general, and organizations.

> "When you engineer early success, what you are really doing is engineering hope. Hope is precious to a change effort. . . . Once people are on the path and making progress, it's important to make their advances visible. (p. 141)

Re-Direct: The Surprising New Science of Psychological Change by Timothy Wilson

Chapter 3: "Shaping Our Narratives: Increasing Personal Well-Being"

This book explores how so much of our personal happiness and well-being is dependent on how we view the world and our role in it. Wilson explains that since how we feel is based on who we think we are, we can "re-write" the stories we tell ourselves, thereby, creating a greater sense of well-being and happiness.

> What kinds of perspectives make us happy? Research reveals three key ingredients: meaning, hope and purpose. First, it helps to have answers to the most basic questions about human existence and our place in the world, in a way that allows us to make

sense of why bad things sometimes occur. Second, it helps to be optimistic—not because positive thoughts magically attract things to us, but because optimistic people cope better with adversity. Third, it helps to view ourselves as strong protagonists who set our own goals and make progress toward them; in other words to have a sense of purpose. (p. 49)

Research Article

"Improving the Academic Performance of College Freshman: Attribution Therapy Revisited" **by Timothy Wilson and Patricia Linville**

College freshman were shown survey results indicating that many students have academic problems in their first year, but that these problems get better over time. They were also shown video interviews with upper-class students who conveyed a similar message about how they improved their grades over time. These students showed significantly higher grades and were less likely to drop out than students who did not receive this type of information. *The students who were told stories of hope performed better than the ones who received no such stories.*

ACTIVITIES

Video Clip Discussion

Show a YouTube clip from the movie *Moneyball*, directed by Bennett Miller and starring Brad Pitt.

This particular scene illustrates how showing a video clip can affect how another person views and ultimately feels about a problem. In this clip, Jonah Hill plays Brad Pitt's assistant. Pitt is discouraged because his new system for managing a baseball team doesn't seem to be effective. Hill thinks that it is and that Pitt is overlooking his successes. Instead of lecturing or just telling Pitt that he is mistaken, he invites him to view a video clip of a player who falls down rounding first base and appears discouraged because he failed to make it to second. What the player doesn't realize is that he hit the ball over the fence for a homerun, so his falling is of no consequence. His teammates have to cheer him on to continue around the bases. Pitt watches this clip and thanks Hill for the message without even having to talk about it. All Hill says to him is that it is a "metaphor." Pitt replies that he "got it" and told Hill he was a "good guy." Hill reframed Pitt's failure into a success; it gave Pitt hope to continue to manage the club in the innovative way that he had been.

Discuss the clip with students and staff and talk about how *Show Hope* can make a significant difference in helping people persevere during inevitable times of disappointment and discouragement.

Text-based Discussion

Read *Thank You Ma'am,* a short story by Langston Hughes. It is a story about a young boy who attempts to rob an elderly woman on a city street. The woman realizes that the boy is from a troubled background and brings him back to her small apartment. She ends up feeding him and taking care of him. The boy is surprised by these acts of kindness especially from someone whom he attempted to rob. The woman's act of kindness touches the boy and gives him hope for changing how he lives in the world.

This story provides a contrast to traditional ways of treating people who do wrong. It shows how kindness and caring (showing hope) can have a positive impact on those in need.

ACTIVITY: ON THE LOOKOUT

Purpose: Comparing the Impact of Positive and Negative Events

Have students and staff learn about how negative events have a greater impact on how we view the world, much more so than positive events. Tell them that in order to counteract this negative impact that positive events and experiences need to be noted, recognized, and shared. Ask people to commit to being on the "lookout" for such positive acts and to write them down for at least a week. Reconvene the group and spend time sharing these positive stories and how it felt to be on the lookout for the positive.

Recommendations for *Showing Hope* in Schools

- Devote a bulletin board for posting stories of positive actions that help others. All members of the community can post stories. There should be guidelines for what type of stories get posted and someone needs to be responsible for reviewing submissions. If students and staff are only exposed to the negative stories in the media, *hope* can easily be lost—the sense that nothing can ever change for the good takes over. Having a designated spot in the school for sharing stories of hope at least demonstrates that the school values the importance of finding the positive in the world.
- Establish protocols for meetings so that positive aspects of the topic of discussion are shared prior to examining the negative. For example, when teams are meeting about students make certain that the strengths and assets of the students are described and understood before analyzing their needs or problems.
- Make sharing good news a prominent feature of classroom meetings and staff meetings. Devoting even a small amount of time to letting people share the good things happening in their lives with others can lift the spirits and morale of all the participants.

- Have students make PSA videos showing students performing small, but meaningful acts that help others. These videos can also include brief interviews with the students or staff who were the beneficiaries of the kind and helpful acts. They can briefly recount their feelings both before and after someone said a kind word or reached out to help them.

STRATEGY THREE: CONNECT THE "I'S"

> "The longer we listen to one another—with real attention—the more commonality we will find in all our lives. That is, if we are careful to exchange with one another life stories and not simply opinions."
>
> —Barbara Deming

I am going to make a statement that could possibly alienate many readers, so please refrain from putting down this book or dismissing what I have to say until I explain the statement. This statement is an irrational one, but it does reflect a relevant truth related to facilitating change.

I never met a Yankee fan I didn't like; and therefore, I often think that all Yankee fans must all be good people.

I love baseball and grew up in New York City rooting for the Yankees. It is part of who I am and it connects me to my past. It is source of immediate connection with many people with whom I might have nothing else in common. Discovering this simple fact about someone I just met puts me at ease with them and predisposes me to see them in a positive light. From that sharing of common interests and identities, that stranger and I can then discover other aspects of who we are and how we might be different as people. This commonality also sets the stage for having other future conversations about more serious topics.

I have also discovered that even if I meet a Red Sox fan (a bitter rival of the Yankees) that we at least have this "rivalry" in common and share a love of baseball and the ups and downs of identifying with a team and following them from day to day.

In my mind, I know that there are probably Yankee fans that I would dislike if I really got to know them. Of course there are Yankee fans that do things that I disapprove of, but having this seemingly trivial connection and association with them, allows me to give them the benefit of the doubt before I come to some other perhaps negative conclusions about them as people.

Finding a connection, something in common with someone has a profound impact on how we perceive a person and how we relate to and treat that person. When individuals are connected in any way, their relationship usually changes for the better; therefore, *connect the "I's (individuals) shouldn't be left to chance, especially in a school!*

Connect the "I's": What Does It Mean?

As discussed in the early chapters of this book, the current frame of school is designed for individual work: to get individuals to do their work with minimal distractions. *Connections* among individuals only produce unnecessary conversations that lower each individual's productivity. With this as the governing frame, schools and the people who live in them are caught in this terrible dilemma: their natural tendency is to be social, yet the structure of their environment tells them to suppress this and get to work.

Teachers and students are too often caught up in the inherent tensions of this conflict. Teachers fight to keep conversations among students to a minimum. Language, however, is social; it exists to connect people and to allow them to share meaning with each other. How is it that a kindergarten teacher, a well-intentioned, hardworking professional told me that her biggest problem with her class was that the students talked too much with each other? This teacher worked in a low-performing school, where the students scored poorly on standardized state tests. And the main reason for these results? Many students had language deficiencies.

Since it seems that improving students' comprehension and facility with expressing ideas and concepts is directly related to academic achievement, it makes sense that the "way to raise test scores" (sadly the primary concern for many low-performing schools) is to let students talk and think more with each other. But sadly, that is not the case. In most schools, the desire that students have to talk and interact is too often viewed negatively, as something that a teacher needs to suppress. (This is another example of how the *frame* determines the *game*: the need to control student behavior actually interferes with learning.)

Connecting the "I's" is a strategy for reframing that serves many purposes. It acknowledges the social need of students to connect with others, and in the process to discover their own identity. It uses the social aspect of learning to support academic learning, connecting these *two worlds* that are unfortunately separated in most schools. When students connect socially within the classroom (not just outside in the hallways) with teacher guidance and support, they can discover what they have in common with other students who might not be in their social circle.

Teachers who integrate the social with the academic can create new and more inclusive social circles and allow students who have difficulty connecting socially on their own to find a connection in the classroom. *Connecting the "I's"* is not just an essential strategy for reframing bullying prevention, it can reframe teaching and learning in schools.

Connect the "I's": How Does It Work?

People make very snap judgments about other people usually based on many unconscious factors. Therefore, a student might think that an unpopular student is very different, when in reality they might have a lot in common. Discovering commonalities with others can override the automatic and usually inaccurate assessment that students make of their peers. Very often, even finding one commonality with an unpopular student can be enough to prompt a bystander to conclude that the unpopular student, although maybe not a friend, should not be mistreated. If the more "unlike me" is what prevents helping, then the opposite is true, the more "like me" is what will prompt helping.

The more commonalities that students discover with each other, the less likely they are to exclude other students in the first place. Students who might be tempted to bully other students find it harder to select easy targets or students with no allies or defenders.

When students begin to feel connected and supported, they are more relaxed and able to perform at their best, which decreases the negative image that they might otherwise project to their peer group. These students participate more fully in all aspects of school life and become less and less vulnerable to bullying or mistreatment.

Students have a remarkable capacity to accept differences once they discover that they don't have to be afraid of people who initially appear different. This is what occurred when students with disabilities were included in the schools. Students in wheelchairs or with other visible disabilities became commonplace and the range of acceptable difference expanded in the school environment. *Different* didn't seem so *different* anymore. This same process of expanding the range of acceptance of differences in an environment can and should happen for all individuals.

Since many students who are selected as targets often don't appear very "likeable," it is difficult to hold bystanders responsible for not helping because like most people, they typically only help the people they like or know. Left to chance and without adult guidance and support, students decide to help others simply based on the criterion of whether or not they like a student. When educators help students discover commonalities with each other and thereby strengthen the sense of community in the classroom, they provide students with another criterion for whether they should help others or not. *Connect the "I's"* at least provides a clearer choice for students to make.

RESOURCES FOR SUPPORTING AND EXPLORING THE STRATEGY OF CONNECT THE "I'S"

Influence: Science and Practice **by Robert Cialdini**

Chapter 5: "Liking"
    This is a foundational text for those interested in how to influence people's behavior. In this chapter, Cialdini explores how the simple act of liking someone influences how a person responds to everything that the "liked" person says or does. He explains the perception of similarity that

determines what people like or don't like. Ironically, he cautions consumers to beware of situations where false commonality can fool them into buying products or services that they want or need. If this influence can be used so effectively to affect consumer behavior, educators must understand and use it to promote prosocial and helpful behaviors.

> Because even small similarities can be effective in producing a positive response to another and because even a veneer of similarity can be so easily manufactured, I would advise special caution in the presence of requesters who claim to be "just like you." (pp. 151–152)

The Progress Principle: Using Small Wins to Ignite Joy, Engagement, and Creativity at Work **by Teresa Amabile and Steven Kramer**

Chapter 7: "The Nourishment Factor: The Power of Interpersonal Support"
This chapter explores the essential need that people have for human connection. This sense of being connected to other people actually nourishes people and provides meaning and purpose to them, even if the content of the work might not engage or excite them. Educators and students are more likely to persist through difficulty and accept challenges when they don't feel alone, but instead feel the support of those around them.

> The nourishment factor refers to something that everyone craves at work: human connection. You nourish the inner lives of your subordinates when you reward or recognize their good work, encourage them, or offer emotional support. You might also help resolve interpersonal conflicts, provide opportunities for people to get to know each other, or simply let them have some fun. Our guess is when you think about your best days of your work life, many of them are days when you enjoyed that human connection. (p.130)

Teaming: How Organizations Learn, Innovate, and Compete in the Knowledge Economy **by Amy Edmondson**

Chapter 6: "Teaming Across Boundaries"
In this chapter, Edmondson explores both the critical necessity and the difficulty that individuals and teams have in overcoming a variety of differences that initially separated them. She explains the role of leadership in creating the right conditions for people to overcome differences (real or imagined) and to work together to achieve high levels of learning and problem solving. Given the challenges facing students to meet higher standards, educators must also find ways to get students to support each

other in their learning. Every organization (including schools) can only meet the challenges of the complex world today when people team together rather than work independently of each other.

> Communication with anyone from a group, whether the difference is demographic or organizational is fraught with small hurdles. . . . This requires discovering and revealing taken-for-granted assumptions to avoid misunderstanding and error. (p.195)

To Sell Is Human by Daniel Pink

Chapter 4: "Attunement"

This chapter describes the benefits of being able to connect with other people. Pink calls this *attunement*: the ability to bring one's own actions and perspectives in harmony with other people and the social context.

> Searching for similarities—Hey, I've got a dachshund, too!—may seem trivial. We dismiss such things as "small talk." But, that's a mistake. Similarity—the genuine, not the manufactured—variety is the key form of human connection. People are more likely to move together when they share common ground. (p. 94)

Research Articles

Enacting Cultural Interests: How Intergroup Contact Reduces Prejudice by Sparking Interest in an Out-Group's Culture by **Tiffany Brannon and Gregory Walton**

When students from different ethnic groups discover common interests, they are more likely to show an interest in a minority group's culture. Participation in cultural activities ultimately improved attitudes of the students in the majority group toward the minority culture.

> To illustrate, suppose a shared interest in mystery novels facilitates a social connection between Karen, a White American, and Liliana, a Mexican American. As the two become friends, Karen may learn about Liliana's personal interests, including those related to her Mexican heritage, and come to share these interests herself. If Karen has the opportunity to participate in relevant cultural activities, such as watching a Mexican telenovela or making the Mexican dish *sopa seca* with Liliana, this openness to Mexican culture may lead Karen to participate fully and enthusiastically. Doing so may seem to Karen to reflect and express her interest in Mexican culture and feel inconsistent with holding negative attitudes toward Latinos. (p. 2)

Mere Belonging: The Power of Social Connections by **Gregory Walton, Geoffrey Cohen, David Cwir, and Steven Spencer**

This research shows how even an unrelated social connection among individuals can affect academic performance. In one study, undergraduate students read a report written by a student who graduated with a major in math. The report recounted positive experiences in the math department that led to the author's success. For some of the students who read the report, the author's birthday was manipulated to match the birthday of the participants. Subsequently, all the students were given a similar math task to perform and asked questions probing their own motivations for learning math. Those students whose birthday's matched the author's birthday persisted significantly longer on the math task and reported a higher motivation for learning math.

> The conclusion that motivation is highly sensitive to social relationships is consistent with research on social identity threat, which finds that subtle cues that convey to students that they do not belong or that their group does not belong in a field of study can undermine motivation. (p. 529)

ACTIVITIES

Video Clip Discussion

The movie *October Sky* is directed by J. Johnston, stars Jake Gyllenhaal, and is based on a true story about the NASA scientist Homer Hickham. While in high school, he became obsessed with rocket science and gathered a group of his friends to build a rocket. Finding that the group lacked the expertise to achieve their goal, he had to reach out to an unpopular student. This scene occurs about ten minutes into the movie where he spies this unpopular student sitting alone in the school cafeteria. He decides to approach him, but his friend cautions him that if he does, "he can kiss his social life goodbye." He takes the risk and approaches the student who is at first suspicious of Homer, but eventually joins the group and helps them build a rocket.

Discuss this clip with students and staff to show the impact of finding common interests among students. It illustrates how people can learn to overcome social differences while working together on projects.

Text-based Discussion

Read and discuss: *One Teacher's Brilliant Strategy to Stop Bullying* by Glennon Doyle Melton in the June 2014 *Reader's Digest*.

She describes a teacher who finds out which students in her class have the fewest friends and then designs activities and learning experiences to build relationships among the students.

ACTIVITY: EXPANDING CIRCLES OF COMMONALITY

Purpose: Discover Commonalities in Groups

This activity can be done with any type of group.

Sort people into pairs. Give each pair 2 to 3 minutes to write down on a sheet of paper all the things that they might have in common with one another.

Have that pair find another pair. Now give the group of four 2 to 3 minutes to compare their list of commonalities and find the ones that all four of them share. They can also use the time to discover new things that all four may have in common.

Keep doubling the group (four becomes eight; eight becomes sixteen, etc.) until the final group matches the size of the entire group. Have a circle drawn on a sheet of chart paper and in that circle have someone write all the things that the entire group have in common.

Place that circle in a central location in the room and have each person sign their name in the space around the circle.

Ask each person to write down thoughts and feelings while participating in the activity. After this reflection, open up the discussion asking participants to share their thoughts and feelings with the whole group.

Recommendations for Connecting the "I's" in School

- Post photographs of people shown together in groups on prominent bulletin boards in the building. People need to see people connected.
- Have all staff make a commitment to devote time in the beginning of the year to inventory the commonalities (things in common) in each class. Post the list in the classroom and make available space on it to add new things as the year progresses.
- Have a visual display somewhere in the building with categories of "likes": likes to run for exercise, likes to go to the movies, likes to vacation at the beach, likes country music, and so forth. Students and staff then add their names under the category of "likes" that pertain to them.
- Birthdays are a great way to discover what people have in common. If a school has regular assemblies, devote time to ask those who celebrated a birthday prior to the assembly to stand up. The entire school could give them a round of applause or even sing to them.
- Develop a resource library of books that contains activities that help people get acquainted, communicate about experiences, and share stories with each other.
- Designate a day where every person in the school agrees to wear a particular color.

- Intentionally use humor as a way to connect to people. Showing a video clip of something funny, no matter how brief, can connect people in laughter. With smart boards in many classrooms, teacher can start almost every day with a laugh as a way to put everyone in a good mood and ready to work together.
- If connecting the community becomes a valued goal for the school, a planning committee or an already established committee or group can be charged with the task of finding and recommending ways to strengthen the connections and ties among all members of the school.
- When an entire school commits to a service project, make sure that there is a visible sign of the progress that the school is making in achieving this goal. Adding photos of people actually participating in the service project is a good idea as well.

SUMMARY

These strategies for reframing are designed to facilitate the change process not to mandate or impose change.

Their aim is to get people to think and feel differently about their experiences in school and to support a process where people can change and influence each other.

There are three categories of strategies: *heart* strategies designed to remind people of the human element of school; *"who"* strategies designed to change people's identities and how they view their role in school; and *"do"* strategies designed to provide specific words and actions that leverage positive change in school.

Heart strategies include (1) **Find the Human Why**—emphasizing the role of moral purpose in everything that happens in school; (2) **Show Hope**—emphasizing the importance of highlighting the positive that is already occurring in schools and how it affects people; and (3) **Connect the "I's"**—shifts from the traditional default emphasis on just the individual to the connections and commonalities that exist among all members of the school community.

9

"Who" Strategies for Reframing Bullying Prevention

"WHO" STRATEGIES

1. Change Identity
2. Require Assembly

STRATEGY ONE: CHANGE IDENTITY

> "If you treat an individual as if he were what he ought to be and could be, he will become what he ought to be and could be."
>
> —Johann Wolfgang von Goethe

Kevin was a very quiet and unassuming student. Usually the most emotion he ever expressed was a slight smile that disappeared after a brief second. He worked hard, especially when it came to reading and writing as these skills didn't come easily to him. However, no one was surprised when he took his first standardized state test in the third grade and scored at Level 1, the lowest of the four levels.

On a daily basis, Kevin had to confront the very things that posed the greatest difficulty for him: reading and writing. I often wondered what he felt when he looked around and saw other students reading and writing with less effort and struggle. Although he probably couldn't verbalize it, he must have constantly thought about what was "wrong" with him. He accepted the help from his teachers and worked hard for them, but in a way this extra help and attention only underscored the fact that he was different from the great majority of students. As much as we tried to be positive with him, it was almost impossible for him not to interpret this "difference" as "not as good." Also, praising his effort wasn't enough to make school a place that produced smiles for him; he knew that he worked harder than his peers and still made less progress than they did. Our encouragement couldn't erase what he saw happening around him, and sadly, what he started to think and feel about himself.

One day all of that started to change when a teaching assistant, who supervised the school store (a little space we had in a storage closet where we sold school supplies a few days per week) asked Kevin to volunteer in helping her. He readily agreed and quickly became a wiz in all aspects of running the store. He could describe in detail every item sold and mentally keep track of the inventory. He gave advice on what pencil or eraser worked best for what school task. He quickly made change in his head and he even started to make small talk with others in the store. As principal, I periodically stopped in to buy a pen or pencil, and Kevin (who normally didn't say too much to me because I think he was nervous around the principal) gave me advice on what I should buy. We all saw him become a new person who talked, acted, and even looked very different from before.

Kevin continued to struggle in reading and writing and continued to get quite a bit of help, but he also smiled more and talked more. He was no longer defined by his struggles, but had *someplace* in school where he excelled. It was as if a burden or a weight had been lifted off his shoulders; the school store experience gave him a new identity. His new identity gave him confidence that spread into his social interactions and other aspects of his school life. Reading and writing never became easy for him, but they no longer defined or limited him. His test scores consequently improved from a Level 2 in the fourth grade to a Level 3 in the fifth grade. However, even if his scores hadn't improved so dramatically, there were many other clear signs that Kevin's school store experience transformed what school meant to him and who he was to himself and to others.

Maybe Kevin might have jumped two levels on the standardized reading test without the school store experience. Maybe his improvement was because the extra help he received finally paid off. No one can really know for sure, but I saw a "new" Kevin once he found the school store as a place where he could succeed. It gave him a new identity and with it a confidence that he could succeed at something; whereas, before I doubt that he thought he could succeed at anything in school. He carried this new identity into new situations, including testing situations. His new identity and confidence allowed him to perform at his best on these tests, while his former identity—before the school store experience—suppressed his performance on tests. His *new identity* reframed how he viewed the academic assistance he was receiving: it was no longer an indication of what was wrong with him, but became an opportunity for him to improve, just as each day in the school store helped him improve.

Once his school experience gave Kevin a new identity, school itself became a very different place for him; it opened horizons instead of closing them. Kevin changed from being someone who had something *wrong with him that needed to be fixed* to someone who was fine and could always get better, just like everyone else. He also became a benefactor, someone who helped the school become a better place rather than just being a beneficiary, someone who just received assistance all the time from the school.

As a group of educators who desperately wanted to help Kevin, we stumbled on a different and a better way of helping him. Instead of trying to motivate him to change (ironically, he always wanted to do better), we treated him differently and this change in treatment gave him an experience that *changed his identity*. Subsequently, he acted in accord with this new identity; he was someone who just kept getting better all the time. As it turned out, he was just waiting for us to view him and treat him that way.

This lesson we learned with Kevin gives me great pause; I wonder how many other students are waiting for these new opportunities (and different identities) and sadly never receive them.

Change Identity: What Does It Mean?

Most educators care deeply about students who are having problems in school, but this caring can inadvertently project an identity onto the student that limits and shapes how they ultimately perform in school. Students absorb (by osmosis) the attitudes and conclusions that educators infer about them from observing how they act. So, when students demonstrate any behavior that deviates from the expectations of school, many educators quickly conclude that those students need to change in some way and that something might be "wrong" with them. The bottom line of that message: *the student is the one who needs to change (not the school environment)*.

The *change identity* strategy means that educators and all adults who interact with students must constantly keep the focus on their strengths and abilities. This means that adults must put aside their desire to fix or change students and instead project a confidence that all students want to learn and will learn when given the right conditions and support by the people around them. If the students *get stuck* and fail to make progress, the problem rests in the circumstances, the conditions around them, and not in anything within the students themselves. *(Adults need to refrain from making the fundamental attribution error [FAE] about students.)*

The *change identity strategy* is directly connected to the growth/fixed mind-set concept described by Carol Dweck and colleagues (2011). Instead of projecting onto students that their problems are related to a fixed ability, and therefore a sign that something is wrong about them, educators should *reframe* any problem a student has as an inherent and natural part of the learning process that all people experience. Problems are only opportunities for all people (teachers included) to grow and learn more; they are not signs of something being wrong or to be regarded as events that shouldn't have occurred in the first place.

When problems or struggles occur (they always do), students can try many different strategies and adjustments to work through them. This sense of agency for learning cannot magically appear in students; it has to be developed by how the adults they interact with view and treat them on a daily basis. Adults cannot just tell students what to do and how to do it and then expect them to feel in control of their own learning. When adults change their identity from being controllers or managers to coaches and mentors, their students naturally assume identities that reflect a greater sense of agency and self-efficacy.

The *change identity strategy* requires adults to stop asking what they can do to motivate students to change (usually by limiting options with rewards and consequences) and instead begin asking what opportunities do students need that will reveal and affirm those positive identities of themselves.

The *change identity strategy* emphasizes the positive words and actions from adults that can affirm students as responsible and caring members of a school community. This also includes *how* adults talk to students: that they talk with them, with a respectful tone of voice, and refrain from talking at them.

Adults need to demonstrate the same respect and courtesy to students that they show to those with more power and authority over them. When adults intentionally choose not to automatically rely on their institutional authority as the primary way of affecting change, they are modeling how to treat all people regardless of their social status or power. By doing so, they hold up a different identity or example for the students to emulate. When students are respected, they are given the identity that they truly want from adults; an identity that says that they are people worthy of respect. They prefer this identity to one that only tells them what they shouldn't do or what rules they shouldn't break.

The *change identity strategy* recognizes the developmental and human need to discover one's identity as an integral part of the process of becoming a person. Students look to adults to tell them who they are. *They need the adults in their lives to recognize their potential to be Superman, and not just Clark Kent.* They respond positively to messages that offer hope and emphasize what they are capable of rather than messages that focus on their limitations and their failures.

Instead of being places where identities are shaped by the fear of failure and negative judgment, schools need to be places of hope that give students identities shaped by the confidence that students can persist through difficulty and adversity to achieve success.

Change Identity: How Does It Work

Relationships create and define identities, so they are the way to change identities.

Students should not be locked into the identities of bully, bullied, and bystander, but be given the knowledge, skills, and attitudes that support them in exploring who they are beyond the limits of defined roles and identities. When the school creates opportunities for students to try out different identities, they are able to view their peers differently and act differently toward them. When educators change how they view students, the students can begin to change how they view themselves. As more and more students view themselves as active agents for their own learning and for their community responsibilities, the cultural norms of the school change in a positive direction toward greater caring and respect toward each member of the community.

When educators deliberately and intentionally decide to project a positive identity on to students, then they are telling students that they believe in their ability to become that type of person. Students are more likely to make moral, altruistic, and even heroic choices when they get this vote of confidence from adults whom they trust.

Students who are more likely to be bullied benefit greatly when they receive positive and affirming messages from adults. Very often their failure to self-report bullying is because they feel that they deserve it, or mistakenly infer that adults might believe they deserve it. They need positive messages that can reframe their school experience and help them see school in a positive light.

When school staff appear too authoritarian and controlling, then students who bully can demonstrate their ability to elude adult control and feel that they gain enhanced status in the eyes of their peers. However, when adults change their "power over" identity and become more trustworthy and supportive, they project a more positive identity on to students and lessen the sharp divisions between the student world and the adult world. (Accordingly, the nature of student staff relationships then shift from an "us against them" perspective to a "we" perspective.) In this more cooperative and collaborative environment, students who witness bullying are less likely to view students who "dupe" adults as attractive or *cool*. Students who use bullying to gain greater peer status discover that many peers do not approve of their actions.

When students assume the identity of active citizens, they act in a way that is consistent with that identity. They accept responsibility for creating the type of school and community they want. Their words and actions as a citizen or community member are more in alignment with the values of respect and caring rather than of compliance and conformity.

By providing students a set of values rather than just rules, schools help students assume *identities of people who make moral decisions based on what they believe to be right*. This makes it harder for students to dismiss or ignore words or behaviors that conflict with their values. When rules are explicitly connected to values and principles, students, who witness mistreatment of others are presented with moral choices. Although some students might still decide not to help, this situation is preferable to one where students see mistreatment as a normal part of school life and automatically opt to stay safe and preserve their own status when they observe others in need.

When students feel a sense of ownership for their school because adults offer many opportunities for choice and voice in shaping the school environment, they develop the courage to speak up if they see or hear of any behavior that detracts from the school as a place that makes them proud. This identity helps students shift away from a self-protective way of thinking. It propels them to look out for others because they care too much about what happens in the school regardless of how they feel about the person who is being mistreated. They are more likely to think: "this is not the way anyone in *our* school should be treated."

Very often students who witness bullying are unsure of what to do or say, therefore the uncertainty and ambiguity freezes them in place. If students have to stop and think about what to do, the situation could be over before they have made a decision or have time to take even a small step to help. Their inaction is interpreted as a tacit approval of the bullying, which gives the students who bully a false self-identity based on the mistaken assumption that the bystanders think well of them. Inaction can inadvertently create and sustain identities that would fade if the truth (what people really feel) had the opportunity to surface.

In reality, most bystanders don't approve of the bullying and they are not proud of their own inaction. Not being able to act in accord with one's values or conscience becomes troubling and disheartening for students. Providing students with a clearer and more defined identity as a citizen, community member, teammate, or caring (moral) person removes much of the ambiguity and uncertainty from the situation. When students assume these roles, they accept the actions that accompany those roles:

doctors treat people who are sick, coaches help people, citizens vote, and so on. A positive identity makes helping behaviors more automatic. (In Chapter 10, the identity of a first responder is discussed as an identity that all students can assume.)

The *change identity strategy* adheres to the self-affirmation theory explained in Chapter 7. When adults act on the assumption that students want to help others and contribute to the common good, they project a positive, affirming identity onto the students. This decreases the tendency that students have to "tune out" critical or negative messages and devote their energies to defending themselves. Adults who project positive identities onto students (even those whom they observe behaving to the contrary) are more likely to gain the trust and respect of these students. *Many of these students need to have an adult believe in them and to view them in a favorable light before they can believe it about themselves. The identities that adults have for children become the ones that they grow into and become—for better or for worse.*

Students who feel respected by adults are more likely to trust that adults will help them if they ask for advice and guidance on how to handle any bullying they encounter, either as a target or a bystander. Students can also develop greater confidence in taking risks and stepping into ambiguous bullying situations when they are not fearful of adults automatically criticizing them for not deferring responsibility to those in positions of authority.

When issues about how people are treated and the responsibilities that individuals have toward each other are routinely discussed in school, students can continue to develop their identities as moral people who act in accordance with values and principles. When these issues are not addressed or discussed, students are more likely to embrace the "nonidentity" of being part of the majority without thinking about what they are doing.

When helping others and supporting the school community become publicly valued and recognized activities, success is not dependent on demonstrating a skill set in comparison to others, it becomes available to everyone. In contrast to school environments where some identities are viewed as better than others, schools that strive to become communities allow all students to develop equally valid and important identities. In this type of school environment, students no longer have to try to fit into the more approved or desirable group *because the entire group has become one community with room for all members*. In this type of school environment, bullying no longer serves the social function of protection and promotion that typically happens in the stratified social environment of most schools.

The *change identity strategy* is essential for promoting positive change in individuals and organizations. *Schools, therefore, need to dramatically change how they articulate and approach their core mission: instead of asking how to control student behavior to do or not do something, they should ask how can they create opportunities that allow students to become the people that they aspire to be and help to create student identities that empower them.*

RESOURCES FOR EXPLORING AND SUPPORTING THE STRATEGY OF CHANGE IDENTITY

Here are various books, chapters, articles, and research that can be used to learn more about this strategy, why it is so important, and how it supports positive change.

Switch: How to Change Things When Things Are Hard to Change by Chip Heath and Dan Heath

Chapter 7: "Grow Your People"
    This chapter summarizes how an *identity* model of change differs from a *consequences* model of change. The authors explain how small steps or actions a person takes can gradually evolve into a new identity that then governs how one responds to many other situations. The motivation to act consistently with an identity is much stronger than other external motivations.

> Identity is going to play a role in nearly every change situation. Even yours. When you think about the people whose behavior needs to change, ask yourself whether they would agree with this statement: "I aspire to be the kind of person who makes this change." If their answer is yes, that's an enormous factor in your favor. If the answer is no, then you'll have to work hard to show them that they should aspire to a different self-image. (p. 156)

Influence: Science and Practice by Robert Cialdini

Chapter 3: "Commitment and Consistency"

Re-Direct: The Surprising New Science of Psychological Change by Timothy Wilson

Chapter 4: "Shaping Our Kids Narrative: Becoming Better Parents"
    In both Cialdini's chapter and Wilson's chapter, the authors describe empirical experiments that demonstrate how strong external threats or rewards only gained temporary compliance with directions or rules. Once these external forces were removed, or the adults who presented them were not present, the subject children acted with disregard for the

previous directions or rules. The chapters also describe what happens when alternative approaches with less reliance on external motivators are applied.

The authors of both books recommend parenting and educational practices that rely on explaining the reasons and purposes for rules as a way to help children internalize the values. These approaches help children attribute their positive behaviors to who they are or their identities. This also allows them to feel more in control of their lives and less like victims when they encounter problems or difficulties.

> Social scientists have discovered that we accept inner responsibility for a behavior when we think we have chosen to perform it in the absence of strong outside pressure. A large reward is one such external pressure. It may get us to perform certain actions, but it won't get us to accept inner responsibility for the acts. Consequently, we won't feel committed to them. The same is true of a strong threat; it may motivate compliance, but it is unlikely to produce long-term commitment. (Cialdini, 2001, p. 82)

> From a story editing perspective, however, the critical question is how the children explained to themselves why they weren't playing with the toy. In the severe threat situation, the kids were likely to attribute their behavior to the threat . . . the kids in the mild threat condition . . . they found another way to explain their good behavior, namely, they must be especially honest kids who are good at avoiding temptation. (Wilson, 2011, p. 85)

David and Goliath by Malcolm Gladwell

Chapter 4: "Carolyn Sachs"

In this chapter, Gladwell explores the idea that identity is determined by how a person views him or herself in relation to others. He uses the example of high achieving high school students who go to prestigious Ivy League colleges and end up becoming very discouraged because they are no longer at the top of the class.

> Students who would feel that they have mastered a subject at a good school can have the feeling that they are falling further and further behind in a really good school. And that feeling—as subjective and ridiculous and irrational as it may be—*matters*. How you feel about your abilities—your academic self-concept—in the context of your classroom shapes your willingness to tackle challenges and finish difficult tasks. It's the crucial element in your motivation and confidence. (p. 80)

"Expandable Selves" by Gregory Walton, David Paunesku, and Carol Dweck. In M. R. Leary & J. P. Tangney (Eds.), *Handbook of Self and Identity*

Chapter 7: "Expandable Selves"

This chapter explains that people have many selves or identities that are specific to certain domains of life: family, school, sports, church, to name just a few. Each person has a different identity depending on where or what he or she is doing. People who see themselves as having different identities in different situations (e.g., "I am a good golfer, but not too good at public speaking") are less prone to stress or depression when they have difficulty in one domain. Conversely, those people who view themselves globally as only having one identity are less able to cope with difficulties encountered in any domain. The authors suggest that a way to help people deal with threatening situations is to broaden their view of themselves by reminding them of the domains where they perceive themselves as more successful.

> It is intriguing to think that the more people are aware of their expandable selves, the more they may be able to evoke more complex and varied selves in challenging situations and thereby harness more resources to perform effectively. (p. 151)

How to Get People to Do Stuff: Master the Art and Science of Persuasion by Susan Weinschenk

Chapter 2: "The Need to Belong"

The book is designed to give people in leadership or sales positions strategies on how to get people to change their behaviors the way that you want them to change. Although it might sound a bit manipulative, the book does present a lot of the social psychological research that is accessible and easier to understand than more scholarly texts. The author uses the subheading of "use nouns, not verbs" to connect the need people have to belong to social groups to the labels or names given to the group. Calling people *voters* rather than *people who vote* makes them more likely to identify as part of a definite group of people and then begin to act like those people do.

> When you ask people to do stuff, use nouns rather than verbs. Invoke a sense of belonging to a group and people are much more likely to comply with your request. (p. 11)

Research Articles

"'Helping' Versus 'Being a Helper'": Invoking the Self to Increase Helping in Young Children" by Christopher Bryan, Allison Master, and Gregory Walton

In this research, preschool age children were put into two groups. In one group, the experimenter engaged them in conversation and mentioned how the child was good at helping others. In the other group, the experimenter referred instead to them as "helpers." Briefly after these conversations, the experimenter accidentally dropped items on the floor while the child played with a toy. The students who were referred to as "helpers" stopped their play and helped the experimenter much more than the students who were not called "helpers." The authors concluded that the students called "helpers" helped because they saw it as an opportunity to assume a valued identity.

The authors make a very significant point about when and where to use nouns and verbs with children: "Noun wording may undermine motivation when the prospect of failure looms large because the noun threatens to tie that failure to the self. In contrast, noun wording may enhance motivation when failure is not a relevant concern" (p. 5).

Using a noun for a task that could pose difficulty is similar to praising a student for being smart instead of acknowledging their effort. A student would be reluctant to try something challenging because failure would contradict the identity they want to maintain in the eyes of the world. Using nouns for tasks that are well within a child's ability increases the likelihood that they will perform any action that is consistent with that identity.

"Reducing the Racial Achievement Gap: A Social-Psychological Intervention" by Geoffrey Cohen, Julio Garcia, Nancy Apfel, and Allison Master

In this study, at the beginning of the school year Afro-American college students were asked to write about a personal value and why it was important to them. Students in the control group were asked about values in general (without making any personal connection to the values). The students who wrote about positive personal values had significantly higher grades than the students in the control group. The researchers concluded that affirming personal values helped these students expand their identities beyond the academic domain. By viewing themselves positively as people with strong values, they were better able to handle the academic challenges they faced. This expanded identity offset the stereotype threat that typically depresses academic performance in minority students.

> What appear to be small or brief events in isolation may in reality be the last element required to set in motion a process whose other necessary conditions already lay, not fully realized, in the situation. The flicking of a switch viewed in isolation may seem a quick and minor physical movement, seemingly out of proportion with the effect of having a room or a city block flooded with light. (p. 1309)

"Pawn or Origin? Enhancing Motivation in Disaffected Youth" by Richard deCharms

In this summary of his research, deCharms describes the "pawn" identity as feeling pushed or controlled by external forces and the "origin" identity as feeling in control of one's own behavior. His findings are quite clear: students who feel that they have some control over their own learning perform better than students who feel like they have little or no control. When teachers were trained to develop classroom environments where students had choice and control over aspects of their learning, the students' academic performance improved as well as their positive feelings about school. *The idea that identity is critical to learning is not a new one.*

> Slow and careful nurturing of the ability to make choices about how to go about the business of school, and allowing more choice as the ability to assume responsibility is learned, was the major characteristic of teachers who enhanced motivation and augmented academic achievement. (p. 446)

ACTIVITIES

Video Clip Discussion

Show the video clip of the National Anthem being played at the start of the NBA playoff game (Shapiro, 2003).

Although used in the activity in Chapter 7, this video clip can illustrate many points. In the clip, Mo Cheeks, the basketball coach extends his identity beyond basketball to coach the girl singing the National Anthem.

Discuss how one person's identity can change the identities of others.

Discuss how identities can change and how identities affect the culture and climate of any social environment.

Discuss how this situation can mirror a bullying situation. How can the *change identity strategy* be applied to all the participants in bullying situations?

Text-based Discussion

Read and discuss the article "Raising a Moral Child" by Adam Grant in the April 11, 2014, *New York Times*.

This is an excellent article that cites some of the current research on the role of identity in child rearing. It addresses the differences between using guilt and shame in responding to children's inappropriate or hurtful behavior. The author discusses how *shame* makes children feel bad about themselves as people whereas *guilt* makes them feel bad about how their actions hurt others. This is an important distinction to make when disciplining all children.

ACTIVITY: THREE QUESTIONS

Purpose: Use Positive Presuppositions to Change Identity

This activity can be used with staff, students, or any group connected to an organization.

Question One: Ask people to reflect on the following question: "What do I currently do to help our school or that helps to make it a good place?"

This presupposes all the participants are already people who not only care about the school, and are people who take specific actions that demonstrate caring and helping. Even though there are some people who might not do much or anything to help their school, they are being treated the same as the people who do care and help. They might have to search their memories a bit, but they should be able to find something positive in their histories. The question projects a positive identity on each participant.

Make certain that people have individual reflection time and that they write down their answers.

Depending on the group size and comfort level with sharing, determine the best way to disseminate the answers. Some options could be

- to have people work in pairs to share;
- a round-robin sharing with each person getting a brief amount of time to state what they do to help and care; and
- post what they wrote on a sheet of chart paper and allow everyone to view it once they are all posted.

It can be left up to the participants to decide whether they want to put their name on their statements.

Find a way to collect and keep a permanent visible record of all of these actions.

Question Two: Repeat the same procedure for the second question: "What else are you prepared to do (in addition to what you do now) to help the school and make it an even better place?"

Question Three: Repeat the same procedure for the third question: "What is one thing that *you would want every person to* do to make it a better place?" An additional option is to ask participants to explain how and why this one thing would make the school a better place.

The answers to this last question could become the basis for goal setting for the entire school community. A planning group could review these recommendations and look for similar suggestions. A list of three to five recommended actions could be presented to the school community for a vote to determine the one people would commit to enacting.

This activity can be done with students and staff, either separately or together. By sharing a common identity as community members, the students, staff, and parents can join together to actively make the school a better place. Bullying prevention can be reframed from simply responding to a singular problem to actually creating a better environment for everyone.

Recommendations for Change Identity in Schools

- Encourage students, staff, and parents to work on any type of project that can improve the school in any way. In addition to connecting the separate identities of the groups within the school, these types of activities produce tangible signs of progress.
- Find ways to use stories, rituals, and visible ways of emphasizing the school's values and recognizing the words and actions of community members who act in accordance with those values.
- Find ways to involve all students in volunteer activities in the school. Avoid dispensing jobs and responsibilities to the students who earn them. This only reinforces the stratification of the school instead of helping and supporting the school in an activity for all students.
- Make it a regular practice to have students offer advice in writing and/or videos to those students who are coming into their grade the following year. When students are able to translate what they have learned into information that benefits others, they assume the identity of benefactor, someone who acts in a way that benefits the common good.
- Teachers and staff need to become comfortable with asking students for their help in solving problems. Adults who show their humanity to students become more real, trustworthy, and tend to go up (not down) in their students' estimation and respect.
- Have staff get in the habit of talking about community and referring to students and colleagues as citizens and community members.
- Expand the range of clubs or afterschool activities beyond the traditional ones offered. For example, a builders club could be formed to allow students to work on Lego projects where students can work together on an equal basis without the need for special skills or abilities.
- Have periodic focus groups asking students for their input and advice on how to make the school a better place. The act of inviting students to give input to staff changes their identity and confers respect and positive recognition on them.

STRATEGY TWO: REQUIRE ASSEMBLY

> "Respect your fellow human beings, treat them fairly, disagree with them honestly, enjoy their friendship, explore your thoughts about one another candidly, work together for a common goal and help one another achieve it."
>
> —Bill Bradley

When I first became a principal, the president of the Parent Teachers Association (PTA) asked me what I thought about Christmas. I was a little surprised by the question, but it was simple enough to answer. I replied, "I enjoy spending it with my family; it is a nice time of year." She smiled back and said, "I mean what do you think about it at school?" I didn't have a ready answer for that question because it wasn't one that I had really thought a lot about. It didn't take long for that to change: how to celebrate or not celebrate Christmas (and any holiday in school) became an issue that our school lived with and struggled with for over five years. Although it was a problem that threatened to divide our school community, and one that I often wished would just go away, in retrospect, it brought the community together and helped me become a better school leader.

Our school was not located in a very diverse community. The large majority of families were Christian and were used to a typical Christmas and the nonreligious way of celebrating it in school. The principal who preceded me thought that his predecessor had celebrated Christmas too much and decided to de-emphasize any type of Christmas recognition or celebration. When I became principal, the community needed to know which way I would lean, whether toward the Christmas side or the non-Christmas side.

All I knew was that I didn't know much about the problem and needed to learn more. I also knew that I couldn't learn about it by myself; the community needed to learn about it together with me. That is what we did—and it wasn't easy. It took a while, several years, for many community members to realize that there was something to learn about the problem. Most people just thought that the problem was simple and straightforward and that I should just declare that their approach was right and that those who disagreed with them were wrong. Once a committee of parents and staff met together (fortunately people on both sides of the issue made sure to volunteer), they realized that although they might have been initially frustrated with the debate, they soon discovered that if either side "won" and got their way, then the school would ultimately lose because of the bad feelings it would generate for those who "lost." After much reading, discussing, consulting, researching, debating, and deliberating, the committee drafted a set of guiding principles and beliefs that represented what the committee thought was best for the whole school community. We also developed a series of Q's and A's that addressed particular issues and explained how the school would approach them. It took a while, almost a total of five years, for the issue to be understood and for our approach to be accepted, but by the time we as a school community had finished our work on the problem, we were a stronger school, had a process for addressing other problems, and had confidence in our collective teamwork. The struggle to work together, at times through strong differences of opinion, had forged a genuine atmosphere of trust and respect among all of us. As it turned out, our differences and our desire to not let our differences split us apart, led us to discover enough solutions in common to work out a plan where no side won or lost: an approach that represented *shared values and beliefs* for our school.

Looking back, the work that was done by the entire school community paved the way for many other creative ideas that often seemed to flow naturally from the processes that we established in confronting that seemingly intractable and emotional problem of Christmas in the school. The school community had developed a solution together for one problem that transferred the process to future problems. Our school learned that any positive change for us *required that same type of assembly (putting together the solutions we needed)* and that involved the whole community.

Require Assembly Strategy: What Does It Mean?

The *require assembly strategy* goes hand in hand with the *change identity strategy* because identities evolve from the words and actions of individuals working together. When people collaborate to solve problems and achieve common goals, they start to see and know each other differently. How they view and treat each other then influences and shapes the identity that each individual assumes within that community.

The *required assembly strategy* is related to the social psychological phenomenon known as the Ikea effect: "The IKEA effect is a cognitive bias that occurs when consumers place a disproportionately high value on products they partially created" (Norton, 2009, p. 30). When people are involved in the process of addressing a problem, they are more likely to take greater ownership for contributing to the solution; they value both the process of addressing the problem, and the solutions that emerge from the process.

When staff and students are involved in learning about the problem of bullying, they are more likely to change how they see the problem. Being part of the process to address the issues creates the conditions where the students start to "reframe" the problem from a rule infraction to a moral issue involving how people should treat each other.

The *require assembly strategy* assumes that if people work together and follow a process that

- respects each individual's voice;
- allows time for reflection and dialogue; and
- avoids jumping to quick solutions based on preconceived ideas; then not only is the problem addressed in a creative way, but the overall culture and climate of the school is enhanced as well.

The *require assembly strategy* means that those in leadership positions or wise educators who have the courage to speak up to those in leadership positions, devote time and thought to who should be involved and how the problem solving and decision-making process should be designed.

The *required assembly strategy* also means that those in leadership positions are able to facilitate (not micromanage) the process of addressing a problem. Effective facilitation means insuring the full and equal participation of members involved in the process.

Require Assembly: How Does It Work?

This explanation focuses on the inclusion of students in the process of addressing the problem of bullying and improving the school's culture and climate. I emphasize the student role since they are often overlooked and become recipients of services or programs determined by adults. However, I realize that staff also must be included in the process of learning about bullying and determining the right approach to take. Their input is essential and their role should be more than implementers of plans and strategies handed to them by a higher authority. The comments that follow really apply to all members of the school community.

When adults involve students in the process of addressing the issue of bullying prevention, a very different message is sent to them: they are part of the solution and are no longer viewed as part of the problem. Just telling students that they are part of the solution is not enough to change student identity. Actions speak louder, more convincingly and truthfully than words; students need to be personally invited to be part of the solution.

Students need to be given concrete ways to contribute to the well-being of the school community. They need to feel that they are true partners with the staff in making the school a better place. When students feel they are part of the solution, they act that way. They assume the identity of a responsible community member. Someone with that identity acts in a caring and responsible way toward the mistreatment of any member of the community.

If you want students to act in a different way, create the conditions for them to assume a different identity. For students to believe that the positive identity given to them by adults is genuine, they need to be invited to fully participate in actions that are associated with the new identity. In this way, they receive the identity and learn the skills that come with that identity all at the same time. For example, citizens becomes a jury members when they are first invited to serve on a jury and they learn how when they experience and actively participate in the trial itself.

Part of participating in any problem-solving process includes gaining knowledge and insight about the problem and how that problem affects people (including each participant on a personal basis). As students are involved in learning about bullying and receiving information about broader issues related to people's moral commitments to each other, they have a great opportunity to learn about themselves and other members of the school community. For example if in the past, a student might have been reluctant to speak up when witnessing a bullying situation, he or she might gain insight about why they were hesitant in the course of being involved in the process of addressing school bullying. That same student might also hear and see strategies that can be used effectively when encountering bullying.

Being able to intervene or report bullying can be a daunting task for any student. When students are involved in the process of addressing school issues, they can "pick up" ideas and strategies for how to help and support their peers. Talking with a peer about how to help a mistreated student expands the range of options that any one student has when witnessing bullying. Bystanders can gain the courage to do the right thing even in the face of social pressures constraining their helpful actions when they discover like-minded peers who also want to do the right thing. These students can give each other advice and encouragement. Intervening and reporting bullying is easier to do in pairs than alone.

Adults can forget that students are often not able to understand their own motives for bullying others or for not helping others in need. When students become involved in learning about the social dynamics of bullying, they are learning about their own developmental needs to conform to the social group. Very often just this added knowledge and awareness of *what might be going on inside of them* helps students understand their feelings and motives. This understanding can lead to their making better moral choices when presented with an opportunity to bully more vulnerable students or to help a student who is being bullied.

Staff can intentionally design the composition of small problem-solving groups of students in order to give students the opportunity to become familiar with students who are not typically in their social circles. This does not mean putting together a potential target and a student who might tend to bully. Instead, it can be an opportunity for students who typically don't bully other students and are well liked by peers to develop more meaningful relationships with students who are vulnerable to being bullied. When an unpopular student who doesn't have many friends can form a positive relationship with a more popular student, then the protective factors for that vulnerable student against bullying increase dramatically.

Students are used to working in small groups on assignments in class. Many times this work has little meaning or purpose beyond getting the assignment done. When students work in small groups to address a problem, the work takes on a very different meaning and purpose. Many students who otherwise might appear unmotivated or lacking in academic skills can very often "shine" in the eyes of their peers when they view their work as meaningful and purposeful. Since there are many ways of helping and contributing to the school community, "success" is not dependent on academic skills or knowledge. Students who might feel inferior to students who achieve academically can often contribute as well, if not better, than the students who typically succeed in school. Since these students are more vulnerable to being bullied, anything that can showcase them in a better light in school decreases their attractiveness as easy targets for bullying.

On a very practical level, students can bring great ideas and effective strategies to the table. Since students often see and hear bullying when adults aren't present, they know how bullying functions in the school environment. They are truly the experts on the subject, more so than the adults. Students know how their world operates and what messages would strike a meaningful chord with most students and what ones would be ignored. Solutions and strategies designed by students are perceived more positively than ones that just come from the adults in charge. And they are more likely to work!

Getting students involved in the process of addressing bullying prevention requires more than assemblies or students wearing anti-bullying shirts. Students should be given meaningful tasks and assignments that challenge them to think and solve problems. The more effort and time they invest in helping, the more they value the work they do. Giving them authentic tasks that can visibly improve the school environment increases their sense of accomplishment and their commitment to making the school a better place in the future.

The *require assembly strategy* means that all members of the school community work together to make their school a better place: using community to build community. Identities, skills, knowledge, meaning, and purpose flow out of people coming together to support the common good, and where every person has something to contribute. In this type of school environment, success and well-being are available for everyone and not limited to a select few.

RESOURCES FOR EXPLORING AND SUPPORTING THE STRATEGY OF REQUIRE ASSEMBLY

Influencer: The Power to Change Anything by Kerry Patterson, Joseph Grenny, David Maxfield, Ron McMillan, and Al Switzler

Chapter 7: "Find Strength in Numbers"

This chapter explains how to use the power of the group to change the group. It offers examples of how sharing the problem with the people who are often considered the source of the problem is a very effective way of changing their identities and solving the problem.

> When the people surrounding you are causing or contributing to the problems—playing the role of the disabler rather than enabler—fight the urge to attack your detractors for their contribution to your pain. Instead, co-opt them. Turn a *me* problem into a *we* problem. Build social capital in order to resolve persistent and **resistant problems**. (p. 181)

The Multiplier Effect: Tapping the Genius Within Our Schools **by Liz Wiseman, Lois Allen, and Elise Foster**

Chapter 2: "The Talent Finder"

This excellent book provides a framework for understanding two basic types of leaders: diminishers and multipliers. The authors describe the mind-sets, assumptions, and disciplines of each type. They assert that leaders who are multipliers build leadership in others, thereby, increasing the overall capacity, productivity, and well-being of each individual and the overall organization.

> They see genius all around them. They see it and they put it to use, stretching and strengthening the talent. People can't help but grow around them. These leaders see talent in others because they are oriented outward, focused on other people, seeing each person as a unique treasure waiting to be discovered. . . . Multipliers hold a deep belief in the intelligence that exists in abundance. They believe that everyone has talent and intelligence and something to contribute. They see intelligence in high definition. (pp. 26–27)

Helping: How to Offer, Give and Receive Help **by Edgar Schein**

Chapter 7: "Teamwork as a Perpetual Reciprocal Helping"

Involving students and staff in the process of improving the school culture and climate, is a way, in essence, to help each individual learn and grow as the entire group works together to "help" the school. The great benefits of involving people in this helping process can only be realized if the group functions well. This book is excellent because it provides a clear explanation of what needs to happen for a group to be able to help the organization and its members.

> I am defining teamwork as a state of multiple reciprocal helping relationships, including all the members of the group that have to work together. Building a team, therefore, is not just creating one? client/helper relationship, but simultaneously building one among all the members. (p. 108)

Join the Club: How Peer Pressure Can Transform the World **by Tina Rosenberg**

Introduction and Chapter 4: "Corporate Tools"

This book chronicles how many traditional approaches that use rational arguments and fear tactics to change people's behavior often produce the opposite effect and actually increase the behavior targeted for change. The author describes how approaches that "use the group to change the group" have achieved remarkable success.

> The typical attempt to solve a social ill focuses on giving people information, or it tries to motivate people through fear. But these strategies tend to fail exactly when the issue becomes most salient and emotionally fraught. The more important and deeply rooted the behavior, the less impact information has and the more people close their minds to messages that scare them. (p. xix)

Chapter 4 describes how involving teenagers in the anti-smoking campaign produced a significant reduction in teen smoking.

> Florida then took its campaign for the teenage mind a step farther: it reinforced the notion of rebellion (against the tobacco companies) by using the social cure. SWAT (Students Working Against Tobacco) recruited thousands of youngsters and trained them in leadership skills and organizing. The SWAT kids created some of the "truth ads themselves and had approval over all of them." (p. 71)

Research Article

"The IKEA Effect: When Labor Leads to Love" by Michael Norton

This research demonstrates that people value products that they helped create more than fully assembled products. Although participating in the process of addressing the problem of school bullying is different than assembling a product, it makes sense that active participation in any endeavor increases a person's investment and commitment to any plans and solutions produced by that process. This research also shows that the increased value of a product is dependent on the participant perceiving it as completed. Similarly, staff and student involvement in any problem-solving process should produce achievable goals that when met provide them with a sense of accomplishment.

> Participants saw their amateurish creations—of both utilitarian and hedonic products—as similar in value to the creations of experts, and expected others to share their opinions. Our account suggests that labor leads to increased valuation only when labor results in successful completion of tasks; thus when participants built and then destroyed their creations, or failed to complete them, the IKEA effect dissipated. Finally, we show that labor increases valuation of completed products not just for consumers who profess an interest in "do-it-yourself" projects, but even for those who are relatively uninterested. (p. 2)

ACTIVITIES

Video Clip Discussions

There are two video clips that illustrate how an entire community can be involved in achieving a goal and solving a challenging problem.

View the barn-building scene from the movie *Witness*, directed by Peter Weir and starring Harrison Ford. This scene shows how the entire Amish community comes together to build a barn for a newly married couple. This clip is often used in training sessions on cooperative learning in order to illustrate positive interdependence: how the different skills and abilities of the entire community are needed for the successful completion of a task.

Next, view the "failure is not an option" scene from the movie *Apollo 13*, directed by Ron Howard and starring Tom Hanks.

This scene shows how the project director challenges the team to meet the difficult task of getting the stranded astronauts home. The scene illustrates the role of effective leadership in helping to define the goal while still empowering all of the members of the team to raise questions, express feelings, and think creatively to achieve that goal. Discuss the concept of interdependence and its effect on each member of the group.

Discuss how working together affects how the participants feel about each other and the work they do.

Discuss how both scenes are applicable to the problem of bullying in schools.

Discuss how purpose and meaning are involved in the challenges facing both communities. Discuss the motivations of each member of the community for participating in both activities.

Text-based Discussion

Read and discuss the article "Peer Influences and Positive Cognitive Restructuring" by Thomas F. Tate in the journal *Reclaiming Children and Youth*.

This article discusses how peer influences usually have negative connotations. In addition, the author states that adults often have a pessimistic view of children and feel superior to them (called "adultism"). These attitudes prevent adults from involving students in problem-solving activities and fail to capitalize on the positive aspects of peer influences. He discusses how essential it is to involve students in these types of activities. Participation in problem-solving activities actually improves students cognitive processing and their social skills.

> Teachers who resist entering into partnerships with students point out that their role is to educate—not raise—children. However,

preparing students responsibly to solve life's problems is a primary function of the educator's role. Failure to recognize the impact of peer relationships on this process only serves to make the teachers' job more difficult and results in more troubled adolescents facing rejection from public school settings. (p. 217)

ACTIVITY: MAKING REAL CHANGE; MAKING CHANGE REAL

Purpose: Putting Ideas into Action

This activity can be considered a test run or a pilot project for taking an idea and making it a reality. As previously discussed, sometimes the greatest obstacle to positive change is thinking that change is not possible. Many school communities seem stuck because too many people believe that change is not possible. Unfortunately, when change is imposed on people they typically resist implementing any aspect of it, therefore, "proving" that change indeed is not possible. Breaking this cycle and creating any type of positive change is an essential first step in making progress to achieve any worthwhile goal.

This activity is based on the previous introduced activity for the *change identity strategy, Three Questions*.

Question Three asked the group to select one thing that they wished everyone would do that could make the school a better place. Designate a group of people (making sure that the group is inclusive of a variety of community members, such as students, parents, teachers, administrators, and support staff) to design a change strategy or plan for having the one behavior—the one action or proposal that received the most votes or was mentioned the most—happen more consistently in the school.

The group charged with this task can begin to learn about the change process by using the resources mentioned in this book or by researching other sources on the change process. They can then design a change plan based on their collective learning and understanding of the change process.

Recommendations for Require Assembly in Schools

- High schools and most middle schools have student councils. Find ways to increase the input of student councils into the decision-making process of the school. Find way to increase the diversity of the members on the council.
- Establish a student council at the elementary level. This provides a good opportunity for students from different grade levels to work together. Each classroom could have a representative on the council.

For the earlier grade levels, there could be a pair of students representing each classroom.
- Now with computers readily available for all students to use, it becomes easier to collect survey data about how students feel about topics relevant to how the school functions. Sharing the data with students keeps them accurately informed about what other students are thinking and feeling.
- Involve students in developing or revising parts of a school's discipline plan. Students might have more creative ways of making restitution for behaviors that show a lack of respect for others.
- If a school has some guiding principles that represent their values and beliefs, they should be visibly posted. Students and staff can add examples on how people in their school have acted in accordance with these principles.
- Make classroom meetings a regular part of each classroom. Having students check in with each other creates a sense of community. Meetings can be times for sharing good news and for addressing problems.
- Have a yearly school theme connected to the school mission statement and values. Students can generate ideas for school themes and the entire student body can vote to select the theme for the following year. Some examples of themes can be: "X School Is Working for Peace," "X School Cares about the Community," or "X School Is Living a Healthy Life." These themes create opportunities for learning beyond separate classrooms and can unite the whole school in learning about topics relevant to each person's life.
- Involve students in planning special events for their classrooms and for the school to recognize the support people in the school, such as the custodians, bus drivers, cafeteria monitors, and secretaries.
- Designate a special day where all the students and staff learn about a topic that is not typically studied in the classroom. Years ago, these special days were called "teach-ins" where an entire school learned about a topic of social importance. Involve students in planning this day. The day could also include watching an inspiring age-appropriate movie together and then having classroom discussions about the movie.

SUMMARY

"Who" strategies seek to create opportunities for all members of the school community to develop a variety of positive and responsible identities. These identities communicate to them and the entire community that students are the solution to the problem of bullying, not the source of it.

People act in accord with the identity that they assume. Student identities are created by their relationships with adults. If adults want to change student behavior, they need to treat them with respect and have confidence in them.

Students who see themselves as responsible and caring community members tend to act in a way consistent with that identity.

Change identity and *assembly required* change strategies are closely connected. Identities are formed by how people interact with each other and the experiences they share together. When people are empowered to work together to make the school a better place, they become benefactors for the school and therefore take greater ownership for the school. This is how positive and prosocial norms develop in a community.

Educators have to value the contributions that all students can make in improving the school environment. Students are truly in-house experts in understanding bullying and can have excellent ideas for how to effectively address it.

10

"Do" Strategies for Reframing Bullying Prevention

These reframing strategies leverage a variety of positive changes that can transform a school's culture and climate. Whereas the previous strategies were aimed at specific goals, for example changing how students think of themselves, and involving all members of the school community in decision making; these strategies point toward broader environmental changes in the school. The resources and activities included should help people envision the ways that schools can change when these strategies are regularly implemented.

1. Make it safe to play.
2. Train "First Responders."
3. Tell the *right* story.

STRATEGY ONE: MAKE IT SAFE TO PLAY

"The principle goal of education is to create men who are capable of doing new things, not simply of repeating what other generations have done—men who are creative, inventive and discoverers."

—Jean Piaget

I was fortunate to grow up in a time and place that allowed my friends and me to enjoy our days on our own during the summers. We knew to be safe, where to go and not to go, and to return home when the streetlights went on. If we stayed within those boundaries, we could pretty much do what we wanted. I loved the summer time.

Compared to my pretty strict, some might say harsh, Catholic school environment, the summer time in my neighborhood offered me great opportunities for creativity and social interaction. I didn't know it at the time, but I learned more in those two months of *play* than I did in ten months of *work* at school.

On really hot summer afternoons, after we played our fifth game of ball or rode our bikes until we were dying of thirst, we returned to a friend's house to take a break. The house had many front steps leading up to the front door, which was perfect because we could play the "game of school."

It was a pretty simple game. One person played the teacher and stood in front of the other kids who sat on the lowest steps. The teacher would put his or her hands behind their back and hold a small stone in either the right or left hand. The teacher presented both closed fists, with one concealing the stone, in front of each student who had to answer the basic question of which hand held the stone. The teacher repeated this question for each student trying to get each player to guess the wrong hand.

Obviously, there was only one right answer and each student had a fifty-fifty chance of getting it right. Those who answered correctly got *promoted* and moved up a step while those who were wrong were *left back* or had to stay on the same step. This game proceeded until one person graduated or reached the top step. As a reward for graduating first, the winning student then became the teacher.

As simple as the game was, it was a frighteningly accurate depiction, boiled down to its essence, of what school was for us: get the right answer and move on, get the wrong answer and suffer the consequences. It was always nice to move up, but the real goal of the game was to avoid watching your friends ascend while you stayed stuck on the lower steps.

We were safe playing this game because we chose to play it and knew it was only a game. We all also knew that the real game of school was not something we chose and that school was not always a safe place: the fear of being wrong and the consequences for being wrong loomed over us and the threat of those consequences hid behind everything we did. Fear was an integral and central element of what it meant to go to school, even though we didn't know it at the time. This made school a place where you couldn't afford to *play* because too much depended on getting the right answers. Fooling around led to trouble in more ways than one. No wonder my school pictures never showed me smiling. I took school very seriously. *School was not a safe place to play. For too many students (and educators) schools are still not safe places to play.*

Make It Safe To Play: What Does It Mean?

My son took piano lessons for many years, so I attended many recitals. Although I had great confidence in my son and I knew he worked hard and was prepared, as I listened to him play I was full of anxiety hoping and praying that he would make the fewest and least noticeable mistakes possible. He could play almost every note just right, but the ones he got wrong seem to wound me right to the bone. Thankfully, these recitals happened once a year and were considered just a tiny part of the experience of learning to play the piano. If they were anything more than that, I am sure he would have abandoned the piano altogether. However, sometimes today it seems like the pressure in school is now more and more like recitals and less and less like rehearsals, practice, or anything remotely resembling karaoke.

I mention karaoke because it is the complete opposite of recitals. It is a fun way to play music; so much fun that the benefits of it are too easily overlooked:

- Karaoke engages people with music in a playful way.
- It is a social activity where every participant gets an opportunity to perform in front of a nonjudgmental audience.
- Participants are given the words and the music to help them sing.
- Mistakes are part of the fun.
- It gives people a chance to try out a different identity for themselves.
- There are no penalties or negative consequences involved.
- People participate in it for its own sake. They don't need incentives.

Karaoke and recitals do not have to be mutually exclusive. People who are involved with music can participate in both activities and both can play a role in fostering a love and appreciation of music. Playing karaoke combined with other forms of rehearsal and practice could conceivably prepare musicians for a time when they have to perform in a more serious venue as a way to demonstrate a level of skill.

There is a time and place for recitals, a time and place when a person needs to be held accountable for performing, but the way to prepare for a recital is not to learn in a recital-like environment. People need the space and time to learn without being held accountable and judged before they are ready and prepared to succeed. If a recital is on one end of the continuum of learning and karaoke is on the other end, then schools as places of learning should be placed more on the karaoke end than on the recital end of the continuum.

When the time comes, people who learn without fear in a safe and playful environment are better able to perform with greater courage and confidence in recital-like situations. They love the process of learning and the opportunity to share what they learned. This is very different from experiencing learning only as a necessary performance to gain approval and to avoid negative judgment; that method is equivalent to learning in a recital-like environment in order to perform in a recital.

When it is *not safe to play* the following happens.

- People naturally become self-protective and self-centered.
- People tend to stay within familiar and reassuring ways of thinking and acting.
- People can view others as threatening to their own safety.
- People are more focused on those who have more power over them than those with equal or less power.
- People become very risk averse and unwilling to try on new identities and ways of acting.
- People are more concerned with complying and conforming (staying safe) and less concerned with helping and supporting others.

The *make it safe to play* strategy means that schools should create an environment for learning that reflects the spirit of karaoke rather than the serious evaluative tone of a recital. It means that schools should be safer places where playing is accepted and embraced as a way to learn, instead of something to avoid or suppress.

The *make it safe to play* strategy means to remove or at least lessen the fear of making mistakes and being judged as the hallmark experience of school.

Make it safe to play means reframing mistakes from aberrations that shouldn't happen to natural and integral parts of the learning process.

Make it safe to play means freeing the experience of learning from the specter of constant evaluation of performance by people who have greater authority and power. It means that the focus should be on learning and not performing for the approval of those with more power and control.

The *make it safe to play* strategy is a difficult one to implement, since educators have been "taught" by the culture of school that playing is not a way to learn and is counterproductive and frivolous. Most educators have been taught *not to play* and that it *is not safe to play*. They are told that they could experience negative consequences for playing and for letting their students play. In fact, a strong case can be made that the reason why schools seem so resistant to change is because they have done such a good job in stifling play and the creativity that comes from it.

The institutions of schools have employed fear very successfully while making this intangible miasma invisible and silent to the people (teachers and students) affected by it.

Unfortunately, educators that embrace play and creativity in their practice often have to do so in covert ways, since such approaches are not sanctioned by current educational policies. Positive school change will come from these creatively subversive educators who can lead their peers toward a different set of practices that make teaching and learning more satisfying and productive. Change is more likely to come from the bottom up than from the top down.

The *make it safe to play* strategy for reframing bullying prevention means understanding the concept of *safety* differently. Most educators would agree that feeling safe is a prerequisite for learning, but this type of *safety* is usually thought of as keeping students safe from the threat of bullying by other students. This concept of keeping students safe is interpreted as keeping some students from threatening other students. With this perspective, students are viewed as the source of the problem and controlling their behavior then becomes the focus of most policies, programs, and protocols.

Make it safe to play means that the educators and adults in the school (the people with greater power and authority) are the first ones to change their behavior, especially if they rely on fear as a means to control students.

The *make it safe to play* strategy means that educators have to expand this narrow view of safety, and instead understand how fear is embedded in the way that schools are structured and function. It means recognizing and understanding how fear manifests itself in school and then taking deliberate and intentional steps to reduce the institutional effects of fear on students.

The *make it safe to play* strategy doesn't mean that all fear has to be removed from the school experience; though laudable, that goal cannot be achieved overnight. This strategy does require that educators become aware of how fear has a negative influence on learning and community. From this awareness, they should first commit to not using fear as a tactic to control students. Although they might not have readily available methods to use as alternatives, they need to commit to learning a new set of skills.

Making It Safe To Play: How Does It Work?

In simple terms, when there is less fear and anxiety in schools, every member of the school community feels better and safer. Less fear and anxiety helps people feel *at home* in school and able to be themselves. Reducing the amount of fear embedded in the traditional practices of school, creates better conditions for nurturing the empathy that students already have. Feeling safer and more secure allows people to cooperate more and become less self-centered. Their attention is freed from worrying about safety, which allows them to explore other aspects of their environment. Feeling safe and secure allows people to play, experiment, and enjoy learning. People are more likely to be at their best and perform to their potential when they are not weighed down with concerns about their status and their place in the community.

Reducing fear and anxiety from the environment does more than just make school settings places without fear; they naturally become better places for learning because people act differently in that atmosphere. Schools characterized as safe places for playing and learning are places where educators learned a different way of interacting with students:

- They talk about learning rather than allocating assignments and work.
- They value what students think and create opportunities for students to learn from each other and not just from the adults.
- They are not afraid of sharing their humanity with students. They tell stories of their own learning—their own successes and failures.
- They make "failing" part of learning and prepare students for the ups and downs of the learning process.
- They explain the reason and purpose for positive and caring behavior (and model it).
- They realize that people tend to overemphasize negative events, so they help students cultivate the ability to recognize and value progress rather than perfection.
- They model humility and confidence: they don't know everything, but are confident in their ability to learn given enough time and effort.
- They convey that the only real failure is not trying at all.
- They acknowledge feelings and doubts as part of learning.
- They look at problems from the point of view of students rather than their own needs or fears.
- They are visible learners themselves and not just teachers.
- They actively seek the positive in people and refrain from judging them.
- They realize that students are works in progress who will make mistakes.
- They are available to help students learn and to learn from them rather than to just correct them or provide negative consequences.
- They believe that each person is always learning and growing with each new experience and challenge. They never "make up their mind" about anyone.
- They create opportunities for students to make choices and have a voice in decision making on a regular basis.

When more and more educators act in these ways, fear is no longer a hidden, predominant, and controlling presence in the school. The simplest formula for positive school change is getting more and more adults to act this way in school until these behaviors become the norm, and not the exception. When educators treat students differently, they help students create new and evolving identities where they can *play* without worrying about negative consequences or the expectations of those with authority. Students also begin to feel more open to trusting adults and to seek their help and advice when they confront problems or challenging situations.

Very often intervening in bullying situations requires a combination of feeling confident to take the initiative, to improvise creative solutions, and to persist when initial attempts are not successful. If students are used to worrying about making mistakes and pleasing those in authority, they cannot be expected to pull these helping behaviors out of thin air; their daily experience of school has taught them to mind their own business. In learning to always *play it safe,* students refrain from the type of playing and experimenting that it takes to help others in many ambiguous bullying situations. If students learn in a safer environment where mistakes are part of learning, they develop the confidence to make their own decisions and learn to take the courageous step of helping others in need.

The more students are used to playing, the less risk adverse they become. They are more likely to learn to empathize and act on their moral feelings, and less likely to worry about what those in authority think about their attempts to help others.

When schools are safer places to play for all students, failing becomes less stigmatizing. When fewer students are stigmatized, the social dynamics of the school change and bullying loses its function of protection and promotion of social status.

If schools become places where every student belongs and no longer has to worry about their membership or status in the community, then the time, energy, and motivation expended to gain the safest or most prestigious social position is freed up for other pursuits and contributions to the community.

RESOURCES FOR EXPLORING AND SUPPORTING THE STRATEGY OF MAKE IT SAFE TO PLAY

Teaming: How Organizations Learn, Innovate, and Compete in the Knowledge Economy by Amy Edmondson

Chapter 4: "Making It Safe to Team"

Since organizations face complex and challenging problems in a fast-paced, ever changing environment, they need every employee's active participation and contribution in order to achieve their goals. The better the organization is at learning to learn the more successful it will be. Learning is optimized when each member feels free to point out problems, raise questions, and challenge assumptions in the natural flow of the work environment. Edmondson describes how difficult it is for people to overcome their fear of authority enough to speak up with confidence. She describes what it takes for organizations to overcome this barrier and to create the conditions that allow for true collaboration and honest feedback.

> In psychologically safe environments, people believe that if they make a mistake others will not penalize or think less of them for it. They also believe that others will not resent or humiliate them when they ask for help or information. This belief comes about

> when people both trust and respect each other, and it produces a sense of confidence that the group won't embarrass, reject, or punish someone for speaking up. Thus, psychological safety is a taken-for-granted belief about how others will respond when you ask a question, seek feedback, admit a mistake, or propose a possibly wacky idea. Most people feel a need to "manage" interpersonal risk to retain a good image, especially at work, and especially in the presence of those who formally evaluate them. (p. 119)

Leaders Eat Last: Why Some Teams Pull Together and Others Don't by Simon Sinek

Chapter 3: "Belonging: From 'Me' to 'We'"

This book explains the essential role of leadership in creating an environment where each individual feels safe and secure from both internal and external threats. The author provides examples of organizations that provide what he describes as the Circle of Safety. This high degree of safety and sense of belonging is the foundation of success because people are inspired to help each other. They also share a collective commitment to the mission of the organization.

> Intimidation, humiliation, isolation, feeling dumb, feeling useless and rejection are all stresses we try to avoid inside the organization. But the danger inside the organization is controllable and it should be the goal of leadership to set a culture free of danger from each other. And the way we do this is by giving people a sense of belonging. By offering them a strong culture based on a clear set of human values and beliefs. By giving them the power to make decisions. By offering trust and empathy. By creating a Circle of Safety. (p. 21)

Free to Learn: Why Unleashing the Instinct to Play Will Make Our Children Happier, More Self-Reliant, and Better Students for Life by Peter Gray

Chapter 4: "Seven Sins of Our System of Forced Education"

This is a powerful book that echoes almost all of the key points that are made in this book. The author is a critic of the entire system of forced education and with great insight he explains how schools stifle and suppress learning. Although his message might be too radical for many educators working in schools, his ideas and arguments cannot be ignored and can be useful in making important changes in how we educate students, even in the current system.

> One of the tragedies of our system of schooling is that it teaches students that life is a series of hoops that one must get through, by one means or another, and that success lies in other's judgments rather than real, self-satisfying accomplishments. (p. 75)

> We are by nature an intensely social species, designed for cooperation. . . . But regardless of the lectures that students might hear in school about the value of helping others, schools work against such behavior. By design, it teaches selfishness. The forced competitiveness, the constant grading and ranking of students, contain the implicit lesson that each student's job is to look out for himself or herself and to do better than others. (p. 75)

Why We Do What We Do: Understanding Self-motivation by Edward Deci and Richard Flaste

Chapter 6: "The Inner Force of Development"

This book, which was previously mentioned in Chapter 5, provides a detailed and elaborate explanation of self-determination theory. In this chapter, the authors specifically address the importance of viewing people as intrinsically motivated to learn and to connect with the social world. The critical choice for educators is whether to treat people in a way that supports and nurtures that tendency or to thwart it by trying to control or manipulate them. When people feel manipulated, either by rewards or consequences, they become more anxious and concerned about complying or defying those who hold power over them. This type of controlled environment restricts a person's play and subsequent discovery of their own authentic inclination to interact with the world in a positive way. This is particularly true of school environments that are constantly telling and manipulating students to be good and kind.

> Controlling environments that demand, pressure, prod, and cajole people to behave, think or feel in particular ways. These are the environments that produce automatons—people who engage in instrumental reasoning, comply with demands, are, in a sense, only half alive, and once in a while are prompted to defy the controls.

> It is truly amazing that if people are ongoingly treated as if they were either passive mechanisms or barbarians needing to be controlled, they will begin to act more and more that way. As they are controlled, for example, they will act more and more as if they need to be controlled. It has led to the call for greater discipline, for more heavy handedness. But ironically, it should call for just the opposite. (pp. 83–84)

Research Article

"Prevention of School Bullying: The Important Role of Autonomy-Supportive Teaching and Internalization of Pro-Social Values" by Guy Roth, Yaniv Kanat-Maymon, and Uri Bibi

This study demonstrated that students who perceive their teachers acting in autonomously supportive ways (non-controlling), bully less frequently and express more positive attitudes toward their classmates. When student felt less controlled and presumably less anxious, they were more likely to act and feel more positive toward their peers.

> In as much as external regulation involves instrumental behaviour enacted to obtain rewards or avoid sanctions by socializing agents, students' aggressive behaviour is liable to continue in places and times where supervision is absent. Furthermore, mere expectations of student obedience to external rules and demands do not coincide with educators' deeper educational goals for their students like profound internalization of considerateness and anti-bullying behaviours. Given that teachers' justification and explanation of pro-social behaviours and attitudes (involving provision of rationale and taking the other's perspective) is straightforward and accessible, an autonomy-supportive context appears feasible. The present findings demonstrate the importance of students' perceptions of AST [Autonomy supportive teaching] that enabled them to identify with values and expectations and integrate them. Thus, according to SDT [self-determination theory], when the behavioural regulation is based on identification and integration external monitoring and external control are no longer needed. (p. 663)

ACTVITIES

Video Clip Discussion:

In this scene from the movie *Hoosiers*, directed by David Anspaugh and starring Gene Hackman, the coach of a small high school basketball team knows that playing in a huge arena could frighten his players. Instead of preaching to them or just telling them not to be frightened, he has them measure the dimensions of the court so that they can discover that the *game* will be the same for them regardless of the size of the arena. He removes the fear from the situation so that they can play their best.

I also highly recommend the documentary *A Touch of Greatness*, directed by Leslie Sullivan and starring Albert Cullum. It is the story of a remarkable elementary school teacher who created a playful, yet challenging learning environment for his students. Although he taught in the early 1960s, many of his classes were filmed, so the documentary is filled with actual scenes from his classrooms. Interspersed with the classroom scenes are comments from adults who were his students. The film shows the rich learning that occurs when teachers make it safe for students to play.

Born to Learn is a short animated five-minute film on YouTube that is narrated by Damian Lewis and is an excellent primer on human development. It describes the value and purpose of play as a foundation for all learning. It advocates for creating an educational system that supports human development.

Discuss and describe an environment that is psychologically safe.

Discuss specific educational practices that can make an environment safe for learning.

Discuss the ways that a school can support human development rather than suppress or control it.

Text-based Discussion:

"Unsolicited Evaluation Is the Enemy of Creativity" by Peter Gray

This blog post describes empirical research that reveals the effects of implied evaluation on creativity. It also describes how a positive environment free of evaluation and judgment leads to higher levels of learning and personal satisfaction.

This post is on his Freedom to Learn blog that can be found at http://www.psychologytoday.com/blog/freedom-learn.

ACTIVITY: CREATING SAFETY

Purpose: Operationalizing Psychological Safety

T-Chart for Psychological Safety

Since psychological safety can be an abstract concept, it needs to be translated into specific words and actions. Participants in this activity can individually reflect on a learning experience when they felt safe and secure to make mistakes and when they could try and fail without negative consequences.

Have participants in groups of four to six people.

Ask them to visualize that safe environment and to recall what was said or not said that contributed to their sense of safety and support.

Have each person take a turn sharing this learning experience.

After each person has shared, the group can work together to create a T chart of what psychological safety "looks like" and "sounds like." For "looks like," participants can include the descriptions of the physical environment that contributed to their sense of safety, such as comfortable furniture, visual references on the wall, people sitting together with no one standing over them, and so forth. For "sounds like," participants can include statements that people could make, such as "I found this difficult also," "how many times would you like to try this," and "it's okay to struggle a bit, we all did when we started."

Looks like	Sounds like

Recommendations for Make it Safe to Play in schools

- Have a schoolwide Safety Day where the entire school community can discuss the concept of safety in all of its forms. All members of the school community can discuss what they need to feel safe to learn. There can also be time devoted to discussing what causes anxiety for people. The school can also gather ideas for how to make the school safer for everyone.
- Have teachers include a discussion about making mistakes in each lesson. Acknowledging the likelihood of mistakes, and discussing productive ways of reacting to them can prepare students for approaching tasks with less anxiety.
- Have students create "hard cards" to help them when they encounter work that is difficult for them. Unfortunately, many students associate being smart with ease and speed of completion. Any time they encounter a task that they perceive as hard, they can often become fearful and anxious, which only depresses their ability. Talking about those times and then preparing strategies to use in the face of perceived difficulty can give students a ready-made plan to use before their anxiety increases. The "hard card" can have the phrase "when something is hard I can . . ."written on it. Then students can generate statements to follow, such as "take a deep breath," "remind myself that I just have to try," "find an example that I can do". These cards are then kept on the student desks for easy reference. This type of concrete support in times of stress is a way to reduce the amount of fear and anxiety in schools.
- Build reflection into the routines of learning. Have students and teachers reserve even two to three minutes at the end of each lesson to jot down thoughts and feelings about what they just experienced. Students create a personal learning history that can become a reference point and reminder of times when they initially were anxious, but persisted and attained positive results.

- Make humor a part of each lesson. Assign students to prepare an appropriate joke of the day. Find a short and humorous video clip to show on a regular basis. The more any group of people laughs together, the safer they feel with each other.
- Have "need to talk" cards readily available in each classroom for students. Teachers can explain that they might appear busy and unconcerned, but really do care about how students are feeling. Stating this explicitly and having a stack of "need to talk" cards available for students to use sends a message to students that adults are there for them as they face the inevitable problems of growing and living. Since it can be hard to verbally initiate requests for help, a simple card indicating a need to talk with a name on it can make it easy for a reluctant student to get help. A student can simply place the card in the designated spot indicated by the teacher. The teacher can then seek out the student at an appropriate time to talk. Knowing support is always available is way to feel safe, even if students never use the card.

STRATEGY TWO: TRAIN FIRST RESPONDERS

"The world is a dangerous place, not because of those who do bad things, but because of those who look on and do nothing."

—Albert Einstein

I knew what it felt like to fight off going to sleep while driving. That was why waking up to the sound of my car crashing into a telephone pole and the continuous beeping of the car horn, left me stunned and totally disoriented. Right before the accident, I didn't sense that I was about to go to sleep; I just suddenly fell asleep only two blocks from my home. When I opened my eyes, there was no alarm clock to turn off; the nightmare was a reality and all I could see was the white airbag inches from my face. When I pushed it away, I also discovered that my car was facing down the hill that I had been driving up just seconds before.

Instinctively checking to see if I could move and for signs of blood (there was none), all that entered my mind was that I was in an accident and not seriously hurt. I turned off the ignition to stop the beeping, unsnapped my shoulder belt, opened the door, and almost stepped into a drainage ditch on the side of the road. By then, other cars had stopped and people in neighboring houses were walking over to me to see if I was okay. I opened my mouth, but wasn't able to talk because I was still so confused and stunned. As I was slowly starting to think about to do next, I heard a siren and the Emergency Medical Technician (EMT) truck pulled up right next to me. A very calm EMT approached me and started to give me clear directives to stay still and not talk. He then explained everything he was going to do and why he was doing it. I was put in a stretcher and my neck and head were immobilized. He was so gentle and efficient that I immediately felt I was in good hands. I vividly recall thinking that this guy knows what he is doing, so all I need to do is let him do his job. I took a deep breath and actually relaxed, knowing that there was nothing I could do at that point except let the EMT help me. Looking back, I am still amazed at how quickly I trusted this "stranger," even in a moment of extreme stress and confusion.

The ambulance took me to the emergency room where a caring "SWAT" or triage team descended on me. Within seconds, they were checking everything they could, only to discover that I was okay except for some sore ribs. I was fine, even though my car was totaled. Although my ribs quickly recovered and I later got a new car, something will always remain with me from that experience: an indelible appreciation and gratitude for the care and skill of these remarkable first responders. *I realized also that we are all first responders to any incident when someone is harmed or hurt in any way.*

Train First Responders: What Does It Mean?

Train first responders is a strategy that views all members of the school community as first responders to any emotional harm and damage that is inflicted on any fellow member of the community. First responders assume the responsibility to help in a crisis, even in the most confusing and frightening situations. They become people who don't wait for someone else to help for they know that waiting only makes the situation worse. They also don't selectively choose whom to help; they help anyone in need. When more and more people no longer ignore a person who needs help, the entire community benefits and everyone feels safer. There is no reason why every member of a school community cannot be given the knowledge and skills to help others in times of emotional distress. A school can be full of first responders; it just has to decide to do it. Although this *train first responder* strategy has great merit, the conditions must be right for it to take hold in a school environment.

By itself, this strategy can be viewed by many as the answer to the problem of bullying in schools. It is a tempting simple prescription: give all students a course in "emotional first aid," similar to cardiopulmonary resuscitation (CPR) and automated external defibrillators (AED) training, so they can be trained as first responders to acts of bullying. When they see or hear bullying, they would simply say and do what they were trained to do. They could be given a few lines to memorize and a simple strategy to report to the nearest adult what they witness. It would be nice to think that this is the "answer" to the problem of bullying, but a closer analysis of how bullying manifests itself in schools presents a more complex and difficult situation requiring more than one simple solution.

For this strategy to be effective, educators and staff need to create the conditions that facilitate its implementation. Educators and members of the school community need to do the following:

1. **Recognize that psychological and emotional harm is just as serious, if not more serious, than physical harm.** People might believe this statement, however, emotional harm is too often not immediately visible, therefore the urgency that happens with a physical injury is often lacking when dealing with emotional and psychological harm. People will not automatically equate the two types or harm, nor will they respond with similar urgency unless schools provide students and staff with the knowledge needed to understand what they cannot easily see. Training people to be first responders does little good if those who receive the training fail to recognize when and where to use it.

2. **Understand that students are the most influential people in reducing and preventing bullying.** Most school policies betray this basic fact of bullying prevention. Most school practices reflect a different belief: that rules, and consequences make the critical difference in bullying prevention. Wedded to this basic belief is that laws and rules are enforced by people in positions of authority, not by people who are supposed to follow those rules and comply with the law. Asking students to become first responders to incidents of bullying at best gives them a mixed message about their role in the school, and at worse comes across as hypocritical by those in authority.

3. **Recognize how difficult it is for students to intervene or report bullying.** As explained in Chapter 4, there are many NOTS that prevent students from helping other students. Many adults forget just how difficult it is to "grow up" and how many conflicting and confusing feelings are generated in the social world of students. Training them to be first responders is like asking fire prevention or police personnel to learn skills without acknowledging the inherent danger and difficulty they face in applying those skills to real situations.

4. **Understand that feeling empathy, though important, does not come with a specific set of skills.** Sometimes adults think that when students fail to act it is because they lack empathy. Wanting to help someone is important, but it is not the same as having the skills and knowledge to help in a productive way.

5. **Recognize that even skilled individuals often fail to use those skills if they lack the confidence to apply those skills to real situations.**

6. **Understand that students have difficulty in accepting any new role or identity if they are not given the opportunity to reflect on and understand their current role and identity in the school.**

7. **Recognize that fear is still part of the structure and function of schools and how it can immobilize positive action, making students more self-protective and less likely to help others.**

8. **Understand that if the school environment itself is unsafe (even if it appears to be safe), then acts of bullying are more likely to blend into the background "noise" of the school and not be a signal that something is wrong or in need of action.** First responders become meaningless in environments that require constant attention, where emergencies are commonplace rather than the exception. If people routinely mistreat other people then being "hurt" is sadly "no big deal" and it won't draw the attention of those around them to help.

9. **Recognize that the motivation to be a first responder is tied to aspirational actions aimed at making the school a better place for all rather than doing something that those in authority want done or doing something that simply stops a problem.** If students are asked to be first responders in the context of following the imposed rules of the school, they lose the important motivation of doing something noble and important. Without this positive volitional aspect, becoming a first responder just becomes a job or another task to do, and not a special calling with distinction.

10. **Embrace *education* rather than *training* as the core mission of schools.** Education differs from training. Education comes from the Latin words *e* and *duce* which translate to the term "lead out of." Therefore, education has to accept and nurture the *whole person* instead of trying to shape that person into *something* that fits the environment. Education should be the process of creating the right conditions for bringing the best out of every student. As students grow into thinking and feeling human beings, they are more open to receiving the first responder training that can help them do what is in their hearts: help others. The best first responders are caring, empathetic people who intentionally choose to acquire a specific set of skills that equip them to do a tough, but necessary job.

As schools move toward reframing bullying prevention and start to change their culture and climate, giving students the identities of first responders can help them overcome a final obstacle in effectively addressing the problem of bullying: empowering students to act when confronting hurtful acts.

Giving students a specific set of knowledge and skills, under the title or identity of first responder, provides the additional boost of prestige and recognition for it in our post-911 culture and society. Students know that first responders are heroes; people who do courageous things. When that identity can be clearly tied to addressing the problem of bullying, then the act of helping others becomes an entirely different act from the way that it is currently perceived in schools.

Changing the identity of bystanders into first responders to harmful acts transforms what it means to be a witness to an act of bullying. Looking the other way becomes less of an option when students know that it is their responsibility to act when others are in need. Helping students know and accept their inherent role as first responders is a way of removing any doubt or uncertainty from their sense of responsibility, thereby freeing and prompting them to help.

Students are more likely to be motivated to learn a specific set of skills when they see it as an opportunity to do an important even heroic job. They can help others and also do something that makes them feel proud about themselves. They believe that they play an important role in making their school a better place. The role of first responder corresponds to the reframing of school as a community, where it is everyone's responsibility to make sure that everyone is safe and protected.

Train First Responders: How Does It Work?

Making schools safer places to *play* sets the stage for giving students the role or identity of first responders to acts of emotional harm. If you follow the analogy of school as the stage for a play, it makes sense to reconsider the current script that too many students unknowingly adhere to in their daily interactions in school. As discussed previously, the current frame of school gives students this basic script to follow: get good grades, follow the rules, and mind your own business. For students to become first responders, they need to be given a different script in order to "unlearn" what their first script trained them to do.

Training works best when it is added to education. The best trained and equipped first responders to a crisis need the will and desire to help—this cannot be trained into them. Sadly, research shows that student empathy actually decreases as they progress through the grade levels into college (Konrath, O'Brien, & Hsing, 2011). If students are trained to just follow rules and to work in order to meet imposed expectations, they will lack the will and desire to use the skills of a first responder. Conversely, as they grow as full human beings they will have the motivation to acquire the skills that will allow them to help others in times of need or crisis.

The *train first responders* as a reframing strategy for bullying prevention can help the students who have empathy to *use it* before they *lose it*. Although the research shows a decline in empathy, the reasons for this decline are not clear. Perhaps, after a while, having empathy and not being able to act on it becomes too disheartening for students, so they learn to ignore their feelings or rationalize their inaction as a way to relieve themselves of this distress. In addition, students can become habituated to subtle acts of bullying and have trouble discerning them from normal interaction in their social world, so giving them a set of skills for intervening or reporting bullying will do little good in those situations. There are students, however, who witness bullying and want to help, but freeze (get tied up in NOTS) in the moment. If lacking the skills and training to put empathy into action is the reason that empathetic reactions decline, it is worth the effort to remove this element as a factor. This is where first responder training can play an important role—it can *operationalize* empathy for many students.

The *train first responders strategy* consists of two key elements: external training and internal training.

Students can learn to interpret the external cues that can alert them to bullying situations. As opposed to the dramatic depictions of bullying they see in the media, they can be taught to look for more subtle cues and indicators of peers being hurt emotionally. In addition, they can learn to look for peers who might be vulnerable to being bullied and to act proactively in reaching out to them.

More importantly, students can learn about what is going on inside of them, their internal cues. They can learn about human development and their growing need to fit in and gain peer approval. They begin to gain the "words" for new feelings that emerge as they interact with peers. The hidden fears that often keep someone from acting are *bathed in light* when they are discussed with others.

After learning more about the external and internal elements of their social environment, students can learn very specific words, phrases, and actions that they can readily access in situations that involve mistreatment. Even the slightest amount of doubt, uncertainty, or ambiguity can impede positive actions in even the most motivated people. Training and rehearsing with a very specific set of words and actions is one proven way of overriding the human tendency to hesitate or freeze in emotional moments. It is the rare individual who can effectively improvise in helping others, especially when there is even the slightest element of self-protection involved. The more training, practice, and rehearsal individuals have then the better equipped they are to act without *thinking* in the face of an emotional situation. (The *thinking* happens ahead of time in the training and the discussions about the training; it gets released later in that moment.)

The *train first responders* strategy can be effective even if it only adds one or two students to the pool of students who help others. As Gladwell (2002) explained, the actual tipping point of change is unknown, but it can be just one or two more people joining the crowd. Culture change is the tipping point in action: people talking and acting in different ways than before. Getting even a few people thinking and acting differently creates the potential for substantive culture change; it can get the ball rolling when change seems stalled or impossible.

RESOURCES FOR EXPLORING AND SUPPORTING THE STRATEGY OF TRAIN FIRST RESPONDERS

Switch: How to Change Things When Change Is Hard by Chip Heath and Dan Heath

Chapter 2: "Script the Critical Moves"
    This chapter explores the role that ambiguity plays in preventing people from changing. When people are in doubt about what to do in any situation, they tend to revert to old habits of thinking and acting. Providing people with a clear set of words and actions to use in anticipated situations can jump-start the change process. Giving students a clear set of things to say and do in bullying situations can make the critical difference between helping and not helping.

> Change begins at the level of individual decisions and behaviors, but that's a hard place to start because that's where the friction is. Inertia and decision paralysis will conspire to keep people doing things the old way. To spark movement in a new direction, you need to provide crystal-clear guidance. (p. 56)

Change Anything: The New Science of Personal Success by Kerry Patterson, Joseph Grenny, David Maxfield, Ron McMillan, and Al Switzler

    This book offers a variety of strategies for making personal changes in behavior. The authors stress the need for translating the desired change into very specific words or actions along with specific descriptions of the consequences that result from making those changes. In addition, when these specific words and actions are linked to aspirational values, people are more likely to stick with those changes.

> It's about keeping in mind some of the more important reasons behind your current actions and sacrifices. The words you use to describe what you're doing profoundly affect your experience of the crucial moment. For instance, when sticking to a lower calorie diet, don't undermine your own motivation by describing your choices as "starving" or "going without." You are becoming healthy; you're sticking to your promise. The difference may sound small, but words matter. They focus the brain on either the positive or negative aspects of what you're doing. (p. 57)

Strangers to Ourselves: Discovering the Adaptive Unconscious by Timothy Wilson

Chapter 10: "Observing and Changing Our Behavior"

Using examples from empirical research, this book explores in detail how so much of what we do and feel is determined by our unconscious mind, yet we continue to think that we are always in control and consciously directing our lives. He suggests that we act or make decisions based on unconscious influences, but have learned to make up reasons or explanations afterward as a way to make sense of the world and ourselves.

This book has relevance to the *train first responders* strategy because students really don't know why they don't intervene or help others, even when they profess to clearly know right from wrong. Wilson suggests that one of the best ways to understand ourselves is to recognize the fact that we are influenced by our unconscious mind and its response to the social environment. Adults can coach students to learn about themselves as a way to reconcile differences between how they think about themselves and how they act.

He recommends a "do good, be good" strategy for change. Since how we think about ourselves and the world is not under our direct control, we can act in a way that then shapes how we think. If people do good things (even if they don't know why), they start to think of themselves as good people, which in turn results in their wanting to do more good things.

This approach only works when educators acknowledge and affirm a positive view of students and help them to acquire the skills required to act in a positive way. If educators project a negative identity onto them, then students are more likely to reject learning those skills, which results in the student interpreting those signs as an indication that they are not "good enough."

> One of the more enduring lessons of social psychology is that behavior change often precedes changes in attitudes and feelings. Changing our behavior to match our conscious conceptions of ourselves is thus a good way to bring about changes in the adaptive unconscious. (p. 212)

Focus: Use Different Ways of Seeing the World for Success and Influence by Heidi Grant Halvorson and E. Tory Higgins

Epilogue

This book provides a useful framework for understanding two basic types of motivation: promotion and prevention. Some people are orientated toward improving themselves and their situation (promotion), while others are more oriented toward preserving what they have or avoiding loss (prevention). The authors state that both motivations are present in all people, and that each serves a different purpose, but also that both are equally important and necessary. Environments produce varying degrees of one of these motivations. However, school environments that emphasis conformity and compliance tend to produce a greater amount of prevention motivation in students. Students in those types of environments tend to be very risk adverse, cautious, and concerned about self-protection and less concerned about others. As schools become psychologically safer for students, they provide a greater promotional motivation for helping others and taking risks.

The *train first responders strategy* offers a combination of prevention and promotion motivation to students. They can take action to prevent harm by helping others and at the same time promote and enhance their school. They can act heroically, thereby, building their skills and confidence while at the same time preventing hurtful acts and keeping the school safe. These two motivations can be useful in helping students understand their feelings and their responses to the world.

> Your life is more empowered once you have learned about promotion and prevention focus and what fits with them. This is true, in part, because you realize how you can be more effective in just about everything you do by working with what fits your focus. Your life is less frustrating because understanding focus allows you to go a little easier on yourself and everyone else. (Halvorson & Higgins, 2013, eBook 3188)

Influence: Science and Practice by Robert Cialdini

Chapter 4: "Social Proof"

This is *the* chapter for explaining a variety of the situational reasons why bystanders don't help others in need. In particular, Cialdini explores how the uncertainty of situations inhibits people from helping others. He offers concrete advice for how to make sure that others don't walk away when someone is truly in need of help. He recommends using very specific language in stating the problem and telling the bystander what to do to help. Unfortunately, students who are victimized are unlikely to use this strategy since they are very reluctant to publicly state that they are in need. It could, however, prompt students who want to help, to specifically think about what a bullied student is thinking and feeling. It is also important to have as many "trained and certain" people as possible in situations where people are in need.

> In general, then, your best strategy when in need of emergency help is to reduce the uncertainties of those around you concerning your condition and their responsibilities. Be as precise as possible about your need for aid.... When people are uncertain, they are more likely to use others' actions to decide how they themselves should act. (pp. 118–119)

Research Articles

"The Drama! Teen Conflict, Gossip, and Bullying in Networked Publics" by Alice Marwick and danah boyd

This insightful and important paper discusses how teens perceive bullying as an adult issue far removed from their social world. They use the term "drama" to cover a wide range of social interactions that can often include series mistreatment or abuse of others. The authors explain that the need for autonomy or agency can drive teens away from accepting bullying as a legitimate issue for them. This results in unfortunate consequences since teens do need to make important distinctions between typical interactions and abusive and harmful interactions. When adults impose the term *bullying,* especially as a way to control teen behavior, they are inadvertently turning off teens and making them less available for learning these important distinctions of social behavior.

This is an example of how the "script" and "roles" of the current school environment make it very difficult for students to intervene when they witness genuine acts of bullying. Adults can start to change this script by coaching students to be first responders to emotionally harmful situations. This is a way to allow students to have greater autonomy and agency while gaining greater competence in navigating their social world.

> Technology allows teens to carve out agented identities for themselves when embroiled in social conflict. And it lets them save face when confronted with adult-defined dynamics, which their peers see as childish and irrelevant. Most teens do not recognize themselves in the "bullying" rhetoric used by parents, teen advocates and mental health professionals. They do not want to see themselves as victims or transgressors, but as mature individuals navigating their world competently. (pp. 24–25)

"A Student in Distress: Moral Frames and Bystander Behavior in School" by Robert Thornberg

This article should be required reading for all educators interested in bullying prevention. Thornberg's research is based on actual interviews with students. The purpose of the interviews was to investigate how and why students behave as they do in school situations when they witness acts of bullying. The author lists a variety of reasons why students are reluctant to help. He makes specific recommendations for what educators can do to help students make better moral decisions.

> [M]oral education should not be reduced to teaching competence in moral thinking by intellectual moral discussions or by merely teaching students to obey teachers and their rules and regulations. . . .In order to educate and promote moral development and prosocial behavior among students, teachers have to consider the school

culture they produce in their day-to-day interactions with students. . . . Teachers have to consider how they unconsciously might devalue and discourage students' real life morals and consciously find strategies to empower them. . . . Prosocial morality has to be practiced so that it can thereby become a significant part of student's sense-making and actions in everyday real life. (pp. 607–608)

ACTIVITIES

Video Clip Discussion:

There are two YouTube video clips from the *Dateline* television program titled "My Kid Would Never Bully" (Keller and Orr, 2011a,b) showing students confronted with bullying situations.

There are four scenarios: two involving a group of teenage girls and two with teenage boys. Two of the scenarios show students either joining the bullying or ignoring it; two show students who try to intervene. Participants can view the scenarios and discuss the following:

What made it difficult for students to intervene?

What do you think the students who observed the bullying were thinking and feeling?

For the students who did intervene, what exactly did they do or say?

What are the differences among the students? Why did some help and others refrain from helping?

What could be done to encourage the reluctant students to help?

Text-based Discussion:

"The Banality of Heroism" by Zeno Franco and Philip Zimbardo

Philip Zimbardo's research demonstrated how easy it is for ordinary people to act in harmful and hurtful ways toward others. After many years of exploring and analyzing the conditions that can provoke such behaviors, he decided to go in the opposite direction and explore how ordinary people can become heroic and even risk their own lives to help others. This article presents his findings and recommendations for creating the conditions for every person to act heroically in everyday life. This article can be found on the Greater Good website at http://www.greatergood.berkeley.edu/article/item/the_banality_of_heroism.

ACTIVITY: WHAT TO SAY AND DO

Purpose: Learning the Right Words for Intervening

Using the video "My Kid Would Never Bully," have the participants write a letter to the students who didn't help the targeted students in the videos.

Write the letters in a positive, empathetic way acknowledging their reluctance to help, provide them with specific things they could say or do to help fellow students in the future to prevent bullying from occurring, if it is happening in front of them, or what they could do or say afterward.

These letters can be used to develop the First Responder cards mentioned in the recommendations in the next section.

Recommendations for *Train First Responders* in Schools

- Introduce the concept of *first responders* and how this role can be applied to the school environment. Introduce the concept on the physical level stating the need for people to help others in physical need. Once this concept has been introduced, members of the community can identify the various ways each member can be a first responder in some way; then this idea can be transferred to the emotional and psychological domain.
- Establish a First Responders Club where students can research and learn about first responders and what they need to be effective. Actual first responders in the community can be used as a resource for more information about what it entails and requires of people. Students can interview first responders to discover that they have many things in common with them. This knowledge underscores the idea that every person is capable of being an effective first responder.
- Substitute the word "mistreatment" for bullying to expand the responsibilities of community members. Establish the collective responsibility of insuring that no person is mistreated. All members of the school community should commit to responding appropriately to any act of mistreatment or disrespect they witness.
- Have staff and students work together to develop a specific set of words and actions that a first responder can use when they encounter any mistreatment of others.
- Be explicit in stating the core value or belief in keeping all members of the school community free of put-downs, mistreatment, or hurtful acts.
- Give all members of the school community first responder cards that simply list words and actions to use in situations where someone has been mistreated or is at risk of being mistreated.
- Make a first responder card for potential targets of mistreatment reminding them what to do if they feel hurt by anyone's mistreatment of them. The card can also remind them that they don't have to accept the negative identity that others want to project onto them.
- Make a first responder card for students who might be tempted to bully or have already bullied another student. List a series of simple

questions for them to ask themselves about why they might be mistreating others. Ask them to imagine how the targeted student might feel or how others might view their mistreatment. This card can also have a catch phrase or statement designed to get them to think about the identity they would like to have in the school community.
- Have students create first responder posters reminding the school community of their responsibilities as a community member. Have the poster inspire rather than warn or threaten them. It can point to a noble or positive ideal they are embracing when they act in a more caring and helpful way, an ideal that is calling them to make their school a better place for all students.
- Make studying about heroism a recurring theme in literature and explicitly stating its connection to their current situation and environment. Research the lives of people who are everyday living heroes and "adopt" them as guides for confronting the problems and challenges of life.

STRATEGY THREE: TELL THE *RIGHT* STORY

More likely education will improve when we stop looking backward in blame and start looking forward with new stories that bring people together around a vision. (Simmons, 2007, p. 37)

I was invited to participate in a conference where experienced principals offered advice and support to aspiring school administrators. It was a great idea to bring these two sets of professionals together. I was more of an observer than a participant; I sat at a table with two veteran principals and two teachers who wanted to be principals. Most of the discussion naturally focused on practical tasks that principals do on a routine basis. As the veteran principals began to talk about teacher evaluations, their comments became very measured and nuanced. Since teacher evaluation is now tied to standardized test scores and instruction that must conform to very strict rubrics, principals have to be highly skilled in how they offer feedback without making teachers defensive or in some cases demoralized.

After the conversation was over, I felt drained just from listening to it. I was struck by how education, which is supposed to be about learning and discovering new ideas, has sadly become devoid of any of these positive emotions. Hearing principals describe how delicately they had to "maneuver" in administering the mandated evaluation system, I felt like they were talking about how to perform root canals or colonoscopies. These were skilled professionals sharing their expertise, but there was a noticeable absence of any sense of their core mission in doing their jobs; instead it was about limiting the amount of pain and damage in carrying out policies imposed on them. I wondered if those teachers walked away from the conference questioning their decision to become school administrators. The story that these veteran administrators told in solemn voices was a very hard one to listen to.

Does the experience of school (for both students and staff) have to be like taking strong medicine, something that is necessary and momentarily unpleasant, but done for future betterment? Life is not fun and games, so shouldn't the preparation for it—school—match that reality? Is another story about school and education even possible to tell without slipping into fantasy?

I think that the answer is very clear: there is a different story to tell. A different story is not just possible: it is necessary. In fact, the seemingly simple act of telling a different story about schools can begin to change the current reality of schools. The fact that there isn't an alternative and more compelling story being told about school and education is a reason why schools seem to stubbornly resist change. The people who live and work in schools, because they don't hear a different, more compelling story to help them understand their experience, mistakenly think that there is only one story possible for them. They also mistakenly think that they are not the ones to create or tell the story, but are merely people who have to accept the story of what school is supposed to be: the story they inherited and not one that they can or should change. It doesn't have to be this way! Schools can create stories that compel people to act and stories that bring people together.

What do the following topics have in common: abandonment, isolation, exclusion, stigmatization, shame, environmental decay, and loss of a loved one? They are all topics of popular movies produced by Pixar: abandonment: *Toy Story*; exclusion: *Finding Nemo*; stigmatization: *Ratatouille*; shame: *The Incredibles*; environmental decay: *Wall-E*; loss of a loved one: *Up*. These are all sad and some might say depressing topics, but millions of people flock to see these movies because they reflect the human experience and offer the hope that when people work together they can overcome obstacles and hardships. These topics are reframed from being tales of gloom and doom to compelling adventures. People want to see and hear these stories because they affirm life, despite inherent problems, struggles, and the times when people treat each other harshly and sometimes even cruelly. These stories don't suggest pie-in-the-sky fantasies offering people false hopes of a problem-free life of ease and convenience. They offer hope and point toward what is possible when people support each other and believe they can change the world rather than accept a fate that is just handed to them. Just like the stories from Pixar, stories also live and breathe in our schools, and we have to realize that they are there, discover them, and begin to tell them.

Schools will change when their stories change. Schools will change when the people who live them tell and create their own heroic noble stories that reflect their hopes and dreams, and not their fears. Schools are not predestined to be tedious work factories that need to be controlled from above in order to keep the *story* of each day the same. Instead, they can become places like the Pixar studio that tells compelling stories that people want and need and even pay to hear and see. Pixar and schools are both about touching and changing hearts and minds, and therefore both need to be grounded in humanity rather than denying it or trying to escape from it.

If Pixar can turn these topics into life-affirming stories that touch the minds and hearts of millions, schools can also tell a different story of what it means to build a learning community where each person is cared for and valued. There is no greater story to tell than that of protecting and nurturing the lives of children and helping them grow into full human beings. This is the story of schools that most educators held in their hearts when they chose their profession. It is the story that needs to be told to the people who are in the story so that they can begin to tell and live it themselves.

This is the core truth, the true story of reframing bullying prevention:

When bullying prevention is just a story for students about following the rules and for staff about implementing a policy and a program, then nothing will ever change; it's a story that will remain the same. When bullying prevention becomes a story that inspires everyone to work together to achieve something great and noble, and to write and tell their own story of their accomplishments, bullying prevention disappears into this bigger more important story about how people do heroic things every day to make life better for everyone.

However, all people, including students, staff, and the entire community have to decide to tell a different story, and to do that they have to believe a different story is at least possible. As Henry Ford said, "Whether you think you can or think you can't—you are right." The people who think it is possible have to begin on their own to *tell this different story—the right story.*

Tell the Right Story: What Does It Mean?

The *tell the right story* strategy is probably the most important one for reframing bullying prevention; it's the one that all of the strategies are intricately related to and depend on. It means that educators first and then students begin to recognize and accept the power of stories to change realities, including how people are viewed and treated, and how groups can be transformed into communities. *It means that the school community can create its own story rather than just repeat an inherited one.*

The *tell the right story* strategy means that there is a right story to tell and that not all stories are the same. Some stories inspire and affirm people while other stories turn people off or cause them to rebel against a story that they have not chosen for themselves. The right story is *right* in two ways if

- it is the *right* fit for the people who hear it and empowers them to join in creating it; and
- it is morally right because it is about respect and caring for every member of the community.

The *tell the right story* strategy means that each member of the school community is actively involved in creating the story of their school. They must believe that they can chart their own course and it is within their power to make their school the type of community they want. When people from outside of the school ask them about their school, students and staff should be able to tell them the school's mission and goals, why they have them, and how they are going about meeting them. They should also be able to relate what they have learned in the process of creating the type of school that they want.

When members of the school community develop a collective sense of agency for creating the type of school they want, they develop a resilience toward the many external hardships that they may face. Working together in the face of these complex and challenging problems defines who they are and shapes their identities. No longer are they passive recipients whose job it is to do what they are told, instead they are actively engaged participants in solving problems together and meeting real and demanding challenges. When people come together in this way, they want to tell their story; they are proud of what they have done and the story they have created.

The *tell the right story* strategy requires people to look for the stories, events, and successes that are already happening, but often get overlooked or overshadowed by negative events. These stories from the background must be brought to the foreground of people's knowledge about what is happening in the school. No school community is ever starting from scratch or has to invent a completely new and different story. However, they do have to be able to discern those instances where people treated each other the right way, the caring and respectful way, from those times when people forgot the right way and felt justified in mistreating others.

The *tell the right story* strategy means that members of the school community become connected by the story of the school; in other words, the school's story becomes their own story that they create together.

Tell the Right Story: How Does It Work?

In most schools, bullying prevention is not connected to any story at all in the eyes of the members of the school community. (There are stories of bullying prevention in schools, but they are not positive or compelling, or viewed as a story at all.) When an organization and how people act in the organization are viewed through the lens of a story, then the story can change. When people think that what happens in the organization is *just the way things are*, then change is not part of the story, so change typically doesn't happen. When certain people in a school begin to view bullying prevention and the organization of school itself through the lens of story then change itself becomes possible, especially when people start to tell another more positive story. When bullying prevention becomes a different story about people caring and respecting each other rather than one about not doing negative things, then all members of the school community are more likely to accept the responsibility for making that positive *story* become a reality.

There are many events and activities that occur in school. Many things compete for everyone's attention. One of the functions of story is to focus attention on certain events. The right story is a way of directing attention toward certain events and interpreting them for people. Any lack of empathy and lack of helpful responses may be a result of people not "seeing" events as opportunities to help because they blend into everything else that is happening. People will also fail to respond in helpful ways if they don't interpret what is happening as significant or different from the norm. *Telling the right story* strategy may be the missing element that can tap into the empathy and caring that already exists in most people. The right story focuses and points people toward what they need to see and helps them understand what is happening around them.

The *tell the right story* strategy can translate the abstract or the broad concept of doing good into specific human interactions. Students and staff know that they are supposed to good and help others, but when those concepts remain vague and nonspecific, it becomes difficult for students to experience what it feels like to actually do good or help.

When students and staff see acts of mistreatment through the context of the right story, they interpret those acts very differently and respond differently. The right story also redefines their identity from just existing solely as a student in school whose job it is to follow the rules, to a first responder, a responsible member of the community whose actions are needed to right a wrong and restore order to the environment. For example, when the story of bullying prevention changes from "not doing a negative" and turns into "help a student feel less alone in the cafeteria" then students learn that little acts are meaningful and important. The right story helps students and staff act heroically when others are in need in the face of everyday events.

The *tell the right story* strategy can give life to people who otherwise feel like they are just going through the motions of being either a student or a staff member.

The *right story* strategy points toward a positive heroic act that appeals to what is best in people; the story calls them to be great.

The *right story* also tells people that they can *write* their own story, direct their own future, and achieve their own goals.

LISTENING IS PART OF TELLING THE RIGHT STORY

There is one important caveat for telling the right story strategy: it takes time, persistence, and retelling for it to take hold in the hearts and minds of people in schools today. Annette Simmons (2007) offered the following advice for telling the right story.

> Fear is a very strong universal pattern. . . . Love, hope, and faith stories seem to need more energy, imagery, even self-discipline to travel as far as fear stories. (p. 185)

> The storytelling process is best begun by asking individual members of the group to tell a story that expresses who they are and why they are here, personally. (p. 190)

The *tell the right story* strategy is not about competing stories, but rather the value of listening to everyone's story, even if the stories might initially be in conflict. Time must be devoted to letting people tell their stories and making sure that those in positions of authority listen to them and acknowledge them. The act of listening to another's story is an act of respect that ultimately models that type of interaction that will represent the collective story of the community: we are people who are different, but who respect and care for each other. There is room for everyone's story in our community. Listening and respecting define who we are. That is our story. That is the right story.

On a personal note, I recently wrote a novel for middle grade students. It was something of a surprise to me because I had told myself that I was not able to write fiction or wasn't creative enough to make up stories. It took seeing a friend write a play, who was also someone who had never written fiction, in order for me to see that I had placed a false restriction or limit on myself. Once I told myself that I could write fiction, the first line of the book almost automatically popped into my head and I was off writing it chapter by chapter. It was hard and unfamiliar work, but I enjoyed it. What made the experience even more enjoyable is this truth that I discovered: when you write your own story there is nothing preventing you from giving it a happy and positive ending. I believe that to be true for schools that decide to write the right story of how they want to treat each other; to write the story of how they want their schools to be. A happy and positive ending for their efforts is not just possible; it is inevitable.

RESOURCES FOR EXPLORING AND SUPPORTING THE STRATEGY OF TELL THE RIGHT STORY

Made to Stick: Why Some Ideas Survive and Others Die **by Dan Heath and Chip Heath**

Chapter 6: "Stories"

Chapter 10 "Do" Strategies for Reframing Bullying Prevention

This book offers practical strategies for communicating ideas in a memorable way. Even the best ideas will fail to have any impact on people if they are not communicated in a way that gets people's attention and sticks in their mind. This chapter offers examples of how stories have solved problems and motivated people to change. They describe the *springboard* story as a way to let people see the possibilities for solving a problem or changing a situation. This approach offers an alternative to just presenting the problem of bullying to students and staff and expecting them to cooperate in stopping it.

> The problem is that when you hit listeners between the eyes, they respond by fighting back. The way you deliver a message to them is a cue to how they should react. If you make an argument, you're implicitly asking them to evaluate your argument—judge it, debate it, criticize it—and then argue back, at least in their minds. But with a story . . . you engage the audience—you are involving people with an idea, asking them to participate with you. (p. 234)

A Whole New Mind: Why Right Brainers Will Rule the Future by Daniel Pink

Chapter 5: "Story"

Pink makes the case that in an age of information at everyone's fingertips, stories are an important way for people to make sense out of the data they receive. In a school environment with so many things happening, bullying prevention can easily become just another lifeless item on a long list of things to do. Stories can elevate *this item* so that it becomes meaningful and central to our identity as human beings in relationship to each other.

> We are our stories. We compress years of experience, thought and emotion into a few compact narratives that we convey to others and to ourselves. That has always been true. But personal narrative has become more prevalent, and perhaps more urgent, in a time of abundance, when many of us are freer to seek a deeper understanding of ourselves and our purpose. (p.115)

Lead With a Story: A Guide to Crafting Business Narratives That Captivate, Convince and Inspire by Paul Smith

Chapter 8: "Define the Culture"

Chapter 9: "Establish Values"

This book describes how stories can be used to accomplish many goals in the business world. It provides examples of business leaders and the stories that they used successfully. The book also explains why businesses are now recognizing storytelling as an essential skill for their top executives. Chapters 8 and 9 describe how the stories of actual events circulate in any organization and can represent its culture and values often contradicting the formal mission/value statement of that organization. Leaders, therefore, need to make sure that they tell the stories of actual events that positively represent the stated mission or values. If a school's stated mission and values are not reflected in the words and actions of educators, it is foolish to expect students to act in agreement with those values. For students to join staff in achieving a school's mission, they need to see adults acting in harmony with those values.

> [C]ompany values are determined by the behavior of its people, and the stories that capture that behavior—not by corporate value statements buried in a file cabinet. If you don't have strong company value stories, then in the minds of your employees (where it matters most) you probably don't have strong company values. (p. 79)

Whoever Tells the Best Story Wins: How to Use Your Own Stories to Communicate With Power and Impact by Annette Simmons

It is difficult to single out one or two chapters in this excellent and practical book. It is a great choice for a book study for any school leadership team. High school students can also benefit from reading and discussing it. At the end of each chapter are a series of exercises designed to build storytelling skills. The essential message of the book is that storytelling can restore humanity to a world that can be dominated by data and impersonal communication.

Reframing bullying prevention is about restoring humanity to a school environment that too often is dominated by the pressures to score higher on tests and comply with rules and regulations. This book is a very useful tool for anyone interested in reframing not just bullying prevention, but the current state of education itself.

> Communication can't feel genuine without the distinctive personality of a human being to provide context.... The missing ingredient in most failed communication is humanity. This is an easy fix. In order to blend humanity into every communication you send all you have to do is tell more stories and bingo—you just showed up. Your communication now has a human presence.... In this ocean of choice, a meaningful story can feel like a life preserver that tethers us to something safe, important, or at the very least more solid than disembodied voices begging for attention. (pp. 4–5)

ACTIVITIES

Video Clip Discussion:

Many TED Talks begin with a story that leads to a key concept or idea. This particular talk shows how a simple personal story can link with the concept of global poverty and human connectedness.

Jacqueline Novogratz's story about her blue sweater and how it influenced her life and career can be a good "springboard story" for students and staff. Viewers of this TED talk can discuss why she used the story of her blue sweater and the larger theme of how we are all connected.

Text-based Discussion

How Stories Change the Brain by Paul Zak

This online article also contains a brief video that can be shown by itself or discussed in conjunction with the article.

This article shares research that demonstrates how the brain reacts to stories. It explains how stories that follow a dramatic story arc engage the brain and release oxytocin, a hormone that makes people more empathetic and caring.

> Emotional simulation is the foundation for empathy and is particularly powerful for social creatures like humans because it allows us to rapidly forecast if people around us are angry or kind, dangerous or safe, friend or foe.

Research Article:

"Origins and Pawns in Classroom: Self-Report and Projective Assessments of Individual Differences in Children's Perceptions" by Richard Ryan and Wendy Grolnick

This research demonstrated storytelling in reverse: the experience of being in a certain type of classroom determined the stories that students told about themselves. In classrooms where the teachers supported student autonomy and offered choices, those students told stories where they were active agents for their own learning—origins. The reverse was true in classrooms where teachers were very controlling and offered less opportunities for autonomy and choice; these students told stories where they were more passive recipients of learning—pawns.

> In particular, the child's perception of *origin* climate of the classroom appears to influence self-perceptions, such that the more the classroom was perceived as origin in nature, the greater the child's self-esteem, perceived cognitive competence, and mastery motivation. (p. 557)

ACTIVITY: WRITING THE NEXT CHAPTER OF OUR SCHOOL

Purpose: Build Agency by Writing and Telling Stories

This activity can introduce the idea that each school community can write its own narrative or story. It affirms that positive events are already happening in the school and asks the participants to envision future events (the next chapter) where more and more people act in accordance with the school's values and beliefs.

Ask participants to reflect on the school's mission statement or core values. If the school doesn't have these statements, then participants can be given the following sentence stem: "When our school is at its best, we see and hear _____."

Participants are then asked to write down their recollections of times when they acted in harmony with the school's mission and values or when they observed others acting that way.

They can write down as many examples as they can recall. These recollections are then summarized and transferred onto index cards or comparable sized sticky notes.

Have participants work in small groups of four to five people.

Participants can lay the cards or sticky notes on a sheet or chart paper.

After the card or sticky notes have been placed, participants sort them by moving them around into categories or types of stories. They can also generate the labels for these categories.

Each group then creates a visual representation of the saying "Our school at its best" or "Our school's mission and values in action."

Each group presents their visual representation to the whole group. Following all the presentations, there is a general discussion on what each presentation or vision have in common. The whole group generates three or four summary statements characterizing the school.

Participants return to their small groups and respond to the following statements: "What do we want our 'next chapter' to look and sound like?" (What do we need to do to insure we continue to consistently meet our mission?)

Each group writes their answers to that question on a sheet of chart paper. After each small group is finished, these are posted on the wall. All of the participants can walk around to view all of the answers on the chart paper.

The whole group then decides the next steps required to make the "next chapter" become a reality, for example designate a subcommittee to develop an action plan, ask a standing committee to work on the plan, and generate several short achievable goals, to name just a few.

Recommendations for Tell the Right Story Strategy in Schools

- Incorporate storytelling into the academic curriculum.
- Have students and staff improve their storytelling skills and provide opportunities for them to practice with others.
- Keep a school log of positive stories of people helping and supporting others. Ask students and staff to submit stories of their own positive acts or ones they witnessed. This helps keep a record of the school's story. Find times to share these stories at schoolwide events.
- Have a bulletin board labeled "Our School at Its Best" where students and staff post positive stories.
- Generate a series of *springboard* stories. These stories can be based on typical bullying situations and serve to illustrate various ways that students can respond to bullying or any act of mistreatment. They can also include what the characters in the story are thinking and feeling. There can be various decision points in the story where each character makes a decision on how to act and the story can play out to a conclusion. This helps those who hear the stories see how the characters in the stories influence the outcome of the story. Have teachers use these stories in classroom discussions.
- Start an afterschool storytellers group that learns more about stories and how they influence human behavior. This includes learning about myths, legends, fairy tales, fables, and their role in helping people learn about themselves and their world. The group shares their knowledge with the rest of the school community.
- Encourage students and staff to keep a journal to record their learning journey, and tell their stories of how they learned or changed. They can record how they learned to do something new and challenging (academically or socially). This recorded story can be a reference for them when they face future situations that might cause them to doubt themselves.
- Make it a school tradition to refer to each school year as a chapter in the school's story and emphasize the idea that all members of the school community are the authors of the story.

SUMMARY

"Do" strategies can leverage a series of changes to gradually transform the school's culture and climate.

The *make it safe to play* strategy is designed to help members of the school community increase their awareness of the hidden and quiet presence and influence of fear in the school environment.

The *make it safe to play* strategy lessens the amount of fear and frees members of the school community to think less about protecting themselves and more about helping others.

The *train first responders* strategy is designed to promote the idea that each member of the school community is responsible for the well-being of everyone in the community. It uses the analogy of the first responder (now venerated in our culture) as a way to promote helpful and even heroic behavior when someone is in need.

The *train first responders* strategy is dependent on putting a variety of other factors in place. It cannot be a stand-alone strategy imposed on students. However, given the right conditions it can provide a set of responses more accessible to students who want to help others, but don't act or are unable to act for a variety of understandable reasons.

The *tell the right story* strategy is essential to reframing bullying prevention because it dramatically changes how members of the school community view bullying and their role in responding to it.

The *tell the right story* strategy helps people make sense of their purpose and role in any organization. It also increases their empathy and motivation to help others.

The *tell the right story* strategy transforms bullying prevention for students from another set of adult imposed rules to follow and for staff from another policy or program to implement into an opportunity to act responsibly and sometimes heroically; it becomes part of a greater, more meaningful and purposeful story of how people can help each other create the type of community they want for themselves and others.

11

Checklists for Reframing Bullying Prevention

Building Community Spirit in Schools

I initially approached the use of checklists in education with a degree of trepidation. Since schools often are looking for a recipe to follow that can by itself "fix" a problem, the idea of providing a checklist for reframing bullying prevention seemed counter to one of my core beliefs: the importance of empowering educators to make wise collaborative decisions rather than blindly follow a series of directives to check off a list. However, Atul Gawande's research prompted me to take a closer look at the use of checklists and to explore how they can apply to reframing bullying prevention.

Since I had read so many of Atul Gawande's articles in the *New Yorker* magazine and had admired his writing, I decided to read his book, *The Checklist Manifesto*. After reading and studying it, I am now convinced that his checklist approach is entirely compatible with my beliefs. Used the right way, checklists can be a very valuable tool in empowering educators to be more creative in solving problems and promoting positive practices in schools. In fact, Gawande (2010) anticipated my concerns and addressed them this way:

> The fear people have about the idea of adherence to protocol is rigidity. They imagine mindless automatons, heads down in a checklist, incapable of looking outside their windshield and coping

with the real world in front of them. But what you find, when a checklist is well made, is exactly the opposite. The checklist gets the dumb stuff out of the way, the routines that your brain shouldn't have to occupy itself with, and lets it rise above to focus on the hard stuff. (p. 177)

The checklists for reframing bullying prevention do not involve a series of mechanical tasks for educators to perform; they provide a list of ideas, concepts, and research that the school community needs to understand to facilitate the reframing process. They also include key goals and specific steps that can create the conditions for building community spirit in schools.

There is a checklist for each of the tenets of reframing described in Chapter 6. The tenets are organized as an acronym for the word SPIRIT. These tenets are interconnected and taken together provide a qualitative description of a strong school community. The checklists can be used as a way to assess progress in improving a school's culture and climate.

Each of the eight strategies in Chapters 8 through 10 are designed to help each school become a stronger school community and should support all six of the tenets of reframing. Many of the items in the checklist correspond to the recommendations made at the end of each strategy section. Planning teams can use the checklists to determine priorities and goals for their school community.

The Six Tenets for Reframing Bullying Prevention to Build Community Spirit in Schools

S=Student-centered

P=Principle-based

I=Integrated practice

R=Relationships central

I=Influence guides

T=Ties strengthened

REFRAMING TENET ONE: STUDENT-CENTERED

- ✓ Staff examine their basic assumptions about students and discuss which assumptions shaped educational practices.
- ✓ Staff work toward the goal of matching their words and actions to the positive assumptions that students want to do well in school and to help others.
- ✓ Staff are given research and information about the greater influence that students have to prevent and reduce bullying (as opposed to the influence of direct adult actions to control it).

- ✓ Students know the definition of bullying and understand it in the broader context of how to treat others and how the act of bullying functions in the social world.
- ✓ Staff give students information regarding the influence they have in preventing and reducing bullying.
- ✓ Staff verbally express to students that they are needed as partners in making the school community a safer place for learning.
- ✓ Student input is actively sought for determining goals, action plans, and any significant decisions regarding the school community.
- ✓ Staff are vigilant in supporting each other in viewing problems through the eyes of the students rather than through their own eyes or concerns.
- ✓ Staff have an opportunity to learn about the research on noncognitive factors and mind-set research particularly related to how students view themselves as learners.
- ✓ Staff are aware of how their attitudes and language they use to address students affects how students think about themselves.
- ✓ Staff are supported in refraining from making statements that blame students and/or their families for the problem of bullying or other school problems.
- ✓ Staff are familiar with and use the four key student mind-sets essential for success in school: I belong to this school/class community; my abilities will grow with my efforts; I can succeed at this task; my work has meaning and value for me.
- ✓ The school uses these four mind-sets on a regular basis for understanding problems and designing interventions to help students answer affirmatively to each of those statements.
- ✓ Staff are aware of the importance of affirming students' strengths and valuing their contributions to the school community.
- ✓ There is general consensus among staff that when it comes to bullying prevention, students are "the solution," not the "problem."

REFRAMING TENET TWO: PRINCIPLE-BASED

- ✓ Staff have opportunities to discuss and explore the school's mission and core values and beliefs.
- ✓ Students are invited to participate in a process for understanding the school's mission and values.
- ✓ Students and staff participate in discussions about how the school's mission and values are translated into specific words and actions.
- ✓ Students and staff understand the distinction and the connection between rules (limiting certain behaviors) and principles (promoting valued behaviors).

- ✓ Goals are established to support all school community members to act in accordance with the school's mission, values, and principles.
- ✓ Students and staff view and understand principles as guides for making decisions and judgments in situations not covered by rules or procedures.
- ✓ Recognition and acknowledgement is consistently provided to those whose words and actions exemplify the school's mission, values, and principles.
- ✓ The school's mission, values, core beliefs, and guiding principles (whatever a school elects to call their basic tenets) are clearly and prominently displayed throughout the school environment.
- ✓ Professional development is designed to give staff the knowledge, skills, and attitudes necessary to ensure that the school community acts in concurrence with its mission, values, and principles.
- ✓ The mission, values, and principles of the school articulate the importance of community and the responsibility of each member to support each other.
- ✓ The mission, values, and guiding principles of the school are explicitly connected to what it means to be a responsible citizen and other key tenets of our Constitution and democratic traditions.
- ✓ Staff understand the importance of modeling respect for diversity and regularly discuss and illustrate how it enhances the school culture and climate.
- ✓ All members of the school community know the school's mission and values and why they are important.

REFRAMING TENET THREE: INTEGRATED PRACTICE

- ✓ Staff understand the concept of school culture and climate and how their words and actions convey their assumptions about students and what they value and believe.
- ✓ Staff understand the negative impact on the school's culture and climate when any person is mistreated or shown disrespect regardless of the nature of the transgressions committed by that person.
- ✓ Professional development is provided to staff to give them instructional tools to integrate academic and social goals in the classroom.
- ✓ Professional development and staff discussion is devoted to supporting each teacher's skills in creating more student-centered classrooms that provide students with greater autonomy and choice.
- ✓ Professional development is offered to help staff build strong learning communities in their classrooms.

- ✓ Staff understand the research on extrinsic and intrinsic motivation and the effect of each type of motivation on the quality of student learning.
- ✓ Students are provided structured learning opportunities in the classroom that allow them to discover similarities and differences among their peers.
- ✓ Students are provided opportunities in the classroom to work collaboratively with peers while practicing and enhancing their social interaction skills.
- ✓ Students are provided time for reflection and self-evaluation of their own learning and behavior toward others.
- ✓ Students are given opportunities in the classroom to support others in learning academic tasks.
- ✓ Students learn to compete against themselves (try to get better) and to cooperate with others in the learning process.
- ✓ Discussion of the purpose and meaning of all learning is integrated into educational/instructional practice.
- ✓ Staff are provided the skills to make learning (not performing to gain teacher approval) the focus of the classroom.

TENET FOUR: RELATIONSHIPS CENTRAL

- ✓ Staff actively seek to be viewed seen as trustworthy by all students.
- ✓ Staff understand and cultivate the skills necessary to be trustworthy to students.
- ✓ Staff are not afraid to show their humanity to students: admitting mistakes, acknowledging doubt, expressing regret for insensitivity, apologizing and asking for forgiveness when appropriate and necessary.
- ✓ Staff willingly share their own stories of learning and growing with students.
- ✓ Staff welcome and appreciate students telling their stories and experiences.
- ✓ Staff are comfortable with asking students for help and support and express their need for student input and voice.
- ✓ Staff realize the importance of persisting in reaching out and connecting with students who are vulnerable and appear isolated.
- ✓ Staff consistently invite students to share thoughts and feelings and then attentively listen to them.
- ✓ Staff actively try to make each student look valuable in the eyes of peers.
- ✓ There are many schoolwide projects, activities, and events that can promote and nurture positive relationships among students and staff.
- ✓ There many opportunities for mixed grades and ages to interact within the school.

- ✓ School leaders are visible, accessible, and approachable on a consistent basis for both students and staff.
- ✓ Students see that school support personnel (custodians, monitors, bus drivers) are treated with respect and are valued by all members of the school community.
- ✓ Students are knowledgeable about whom they can talk to when they are in need, when they see someone else in need, or when they need advice.
- ✓ Classroom teachers periodically set aside time to check on relationships and how students in the class are getting along.

TENET FIVE: INFLUENCE GUIDES

- ✓ Discipline policies and procedures are designed to respect each student as a person while not condoning inappropriate behavior.
- ✓ Discipline policies and procedures are designed to help students understand that inappropriate words or actions are not just rule infractions, but violate the school's values and principles (as well as their own).
- ✓ Discipline policies and procedures are designed to ultimately help students learn better ways of meeting their needs and relating to other members of the school community rather than just seeking to provide consequences as a deterrence for future inappropriate behavior.
- ✓ Discipline policies and procedures recognize the importance of repairing relationships and restoring a sense of community if and when any damage is done.
- ✓ Students are viewed as "works in progress" so mistakes are considered part of learning and not automatically assumed to be a sign of defiance or personal disrespect.
- ✓ Social and emotional learning are afforded the same respect as academic learning.
- ✓ Problems are viewed as an inherent part of living and working together and are opportunities for learning.
- ✓ All staff periodically reflect on and evaluate how they use their power and authority with those who have less power.
- ✓ Staff understand the importance and influence of stories in helping people make sense of the world and how stories can touch hearts and minds.
- ✓ Staff understand the negative effect of fear and anxiety on learning and make the classroom psychologically safe for learning.
- ✓ Staff are sensitive to any forms of disrespect and mistreatment and have the skills to intervene in a respectful manner when they see or hear it.

- ✓ Rules, procedures, and routines are explained to students and are reasonable and flexible to meet human needs.
- ✓ Rules and procedures are not designed to control the exceptional case. They are based on the fact that most students are cooperative and respectful.
- ✓ Students are allowed to question rules and procedures in a respectful way.
- ✓ Staff recognize the importance of trusting students and the negative consequences of automatically suspecting them of possible wrongdoing.
- ✓ Staff and students don't rely primarily on rules and policies to address conflicts and look at various ways to resolve conflicts.

TENET SIX: TIES STRENGTHENED

- ✓ A stated value and goal of the school is to strengthen a sense of ownership and pride in being a member of the school community.
- ✓ The school develops ways of recognizing the value and contribution of each member of the school community.
- ✓ Community service is a valued component of the school's educational program, not just an occasional event.
- ✓ Cooperative efforts are afforded as much, if not more, recognition than competitive endeavors.
- ✓ The school invites members of the surrounding community into the school to participate in school activities and events.
- ✓ Parents are viewed with respect and staff members refrain from blaming or criticizing them in meetings or during any professional interactions.
- ✓ Parents are welcome into the school on a regular basis and have a variety of ways of participating in the life of the school.
- ✓ There are public and visual spaces provided in the school to display information illustrating how students and staff work together to achieve goals.
- ✓ Students and staff collaborate on a regular basis to plan schoolwide events.
- ✓ Staff and students work together to create a friendly and welcoming school environment.
- ✓ The school has a plan for welcoming and orienting new students and their families to the school.
- ✓ There is a conscious and deliberate effort to highlight and communicate positive events that occur within the school.
- ✓ Time and resources are devoted to assessing how students and staff feel about the school's climate.
- ✓ Students and staff work together to develop goals to strengthen the school's sense of community.

12

Questions and Answers

This chapter focuses on issues and topics not specifically addressed in this book in the form of questions and answers. The questions and responses also explain the relationship between reframing bullying prevention and many of the existing programs and strategies currently employed in schools to address the problem.

QUESTION ONE

What can a school do about cyberbullying?

Cyberbullying has received a lot of attention in the media and raises many concerns for educators. Although this issue does pose a different set of problems than the bullying that occurs in schools, it is still an outgrowth of the social dynamics that exist within the school environment. Research shows that cyberbullying does not create a new set of students who are targeted for bullying, but rather extends the social arena beyond the school walls so that these students sometimes cannot escape bullying, even when they are home.

As I describe in this book, the social structure and dynamics of most schools creates the conditions for bullying. If some students within the school environment were less vulnerable and had more allies among students, the conditions that promote cyberbullying would also change. For example, if more bystanders intervened or reported bullying, the more it would decrease or stop. Change the school environment, create more connections among students and it changes how bullying functions in the social world in the school, and its extensions in social media.

However, cyberbullying does pose a serious threat to the current frame of schools that depend on a command and control structure to manage student behavior. As schools respond to bullying and cyberbullying with greater and tighter controls, students are able to use technology to distance themselves from the less technologically savvy adults and operate well outside of the rules and regulations of schools. Cyberbullying is a sign that the traditional attempts to control students' behaviors no longer work. The "power over" approach must shift to a "power with" approach, especially when it comes to cyberbullying. Adults can no longer control student behavior and the students know this better than the adults. This is a great opportunity for adults to enlist students in helping them achieve what they both want: a safer and more respectful school environment.

Educators must remember that most students don't bully, don't approve of it, and use social media very responsibly. These students will readily assist and work cooperatively with adults whom they feel respect them and whom they respect. The greatest allies that educators can find in developing strategies to address cyberbullying are the students themselves. The key tenets of reframing bullying prevention apply even more so when it comes to cyberbullying. The tenets are more necessary if schools are to be effective in stopping any form of bullying. The greatest obstacle for reframing bullying prevention, including cyberbullying, is the *educators' fear* of losing control that causes them to hold tighter to the traditional methods that seemingly worked for other problems.

In researching bullying and cyberbullying, one of the best resources I found is the work of Nancy Willard. She addresses the issue from a perspective that echoes my point of view articulated in this book. Her work is informed by much of the same research that I used that emphasizes social norms and the importance of working with students. Her book, *Cyber Savvy: Embracing Digital Safety and Civility,* and her website, www.embracingdigitalyouth.org are excellent resources that provide sound advice and practical strategies for educators and parents.

Her approach emphasizes the following critical components that are consistent with the reframing approach:

- Reinforce positive social norms and practices;
- Foster effective problem solving and the use of effective strategies;
- Empower and engage witnesses to be helpful allies; and
- Collect local data to guide instruction and ongoing evaluation. (p. 7)

QUESTION TWO

How about bullying prevention programs that are already in place in school? Aren't they worthwhile and effective in addressing the problem?

There is nothing wrong with a well-researched and comprehensive schoolwide bullying prevention program or curricula. Many of them work very well in schools and more schools should implement them rather than rely on one-shot assemblies or other programs that sound good, but have little research behind them. Programs and curricula can either thrive or exist with little positive impact depending on the culture and climate of their schools. To better explain this statement, the best analogy I can use is from my experiences as a gardener.

My brother-in-law's tomatoes drove me crazy! His garden not only produced more tomatoes than mine, but they were bigger and tastier. Our plants came from the same greenhouse—I purchased them for both of us. Both of our gardens were watered, fertilized, and got about the same amount of sun. Why did his garden produce so much better a yield? Here is what I finally figured out: I had a garden for many years; he had one for two years; therefore, my soil was depleted and his was enriched. All the other gardening things I did were necessary, but ultimately *what mattered most was the soil!* The lesson was clear: To get the best tomatoes, you have to start from the ground up.

This lesson can be applied to bullying prevention in our schools: even the best policies, programs, rules, and protocols will fail to reduce or prevent bullying unless they *take root* in a positive caring school culture and climate. Perhaps this is why recent government statistics from 2005 to 2011 show little change in the rate of bullying reported by students, even with anti-bullying laws in almost every state, greater public awareness of the problem, and many available bullying prevention resources (National Center for Education Statistics, 2012).

Bullying prevention, just like any change initiative, must always confront the predominant influence of the school culture and climate on everything that happens in school, or as Peter Drucker, a management/leader expert said, "Culture eats strategy for breakfast."

Policies, programs, protocols, and so forth can be valuable tools for people to use, but they don't change people—only people can change people. Bullying prevention must always start from the ground up—the ground of changing people's hearts and minds toward greater respect and caring (Dillon, 2013c).

QUESTION THREE

How about programs like Positive Behavior Interventions and Supports (PBIS)? Aren't they effective in addressing all inappropriate behaviors in schools including bullying?

Positive Behavioral Interventions and Supports (PBIS) has become a permanent, organizing structure for more and more schools. For schools where behavior problems take time and energy away from teaching and learning, PBIS can be a "lifesaver," bringing stability and order to an often chaotic school environment.

In many of these schools, punishments, threats, yelling, and inconsistent reactions to student behavior often become the norm for responding to student misbehavior. For schools stuck in these negative patterns of behavior, PBIS can start to turn things around.

Here is how PBIS provides order and predictability to the school:

- Eliminates harsh, thoughtless, and emotional responses to student misbehavior
- Provides consistent and positive ways for adults to respond to student behavior
- Changes the focus from what students should NOT do to what they should do
- Makes certain that students learn and practice positive behaviors
- Clarifies the expectation for appropriate behavior for a variety of school situations
- Provides a method for measuring, monitoring, and evaluating progress
- Makes sure that positive cooperative behavior gets the most attention

In short, the order and stability that PBIS provides for some schools can be a necessary first step toward meaningful school improvement. To use a medical analogy, PBIS can do a good job of "stopping the bleeding" or providing emergency room care. However, my concern is that instead of becoming a starting point for schools in trouble, it becomes the final solution for many schools. PBIS can serve as the triage step for schools in crisis, but who wants to consider that this triage step serves as the final solution to long-term health and wellness?

Once a school has "stabilized," it has a responsibility to build on its positive accomplishment. Schools that have succeeded with PBIS should now challenge themselves to change not just how they handle behavior, but to examine how they educate their students.

The best schools have the courage to ask themselves the following questions:

- Would students misbehave if the content of their lessons was more engaging and meaningful to them?
- Would students misbehave if the teachers established more trusting and supportive relationships with them?
- Would students misbehave if the teachers used instructional methods that allowed more student interaction and physical movement instead of long periods of sitting and listening?
- Would students misbehave if they had more choice in what they were learning?
- Is it our goal for the students to comply with the rules of the school? Or is it to help learn how to make wise decisions in situations that are not covered by the rules when there are no adults around to supervise?
- What is the type of environment that students need to be successful in the 21st century world that exists outside of school?

Think of an optimal learning experience where these conditions were present: You felt that you were in charge, you had social support, and it was safe to make mistakes and to learn from them. PBIS can be of value if it helps schools take an important first step toward this optimal learning. Educators, not programs, have the responsibility to educate students beyond just getting them to behave.

If students are going to be empowered to intervene or report bullying in their social environment, then they need active roles in their own learning and need to develop a view of themselves beyond just following rules and expectations (Dillon, 2013b).

QUESTION FOUR

What can the members of the school community do if the principal or other school administrators don't understand what *reframing* **means, and if they remain** *stuck* **just managing the status quo?**

This is a very difficult problem since leadership is the key variable in most successful change efforts. Walk down the aisle of a bookstore and look in the business section and most books are about leadership in one form or another. The same cannot be said of education. Although more attention is being paid to the role of leadership in schools, in many instances principals of schools are viewed as implementers of policies imposed from higher levels of authority. Too often they are judged by how well they implement programs rather than by how well they touch the minds and hearts of the school community. It is an extremely hard job to manage a school successfully, so it is very hard to criticize principals or administrators who are not effective at leading a school to significant positive change.

An important distinction that is often forgotten is that leadership is not the same as holding a position of power and authority. There have been very effective and positive movements of change that have been led by people with zero power or authority, such as Gandhi and Martin Luther King. Therefore, if there are members of the school community who have a different vision of their school and truly want to make it more inclusive and caring, they can first starting modeling the type of behavior that they want to see in others. They can also work together to share ideas and discuss ways to spread more respectful methods of interacting with all students. Although it requires a lot of courage to speak up when people in authority abuse their power, like-minded people can have a tremendous influence on their school when they refuse to look the other way and speak up in respectful and honest ways. Regardless of the ultimate outcome achieved by speaking up, I have to believe it is always preferable and more productive in the long run than to look the other way and do or say nothing in the face of mistreatment. The more that people work together and don't feel alone in speaking up, then the more effective they will be; sometimes it just takes one person to start the ball rolling for positive change to happen. Sometimes one person's courage can touch the hearts of others who just need a signal to reinforce what they know in their hearts has to be done.

QUESTION FIVE

Since it seems like the mental frames have such a hold on how people view the world, how can people with very different frames ever hope to work together?

This is a very big obstacle precisely because the mental frames that separate people are never seen as the real reason why people differ. People end up clashing and in conflict over attitudes or practices shaped by their mental frame. For example, there are teachers who firmly believe that the only answer to students' inappropriate behavior is to be tougher and apply harsher consequences. Someone with a differing philosophy is then faced with the choice of either letting that person advocate and dominate the discussion or confront and challenge those opinions. Part of the problem is timing. Sometimes these differences are only discussed when there is a contentious issue or problem that needs to be solved. A student did something that provokes a strong emotional response that usually makes people cling to previously held assumptions. Professionals need to be engaged in discussions about these issues when the stakes are not as high and a decision is not pending. This is why I advocate for approaches that emphasize the process of decision making and discussion as more important than content-oriented programmatic approaches to problems. When educators can engage in meaningful and respectful dialogue, they discover their assumptions and values about education and hear a different perspective without being threatened by it. Eventually, as people begin to trust each other and perceive different ideas less as threats and more as opportunities to learn, then the *door* to their minds opens up a bit to the possibility that there might be more than one way to view a problem. This is why is it so important for more and more staff to become better listeners so that they can acknowledge another person's point of view without necessarily agreeing with it. I believe that as trust builds among professionals, then people with apparently opposing ideas can discover how to work together with some of their shared values. Very often as people trust each other and *dig deeper* into what they believe, they discover that their differences are more semantic than substantive.

It is for this reason that when I present to any group of people, I welcome strong disagreements when they are voiced and I thank those who share them for having the courage to offer them to me. I find that as I acknowledge and appreciate their trust in me to offer a differing opinion, then we can have a very good discussion on an issue and both walk away feeling as if we learned something from one another. I find that the less I care about changing someone's mind, the better I am at connecting with them and reaching a common understanding on some level.

QUESTION SIX

It seems as if the practice of *reframing* is too critical of schools and by implication the people who work in them. Isn't there a danger in turning off the very people who need to hear the message of reframing?

This is a real danger and I am highly sensitive about criticizing people who work in schools. They are not to blame in any way at all. I was a person who worked in schools, and I have tremendous empathy and admiration for people who work in schools, especially public schools. In general, they are underappreciated and overly criticized by those who don't work in schools. The last thing that I want to do is to be viewed as joining the chorus of those who blame educators for the current state of education. This is why I studied the historical roots of schools and why they are the way they are. I wanted to discover just what it was about schools that all educators inherited, first as students and then as educators. The mental frames of strict parent combined with the factory frame had a very firm grip on how schools have been defined by our culture, so much so that it is almost impossible to see schools any other way. It explains why even the best intentioned and kind-hearted people often end up treating others, especially students, in a way that they wouldn't in other situations. My attempt to point out how we all have been affected by the frame is a way for letting all of us save face and give us an *out* for changing our ways. I know that teachers are extremely sensitive to any hint that they might have not always acted in the best manner toward students. I am hoping that by understanding the history of schools and how mental frames have shaped our perceptions, feelings, thoughts, and actions that we can start to change what we do in schools without having to harshly criticize ourselves for things that we did in the past. That is my deepest purpose in writing this book, and if I imply criticism of the people who have devoted their lives to helping students, I apologize, for that was never my intent.

QUESTION SEVEN

If effective bullying prevention requires that students intervene or report when they witness acts of bullying, shouldn't character education programs that promote courage and compassion be emphasized more in schools?

My daughter has the ideal work location and it's not because it is in a warm climate (it's not), or that her office is so nice (it is). It is because she lives just a little over a mile from her apartment. She walks back and forth to work every day, so the thirty minutes per day of exercise, which is now the recommended amount of exercise, is a part of her daily routine. No need for her to join a gym or buy home exercise equipment, she just has to walk to work every day and then back home. When exercise is built into anyone's day and is no longer an add-on, or another thing to fit into a busy schedule, then someone like her can stay healthy just by living her life and doing her job.

This built-in or integrated approach to meeting basic needs can be applied to our schools, which is why I think that character education and/or social emotional programs are not necessary in schools if we were truly *educating* students instead of *training* them.

Training is a not a bad thing; it is necessary for many tasks, but it is not *education*. People need to be trained to perform technical skills for specific jobs. Their ability to learn is necessary, but it is a means to the end of acquiring the skills for a specific job, not simply improvement for its own sake. Once trained, the training can stop and those who were trained are monitored and evaluated to make sure that they keep their *trained* skills.

In this factory model of schools, character and social/emotional skills are not integrated into the interactions between teachers and students. There is one main social skill: do what you are told. Recognizing that schools are missing this social/character element, policymakers then decided to have character education and social/emotional skill training inserted into the traditional structure of schools.

If our schools shift from *training* inherited from the factory model, to a model that reflects the roots of the word *education*, students will naturally develop the social/emotional skills and the character traits necessary for success in life. If people are learning from each other (all learning is social, even the books we read are written by people), listening to each other, and solving the inevitable problems that arise from living and working together, they develop "character" and learn social/emotional skills in the process of being educated. John Dewey summed it up neatly: "The very process of living together, educates" (Dewey, 1985).

When teachers respect and believe that each student wants to learn and wants do well, they are teaching "character" by example. If teachers are *educating* instead of *training*, then their example and modeling provides the character and social skills training that comes from daily interactions, not add-on curricula or programs.

The difference between education and training is one that we all have experienced. Despite inheriting a factory/training framework, schools have always had some teachers that educate their students instead of training them. Just ask anyone to tell you about some of their memorable and positive experiences in school and you won't hear things like "I had this really great program" or "The curriculum in tenth grade really influenced me." What you will hear again and again are stories of people touching the minds and hearts of other people: teachers influencing the lives of students by letting students know how important and special they are.

Education of the whole person, doesn't need the add-on of character education. Education itself, in the true sense of the word, is what builds character (Dillon, 2013a).

QUESTION EIGHT

Aren't there schools that have been successful in preventing and reducing bullying and all inappropriate behaviors? Can't schools be successful without reframing in the way that you describe in the book?

Of course there are schools that have succeeded in preventing and reducing bullying and these schools might attribute their success to certain programs or strategies that don't require the type of reframing described in this book. Part of the problem with evaluating success is being able to pinpoint the variables that made the difference. For example, a school can implement a bullying prevention program and achieve a reduction in rates of bullying, however, the positive results could stem from other factors at play in the school that were not specifically included in the program. For example, a change of leadership in the school, or a significant number of staff decided to establish better relationships with students. The main point that I make is that people change people and ultimately any positive change in the culture and climate of a school will be because the relationships have changed for the better. Some programs or curricula could be a catalyst for that change. The problem with bullying prevention is that many schools think that bullying is a problem that requires the students to stop breaking rules and therefore don't accept the responsibility for changing adult behavior toward students. These are the type of schools that are typically immune from the positive aspects of any program they might implement.

It does become a Catch-22 situation: those schools that realize that change depends on changing relationships often seek out a program or curricula as a tool and achieve some success that they might have achieved without the program, whereas schools that desire to merely comply with the mandates imposed on them also implement a program and go through the motions, but fail to make any progress. *Those schools that think they need a program, need it less than those schools that think they don't need it, but use the program simply because they have to.*

Another problem with evaluating success is the criteria used. Some schools look at data on suspensions, detentions, and the number of office referrals as the primary criteria to evaluate progress. Although reductions in those areas are valid measures and can be good indicators of progress, too often schools understandably view stability as more of a destination rather than just one step toward a more important goal.

Most schools set the criteria for success as the three Cs: compliance, completion, and conformity. Students need to follow the rules, they need to complete the work they are given, and those students who don't, need to become more like those students who do. Schools run more smoothly as those three Cs increase. Most programs like PBIS claim to be "evidence-based" because they show data that measures those Cs in some way.

What I advocate is changing the criteria for success to a different set of Cs: commitment, creativity, and confidence. Students and staff need to go beyond following rules and become committed to learning that reflects a higher and more important value than merely the smooth functioning of the organization. They need to do more than answer questions posed to them, they need to create their own questions and see beyond the confines of a narrowly defined subject area. They also need to have the confidence to become the people they are meant to be and not judge themselves by how they compare to others. When students develop in these three Cs—commitment, creativity, and confidence—they become more likely to care for others and more able to develop the knowledge, skills, and attitudes needed for success in school and in the world outside of school.

QUESTION NINE

How is it that the research on change reflected in the social psychological resources cited in this book has not been embraced and applied to educational practices?

I wish I knew the answer, but I have some guesses:

- **Habit**: schools are not used to looking in areas outside of behavioral approaches.
- **Fit**: behavioral approaches fit the current structure of schools and are familiar and compatible with the typical ways that schools operate.

- **Perceived lack of need**: despite public perceptions portrayed in the media, most schools "work" (according to certain limited criteria for success) and are perceived to be successful, so why look to new or different areas of research.
- **Requirement that staff change what they do and say**: most schools are more focused on what they should do to change students and not on changing staff practices.
- **Difficult research to accept because people are too uncomfortable "being wrong"**: it is hard for educators who were taught the importance of being right in traditional schools, to admit that many of their basic assumptions about education could be off the mark, which might be too much for them to face and accept.
- **Preference for concrete strategies**: staff often only have time for strategies that fit the structure of their current practices. Theories of change that require some thought are too often considered a waste of time. This fits the prevailing notion that teaching is series of correct actions rather than an integration of thought and action or theory into practice.
- **Behavioral approaches reflect many embedded cultural assumptions**: educators have internalized and incorporated these assumptions into their practice, besides these approaches make perfect "common-sense" to most people.
- **Power and authority can make people change**: rewards and consequences distributed by those in power do *work* in getting people to change, so why should those in power change how they change people. Businesses who have no power over what people buy or choose have to look elsewhere and have turned to social psychology for ways to influence behavior. It is difficult for those in power to perceive the unseen negative results of using power to change people.
- **Educational policy is determined by people who have little if any knowledge of research**: it is typically designed to conform to conventional and traditional ways of viewing the world and practices that are more politically popular. How else could such *solutions* as zero tolerance policies, retention practices, and merit pay for teachers persist in the face of overwhelming evidence that they don't work.

Despite all these reasons why the research on change has a difficult time traveling to the institution of schools, there is a growing number of educators who are reading many books and research on the subject, including the research that I cited in this book. These educators are also connecting through social media across the globe so that these ideas are spreading and taking hold in more and more classrooms. It is most likely that this change will progress from the bottom up.

QUESTION TEN

It seems like most schools are based on a fixed mind-set rather than a growth mind-set. Is that too big of an obstacle preventing the type of reframing that the book advocates?

That observation does pose a tremendous obstacle for those seeking to reframe or redesign how we educate students in our schools. Not only is there a fixed mind-set built into the structure of schools for students, it is also applied to how teachers are now evaluated. Much more time, energy, and money is devoted to managing and evaluating student and teacher behavior based on performance tests rather than on improving teaching and learning.

For example, with students "the answer" has been to get a better handle on how they are doing by testing them with the hope that once the test results are made public, the students and their schools will be motivated to improve in order to avoid the "shame" of being labeled as failing or low performing. When that approach didn't work, the same type of method was applied to teacher evaluations: use evaluation results to motivate teachers to change in order to avoid their being labeled as ineffective or losing their jobs. In both of these scenarios, students and teachers are expected to perform in certain ways within fixed time periods or else suffer negative consequences. For example, a student who passes a course in June is a success, but a student who needs summer school to pass the same course is viewed as failing and not as "good" as those students who learned the material within an arbitrary time period. Teachers also have an arbitrary time period to learn their craft or face negative consequences. In both scenarios, succeeding means limiting the number of mistakes and failure is to be avoided at all costs. Consequently, schools are not inclusive places where people can learn and grow; they are places where people need to perform in order to meet the demands of those with the power to negatively affect one's life and how one feels about oneself. This is the frustrating scenario for change that is making it harder and harder for students and teachers to work together to support each other's learning.

This is why I believe that the problem of bullying may actually be compared to a *Trojan Horse*—something that opens the door to change for one reason, but then creates changes more far-reaching than the initial problem that prompted the need to open the door in the first place. Poor test scores might outrage some, but there is little motivation for the majority of families whose children are doing well, to want to change schools. Low academic performance affects families who tend to have very little political influence in changing schools. Bullying, however, cuts across socioeconomic lines and also affects schools where students do well academically. When bullying persists in schools, it not only touches every student and family, it touches emotions much more than low test scores. Right now, the dramatic and emotional impact of bullying and the desire to make schools safer can be a stronger impetus for school change than academic factors. When rates of bullying stay stuck despite all the laws, resources, and media attention, then the moral imperative to make certain that children are safe could prompt those in authority to push for solutions that might change the "fixed" mind-set that shapes how schools typically function. This is why I wrote this book, infused with the hope that the persistence of bullying as a problem in schools might lead to a different approach to change: an approach that begins by trying to address the problem of bullying, but ends up significantly changing the culture and climate of schools for the better. This might be a situation where the Buddhist saying, "The obstacle is the path" could prove to be true.

Bibliography

Adaptive Schools. (2013). *Thinking collaboratively*. Retrieved from http://www.thinkingcollaboratively.com

Aguilar, E. (2013). *The art of coaching: Effective strategies for school transformation*. San Francisco, CA: Wiley.

Amabile, T., & Kramer, S. (2011). *The progress principle: Using small wins to ignite joy, engagement, and creativity at work*. Boston, MA: Harvard Business Review Press.

Anspaugh, D. (1986). *Hoosiers* [DVD]. United States: MGM Home Entertainment. Retrieved from https://www.youtube.com/watch?v=9Cdc13CU9Fc&list=FLn1sPEq8nRrTJOFeZxxCMSA&index=67

Asher, W. (Director). (1952). *Switching Jobs* [Television series episode]. In W. Asher (Director). *I Love Lucy* [DVD]. United States: Columbia Broadcasting System.

Bazelon, E. (2013). *Sticks and stones: Defeating the culture of bullying and rediscovering the power of character and empathy*. New York, NY: Random House.

Blackwell, L., Trzesniewski, K., & Dweck. C. (2007). Implicit theories of intelligence predict achievement across an adolescent transition: A longitudinal study and an intervention. *Child Development, 78*(1), 246–263.

Bloom, P. (2010, May). The moral life of babies. *New York Times Magazine, 9*, 44.

Brannon, T., & Walton, G. (2013). Enacting cultural interests: How intergroup contact reduces prejudice by sparking interest in an out-group's culture. *Psychological Science, 20*(10), 1–11.

Briceño, E. (2012). The power of belief—Mind-set and success [Vimeo by L. Butler]. *TED X Manhattan Beach*. Retrieved from https://www.youtube.com/watch?v=pN34FNbOKXc

Brown, R. P., & Day, E. A. (2006). The difference isn't Black and White: Stereotype threat and the race gap on Raven's advanced progressive matrices. *Journal of Applied Psychology, 91*(4), 979–985.

Bryan, C. J., Master, A., & Walton, G. M. (2014). Helping versus being a helper: Invoking the self to increase helping in young children. *Child Development, 85*(5), 1836–1842.

The Center for Effective Discipline. (2010). *U.S. Statistics on corporal punishment by state and race*. Washington, DC: U.S. Department of Education, Office of Civil Rights. Retrieved from http://www.stophitting.com/index.php?page=statesbanning

Cialdini, R. B. (2001). *Influence: science and practice* (4th ed.). Boston, MA: Allyn and Bacon.

Cohen, G., Garcia, J., Apfel, N., & Master, A. (2006). Reducing the racial achievement gap: A social-psychological intervention. *Science, 313*(5791), 1307–1310.

Collins, J. C. (2001). *Good to great: Why some companies make the leap–and others don't.* New York, NY: HarperBusiness.

Cooperrider, D., & Whitney. D. (2005). *Appreciative inquiry: A positive revolution in change.* San Francisco, CA: Berrett-Koehler.

Davidson, A. (2012, May). Mitt Romney, bully. *New Yorker.* Retrieved from http://www.newyorker.com/news/amy-davidson/mitt-romney-bully

DeCharms, R. (1977). Pawn or origin? Enhancing motivation in disaffected youth. *Educational Leadership, 34*(6), 444–448.

Deci, E. (2012). *Ed Deci: Promoting motivation for health and excellence* [Video]. TED X Flour City. Retrieved from https://www.youtube.com/watch?v=VGrcets0E6I&index=13&list=FLn1sPEq8nRrTJOFeZxxCMSA

Deci, E. L., & Flaste, R. (1996). *Why we do what we do: Understanding self-motivation.* New York, NY: Penguins Books.

Deci, E., & Ryan, R. (2000). Self-determination theory and the facilitation of intrinsic motivation, social development, and well-being. *American Psychologist, 55,* 68–78.

Deci, E., & Ryan, R. (2002). An overview of self-determination theory. *Handbook of self-determination theory.* Rochester, NY: University of Rochester Press.

Dewey, J. (1940). *Education today.* New York, NY: G. P. Putnam.

Dewey, J. (1985). *Democracy and education.* Carbondale: APA, 6.30, p. 187: Southern Illinois University Press. (Original work published 1916)

Dillon, J. (2012). *No place for bullying: Leadership for schools that care for every student.* Thousand Oaks, CA: Corwin.

Dillon, J. (2013a). Education builds character. *Smartblog on Education.* Retrieved from http://smartblogs.com/education/2014/06/09/education-builds-character/

Dillon, J. (2013b). Problem with success. *Smartblog on Education.* Retrieved from http://smartblogs.com/education/2013/07/02/a-problem-with-success/

Dillon, J. (2013c). Bullying prevention from the ground up. *Smartblog on Education.* Retrieved from http://smartblogs.com/education/2013/10/07/bullying-prevention-from-the-ground-up/

Dillon, J. (2013d). Best antidote to bullying: Community building [Washington, D.C. Commentary]. *Education Week.* Retrieved from http://www.edweek.org/ew/articles/2013/12/11/14dillon.h33.html

Dillon, J. (2014). Untying the Nots of bullying prevention. *Principal, 93*(3), 36–39.

Dweck, C., Walton, G., & Cohen, G. (2011). Academic tenacity: Mind-sets and skills that promote long-term learning. *Gates Foundation,* 1–40.

Edmondson, A. C. (2012). *Teaming: How organizations learn, innovate, and compete in the knowledge economy.* San Francisco, CA: Jossey-Bass.

Farrington, C.A., Roderick, M., Allensworth, E., Nagaoka, J., Keyes, T. S., Johnson, D.W., & Beechum, N. O. (2012). Teaching adolescents to become learners: The role of noncognitive factors is shaping school performance: A critical literature review. Chicago, IL: University of Chicago Consortium on Chicago School Research.

Fassler, D. (2012, February). Adolescent brain development and life without parole. *Huffington Post.* Retrieved from http://www.huffingtonpost.com/david-fassler-md

Franco, Z., & Zimbardo, P. (2006, September). The banality of heroism. *Greater Good Magazine*. Berkeley: University of California at Berkeley. Retrieved from http://greatergood.berkeley.edu/article/item/the_banality_of_heroism

Fredrickson, B. (2009). *Positivity*. New York, NY: Crown.

Freire, P. (2000). *Pedagogy of the oppressed* (30th anniversary ed.). New York, NY: Bloomsbury Academic. (Original work published 1968)

Friesen, S., & Jardine, D. (2009). *21st century learning and learners* (Report prepared for Western and Northern Canadian Curriculum Protocol). Calgary, Canada: Galileo Educational Network, University of Calgary. Retrieved from http://education.alberta.ca/media/

Fullan, M. (2001). *Leading in a culture of change*. San Francisco, CA: Jossey-Bass.

Garmston, R. J., & Wellman, B. M. (1999). *The adaptive school: A sourcebook for developing collaborative groups*. Norwood, MA: Christopher-Gordon.

Gawande, A. (2010). *The checklist manifesto: How to get things right*. New York, NY: Metropolitan Books.

Gawande, A. (2013, July). Slow Ideas. *The New Yorker*. Retrieved from http://www.newyorker.com/magazine/2013/07/29/slow-ideas

Gladwell, M. (2002). The tipping point: How little things can make a big difference. Boston, MA: Little, Brown.

Gladwell, M. (2014). *David and Goliath: Underdogs, misfits, and the art of battling giants*. New York, NY: Little Brown.

Goodman, R. (Director). (2002). *The "in crowd" and social cruelty with John Stossel* [television series & DVD]. New York, NY: ABC News. Retrieved from https://www.youtube.com/watch?v=UrsHp-z08f8

Gopnick, A. (2012, January). What's wrong with the teenage mind? *Wall Street Journal Online*. Retrieved from http://online.wsj.com/news/articles/

Grant, A. (2014, April). Raising a moral child. *New York Times,* Opinion Section.

Gray, P. (2012, October). Unsolicited evaluation is the enemy of creativity [Web log post]. *Psychology Today*. Retrieved from http://www.psychologytoday.com/blog/freedom-learn/201210/unsolicited-evaluation-is-the-enemy-creativity

Gray, P. (2013). *Free to learn: Why unleashing the instinct to play will make our children happier, more self-reliant, and better students for life*. Philadelphia, PA: Basic Books.

Haidt, J. (2010). Wired to be inspired. In D. Keltner, J. Marsh, & J. A. Smith (Eds.), *The compassionate instinct*. New York, NY: Norton.

Halvorson, H. G., & Higgins, E. T. (2013). *Focus: Use different ways of seeing the world for success and influence* (eBook version). New York, NY: Hudson Street Press. Retrieved from http://www.amazon.com/Focus-Different-Seeing-Success-Influence-ebook/dp/B008BM4MM6/ref=tmm_kin_swatch_0?_encoding=UTF8&sr=&qid=

Hanson, R. (2013). Hardwiring happiness: The new brain science of contentment, calm, and confidence. New York: Random House.

Heath, C., & Heath, D. (2007). *Made to stick: Why some ideas survive and others die*. New York, NY: Random House.

Heath, C., & Heath, D. (2010). *Switch: How to change things when change is hard*. New York, NY: Broadway Books.

Heath, C., & Heath, D. (2013). *Decisive*. New York, NY: Crown Business.

Horowitz, J. (2012). Debate on Romney's memory of incident: Bullying activist says his claim could be true. *Washington Post*.

Howard, R. (Director). (1995). *Apollo 13* [DVD]. United States: MCA Universal Home Video. Retrieved from https://www.youtube.com/watch?v=hLZZ_y1xdJg

Hughes, L. (1997). *The short stories of Langston Hughes* (A. S. Harper, Ed.). New York, NY: Hill and Wang.

Jamieson, J. P., Mendes, W. B., & Nock, M. K. (2013). Improving acute stress responses: The power of reappraisal. *Current Directions in Psychological Science, 22,* 51–56.

Johnston, J. (Director). (1999). *October Sky* [DVD]. United States: Universal Pictures.

Kahneman, D. (2011). *Thinking, fast and slow.* New York, NY: Farrar, Straus and Giroux.

Kanigel, R. (1997). *The one best way: Frederick Taylor and the enigma of efficiency.* Cambridge, MA: MIT Press.

Keller, L., & Orr, A. (2011a, June). My kid would never bully (girls group). *NBC Dateline.* Retrieved from https://www.youtube.com/watch?v=Ask9x8gx9Dg&index=5&list=FLn1sPEq8nRrTJOFeZxxCMSA

Keller, L., & Orr, A. (2011b, June). My kid would never bully (boys group). *NBC Dateline.* Retrieved from https://www.youtube.com/watch?v=JyBTap2wudo&index=6&list=FLn1sPEq8nRrTJOFeZxxCMSA

Keltner, D., & Marsh, J. (2010a). We are all bystanders. *The Compassionate Instinct.* New York: W.W. Norton.

Keltner, D., Marsh, J., & Smith, J. A. (Eds.). (2010b). *The compassionate instinct: The science of human goodness.* New York, NY: W.W. Norton.

Kennedy, J. (1960). *The New Frontier speech.* Retrieved from. http://www.wikiquote.org/

King, M. L. Jr., (1992). *I have a dream: Writings and speeches that changed the world* (J. M. Washington, Ed.). San Francisco, CA: HarperCollins Publishers.

Knight, J. (2011). *Unmistakable impact: A partnership approach for dramatically improving instruction.* Thousand Oaks, CA: Corwin.

Konrath, S., O'Brien, E., & Hsing, C. (2011). Changes in dispositional empathy in American college students over time: A meta-analysis. *Personality and Social Psychology Review, 15*(2), 180–198.

Kotter, J. P. (2008). *A sense of urgency.* Boston, MA: Harvard Business Press.

Kreisberg, S. (1992). *Transforming power: Domination, empowerment and dominion.* Albany: State University of New York at Albany.

Lakoff, G. (2004). *Don't think of an elephant!: Know your values and frame the debate: The essential guide for progressives.* White River Junction, VT: Chelsea Green.

Lakoff, G. (2006). *Thinking points: Communicating our American values and vision: A progressive's handbook.* New York, NY: Farrar, Straus and Giroux.

Lane, K. L., Menzies, H., Bruhn, A., & Crnbori, M. (2011). *Managing challenging behaviors in schools: Research-based strategies that work.* New York, NY: Guilford Press.

Lewis, D. (Narrator). (2011, March). *Born to Learn* [Video]. United States: 21st Century Learning Initiative. Retrieved from http://www.born-to-learn.org and https://www.youtube.com/watch?v=falHoOEUFz0

Marwick, A., & boyd, d. (2011, September). The drama! Teen conflict, gossip, and bullying in networked publics. A decade in Internet time: Symposium on the dynamics of the Internet and society. United Kingdom: *Social Science Research Network.* Abstract retrieved from http://papers.ssrn.com/sol3/papers.cfm?abstract_id=1926349 or http://ssrn.com/abstract=1926349

McNeill, L. (1988). *Contradictions of control*. New York, NY: Routledge, Chapman and Hall.

Melton, G. D. (2014, June). One teacher's brilliant strategy to stop bullying. *Reader's Digest*.

Miller, B. (Director). (2012). *Moneyball* [DVD]. United States: Sony Pictures Home Entertainment. Retrieved from https://www.youtube.com/watch?v=xn7C6jgl0RI

Morrison, B., & Marachi, R. (2011, March). *Understanding and responding to school bullying [Webinar]*. In *Safe and Supportive Schools Technical Assistance Center, American Institutes for Research*. Washington, DC: U.S. Department of Education Office of Safe and Drug Free Schools. Available at http://safesupportivelearning.ed.gov/events/webinar/bullying-prevention

National Center for Education Statistics. (2012). *Indicators of school crime and safety*. Washington, DC: U.S. Department of Education, Institute of Education Sciences. Retrieved from http://nces.ed.gov/programs/crimeindicators/crimeindicators2012/tables/table_11_5.asp

National Center for Education Statistics. (2014). *Bullying in school statistics*. Washington, DC: U.S. Department of Education. Retrieved from http://nces.ed.gov/programs/digest/d13/tables/dt13_230.50.asp

Norton, M. (2009). The IKEA effect: When labor leads to love. *Harvard Business Review, 87*(2), 30.

Novogratz, J. (2006). Jacqueline Novogratz: Invest in Africa's own solutions [Video]. *TED Talks: Ideas worth spreading*. Retrieved from https://www.youtube.com/watch?v=8k_XH-ajLo0

Olweus, D. (1993). *Bullying at school*. Malden, MA: Blackwell.

Olweus, D., Limber S., Flex, V., Mullin, N., Riese, J., & Synder, M. (2007). *Olweus bullying prevention program teacher guide*. Center City, MN: Hazelden.

Patterson, K., Grenny, J., Maxfield, D., McMillan, R., & Switzler, A. (2008). *Influencer: The power to change anything*. New York, NY: McGraw-Hill.

Patterson, K., Grenny, J., Maxfield, D., McMillan, R., & Switzler, A. (2011). *Change anything: The new science of personal success*. New York, NY: Business Plus.

Perkins, H. W., Craig, D., & Perkins, J. (2011). Using social norms to reduce bullying: A research intervention among adolescents in five middle schools. *Group Processes & Intergroup Relations, 14*(5), 703–723.

Pink, D. H. (2006). *A whole new mind: Why right-brainers will rule the future*. New York, NY: Riverhead Books.

Pink, D. H. (2009). *Drive: The surprising truth about what motivates us*. New York, NY: Riverhead Books.

Pink, D. (2010). *Two questions that can change your life* [Video file]. Retrieved from http://www.danielpink.com/archives/2010/01/2questionsvideo

Pink, D. H. (2012). *To sell is human: The surprising truth about moving others*. New York, NY: Riverhead Books.

Pink, D. (2013). Our motivations are unbelievably interesting [Video]. *RSA Animation*. Oxford, UK: Edge Initiatives. Retrieved from https://www.youtube.com/watch?v=avnHUxSVfVM

Pirsig, R. M. (1974). *Zen and the art of motorcycle maintenance: An inquiry into values*. New York, NY: Morrow.

Reeve, J., Ryan, R., Deci, E., &. Jang, H. (2007). Understanding and promoting autonomous self-regulation: A self-determination theory perspective. In

D. H. Schunk & B. J. Zimmerman (Eds.), *Motivation and self-regulated learning: Theory, research and application* (pp. 223–244). Mahwah, NJ: Lawrence Erlbaum.

Robinson, K. (2011). *Out of our minds: Learning to be creative*. West Sussex, UK: Capstone.

Rodkin, P. (2011). Bullying: The power of peers. *Educational Leadership, 69*(1), 10–16.

Rosenberg, T. (2011). *Join the club: How peer pressure can transform the world*. New York, NY: W.W. Norton.

Roth, G., Kanat-Maymon, Y., & Bibi, U. (2011). Prevention of school bullying: The important role of autonomy supportive teaching and the internalization of pro-social values. *British Journal of Educational Psychology, 81,* 654–666.

Ryan, R., & Grolnick, W. (1986). Origins and pawns in the classroom: Self-report and projective assessments of individual differences in children's perceptions. *Journal of Personality and Social Psychology, 50*(3), 550–558.

Ryzik, M. (2011, February). Animation advocacy, Pixar style. *New York Times*, p. C1. Retrieved from *A Rare Look at Pixar Studios* http://www.youtube.com

Salmivalli, C. (2010). Bullying and the peer group: A review. *Aggression and Violent Behavior, 15,* 112–120.

Sarason, S. B. (1996). *Revisiting "The culture of the school and the problem of change."* New York: Teachers College Press.

Schein, E. (2009). *Helping: How to offer, give and receive help*. San Francisco, CA: Berrett-Koehler.

Schwartz, B., & Sharpe, K. (2010). *Practical wisdom: The right way to do the right thing*. New York, NY: Riverhead Books.

Self-affirmation theory. (n.d.). *Wikipedia*. Retrieved July 28, 2014 from Wikimedia Foundation http://en.wikipedia.org/wiki/Self-affirmation

Sergiovanni, T. J. (1996). *Leadership for the schoolhouse: How is it different?: Why is it important?* San Francisco, CA: Jossey-Bass.

Shapiro, M. (Producer). (2003, April 25). *Mo Cheeks National Anthem* [NBA Playoff Game on ESPN]. United States: National Broadcasting Company. Retrieved from https://www.youtube.com/watch?v=q4880PJnO2E&list=FLn1sPEq8nRrTJOFeZxxCMSA&index=72

Simmons, A. (2007). *Whoever tells the best story wins: How to use your own stories to communicate with power and impact*. New York, NY: Amacom.

Sinek, S. (2009). *Start with why: How great leaders inspire everyone to take action*. New York, NY: Portfolio.

Sinek, S. (2014). *Leaders eat last: Why some teams pull together and others don't*. New York, NY: Penquin.

Smith, P. (2012). *Lead with a story: A guide to crafting business narratives that captivate, convince, and inspire*. New York, NY: American Management Association.

Sullivan, L. (Director). (2004). *A touch of greatness* [DVD]. United States: First Run Features. Retrieved from https://www.youtube.com/watch?v=jujtkzGiG9U&list=FLn1sPEq8nRrTJOFeZxxCMSA

Surowiecki, J. (2004). *The wisdom of crowds: Why the many are smarter than the few and how collective wisdom shapes business, economies, societies, and nations*. New York, NY: Doubleday.

Tate, T. (2001). Peer influences and positive cognitive restructuring. *Reclaiming Children and Youth, 9*(4), 215–218.

Taylor, C., Manganello, J., Lee, S., & Rice, J. (2010). Mothers' spanking of 3-year-old children and subsequent risk of children's aggressive behavior. *Pediatrics, 125*(5), 1057–1085.

Thornberg, R. (2010). A student in distress: Moral frames and bystander behavior in school. *Elementary School Journal, 110*(4), 585–608.

United States Department of Health and Human Services. (2014). *What bullying is, what cyberbullying is, who is at risk, and how you can prevent and respond to bullying* [website]. Washington, DC: author. Retrieved from http://www.stopbullying.gov/

Walton, G., & Cohen, G. (2007). A question of belonging: Race, social fit, and achievement. *Journal of Personality and Social Psychology, 92*(1), 82–96.

Walton, G., & Cohen, G. (2011). A brief social-belonging intervention improves academic and health outcomes of minority students. *Science, 331*(6023), 1147–11451.

Walton, G., Cohen, G., Cwir, D., & Spencer, S. J. (2013). Mere belonging: The power of social connections. *Journal of Personality and Social Psychology, 102*, 513–532.

Walton, G., Panesku, D., & Dweck, C. (2012). Expandable selves. In M. R. Leary & J. P. Tangney (Eds.), *Handbook of Self and Identity* (pp. 141–154). New York, NY: Guilford Press.

Weinschenk, S. (2013). *How to get people to do stuff: Master the art and science of persuasion and motivation*. Berkeley, CA: New Riders.

Weir, P. (Director). (1985). *Witness* [DVD]. United States: Paramount Pictures Corp. Retrieved from https://www.youtube.com/watch?v=a7kLSk9-TRg

Willard, N. (2012). *Cyber savvy: Embracing digital safety and civility*. Thousand Oaks, CA: Corwin.

Wilson, T. D. (2002). *Strangers to ourselves: Discovering the adaptive unconscious*. Cambridge, MA: Belknap Press of Harvard University Press

Wilson, T. (2011). *Re-Direct: The surprising new science of psychological change*. New York, NY: Little, Brown.

Wilson, T., & Linville, P. (1982). Improving the academic performance of college freshman: Attribution therapy revisited. *Journal of Personality and Social Psychology I, 42*(2), 367–376.

Wilson, T., & Linville, P. (1985). Improving the performance of college freshman with attributional techniques. *Journal of Personality and Social Psychology, 49*(1), 287–293.

Wiseman, L., Allen, L., & Foster, E. (2013). *The multiplier effect: Tapping the genius within our schools*. Thousand Oaks, CA: Corwin.

Yakin, B. (Director). (2001). *Remember the Titans* [DVD]. United States: Walt Disney Home Video. Retrieved from https://www.youtube.com/watch?v=uiqdA1B3_Nc

Yeager, D., Henderson, M., D'Mello, S., Paunesku, D., Walton, G., Spitzer, B., & Duckworth, A. (2014). Boring but important: A self-transcendent purpose for learning fosters academic self-regulation. *Journal of Educational Psychology, 107*(4), 559–580.

Yeager, D. S., & Walton, G. M. (2011). Social-psychological interventions in education: They're not magic. *Review of Educational Research, 81*(2), 267–301.

Zak, P. (2013, December). How Stories Change the Brain. *Greater Good Science Center*. Berkeley: University of California at Berkeley. Retrieved from http://greatergood.berkeley.edu/article/item/how_stories_change_brain

Index

Academic mindset, 95–96
Academic standards, 126–127
Accountability, 149–150
Adaptive Schools, 176
Adolescent brain behavior:
    frame/game of schools, 26–27, 35–36
    invisible character process, 19–20
Aguilar, E., 176
Allen, L., 234
Allensworth, E., 148–149
Amabile, T., 202–203, 209
Anspaugh, D., 250
Apfel, N., 225
Apollo 13, 236
Appreciative Inquiry (AI), 175
Art of Coaching, The (Aguilar), 176
Autonomy:
    autonomous motivation, 105, 106
    autonomy support, 105–106
    autonomy-supportive instruction, 108–109, 250
    defined, 104
    self-determination theory (SDT), 104, 105–106, 108–109
Autonomy Supportive Teaching (AST), 250

Ball, Lucille, 147
Banality of Heroism, The (Franco & Zimbardo), 263
Bazelon, E., 20
Beechum, N., 148–149
Bibi, U., 250
Boarding school incident (1965):
    analysis of, 11–14
    bullying characteristics, 18–19
    description of, 9–10
    Romney, Mitt, 11–14

Boring but Important (Yeager, Henderson, D'Mello, Paunesku, Walton, Spitzer, Duckworth), 197
Born to Learn, 251
boyd, d., 262
Brannon, T., 210
Briceno, E., 148
Bryan, C., 224–225
Building Community Spirit in Schools:
    academic standards, 126–127
    accountability, 149–150
    activities for, 144–151
    anecdote, 113–117
    building dimension, 127–128
    bullying prevention terminology, 117–118
    change process elements, 116
    characteristics of, 141
    community dimension, 128–130
    controlled behavior, 115–116, 138–139
    current bullying prevention approach, 141
    democratic frame of citizenship, 121–124
    dominant parent frame, 122–123, 137, 141
    either/or choice, 142
    factory frame, 122–123, 137, 141
    influence guides tenet, 138–139, 282–283
    integrated practice tenet, 135, 280–281
    mind-sets, 148–149
    moral education, 124–126
    negative messages, 119–121
    positive emotions, 118–119
    principle-based tenet, 133–134, 279–280
    psychological safety, 149–150
    relationships central tenet, 135–138, 281–282

self-determination theory (SDT), 149–150
spirit dimension, 130–131
student-centered tenet, 132–133, 278–279
student empowerment approach, 116
tenets of, 131–140
ties strengthened tenet, 140, 283
Bullying:
basic assumptions, 6
personal anecdote, 2–4
reflection on, 1–6
research overview, 5–6
Bullying incidents:
adolescent brain behavior, 19–20
boarding school incident (1965), 9–10, 11–14, 18–19
characteristics of, 18–19
defined, 16
justification elements, 21–22
questions regarding, 22
reactive response to, 20–21
reframing bullying prevention, 22–23
school bus incident (2012), 10–11, 14–17, 18–19
Bullying (Rodkin), 58–59
Bystander behavior:
external responses, 77–78
Fundamental Attribution Error (FAE), 166–169
internal responses, 78–80
learning experience, 53–55
response limitations, 75–80

Change Anything (Patterson, Grenny, Maxfield, McMillan, Switzler), 259
Change Identity strategy:
activities for, 226–228
anecdote, 215–217
controlled behavior, 219–222
defined, 217–219
mind-sets, 218
moral education, 220–221
process for, 219–222
recommendations for, 228
resources for, 222–226
self-affirmation theory, 221
text-based discussion, 226
video clip discussion, 226
"who" strategy, 215–228
Chaplin, Charlie, 147
Character education programs, 292–293

Charms, R. de, 226
Checklist for bullying prevention:
influence guides tenet, 282–283
integrated practice tenet, 280–281
principle-based tenet, 279–280
relationships central tenet, 281–282
student-centered tenet, 278–279
ties strengthened tenet, 283
Checklist Manifesto, The (Gawande), 277–278
Cheeks, Maurice, 186, 226
Cialdini, R., 160, 208–209, 222, 261
Click-and-whirr approach, 30
Coaching, 176–177
Cohen, G., 210–211, 225
Compassionate Instinct, The (Keltner, Marsh, Smith), 195–196
Competence, 104
Confirmation bias, 31–32
Connect the "I's" strategy:
activities for, 211–213
anecdote, 206
defined, 207
heart strategy, 206–213
process of, 207–208
recommendations for, 212–213
resources for, 208–211
text-based discussion, 211
video clip discussion, 211
Controlled behavior:
Building Community Spirit in Schools, 115–116, 138–139
Change Identity strategy, 219–222
frame/game of student identity, 70–75
Fundamental Attribution Error (FAE), 162
Controlled instruction, 109–110
Controlled motivation, 104–105, 106
Corporal punishment, 25–28, 30, 35–36
Cullum, Albert, 250–251
Cwir, D., 210–211
Cyberbullying, 285–286
Cyber Savvy (Willard), 286

Dateline Television, 263
David and Goliath (Gladwell), 223
Deci, E., 102–103, 249
Deep frames, 35
Democratic frame of citizenship, 121–124
Dillon, J., 46–48, 134
D'Mello, S., 197

Dominant parent frame:
  Building Community Spirit in Schools, 122–123, 137, 141
  frame/game of bullying, 60
  frame/game of schools, 35, 37, 39, 43–44
  frame/game of student identity, 67, 72
  Fundamental Attribution Error (FAE), 162
"Do" strategies:
  Make It Safe To Play, 241–253
  Tell The *Right* Story, 265–275
  Train First Responders, 253–265
Drama! (Marwick & boyd), 262
Drive (Pink), 195
Duckworth, A., 197
Dweck, C., 224

Edmondson, A., 90–95, 149–150, 209–210, 247–248
Enacting Cultural Interests (Brannon & Walton), 210
Expected behavior, 65–67
Expendable Selves (Walton, Paunesku, Dweck), 224

Factory frame:
Building Community Spirit in Schools, 122–123, 137, 141
  frame/game of bullying, 60
  frame/game of schools, 36–38, 43–44
  frame/game of student identity, 67, 72
  Fundamental Attribution Error (FAE), 162
  impact on schools, 36–38
  key features, 37
  origins of, 38
False identity, 69
Farrington, C., 148–149
Fast thinking systems:
  frame/game of schools, 29–33, 34–35, 42, 43–44
  frame/game of student identity, 67
  Fundamental Attribution Error (FAE), 159, 163
Finding Nemo, 266
Find the Human "Why" strategy:
  activities for, 197–199
  anecdote, 191–193
  defined, 193
  heart strategy, 191–199
  process of, 193–194
  recommendations for, 199
  resources for, 195–197
  text-based discussion, 198
  video clip discussion, 197–198

Five Truths of Helping, 177, 179
Flaste, R., 102, 249
Focus (Halvorson & Higgins), 260–261
Foster, E., 234
Frame/game of bullying:
  anecdote, 51–57, 61–62
  bully learning experience, 53–55
  bystander learning experience, 53–55
  current school approach, 59–61
  dominant parent frame, 60
  factory frame, 60
  game board of bullying, 55–59
  reactive response to, 52–53
  redeeming school mistakes, 62–63
  redeeming teacher mistakes, 61–62
  social stratification, 56–59
  student empowerment approach, 63–64
Frame/game of schools:
  adolescent brain behavior, 26–27, 35–36
  bullying prevention approach, 43–44
  bullying prevention impact, 32–33
  bullying prevention strategy, 34
  bullying rationalizations, 25–26
  classroom examples, 39–41
  click-and-whirr approach, 30
  complexity of change, 28–32
  confirmation bias, 31–32
  corporal punishment, 25–28, 30, 35–36
  deep frames, 35
  defined, 28
  description of, 38–41
  dominant parent frame, 35, 37, 39, 43–44
  examples of, 39–41
  factory frame, 36–38, 43–44
  fast thinking systems, 29–33, 34–35, 42, 43–44
  heuristic judgments, 29
  legal approach to bullying, 45–49
  mental frames, 33–34
  reframing bullying prevention, 42–43
  slow thinking systems, 29–30, 32, 42, 43–44, 49–50
  spotlight effect, 30
  textbook examples, 41–42
  WWSIATI approach, 30
Frame/game of student identity:
  anecdote, 65–67
  behavioral expectations, 65–67
  bystander response limitations, 75–80
  compassionate influences, 69–70
  controlled behavior, 70–75
  dominant parent frame, 67, 72
  external responses to bullying, 77–78

factory frame impact, 67, 72
false identity, 69
internal responses to bullying, 78–80
mistaken student assumptions, 67–69
negativity bias, 68–69
reframing bullying prevention, 80
Franco, Z., 263
Free to Learn blog, 251
Free to Learn (Gray), 248–249
Freire, P., 37
Friesen, S., 38
Fundamental Attribution Error (FAE):
avoidance of, 159
behavioral approach, 164–166
bullying behavior, 161
bullying context, 161–162
bystander behavior, 166–169
controlled behavior, 162
defined, 159
dominant parent frame, 162
empirical research, 166
example of, 162–164
factory frame, 162
fast thinking systems, 159, 163
organizational example, 159–160
recognition of, 159–161, 169–170
recommendations for, 169=170
reframing bullying prevention, 158–170
slow thinking systems, 161
social psychological approach, 164–166
stereotype threat, 166

Game board of bullying, 55–59
Garcia, J., 225
Gawande, A., 277–278
Gladwell, M., 223
Grant, A., 226
Gray, P., 248–249, 251
Greater Good Magazine, 263
Grenny, J., 195, 233, 259
Grolnick, W., 273
Group decision-making, 171–174
Gyllenhaal, Jake, 211

Hackman, Gene, 250
Halvorson, H. G., 260–261
Handbook of Self and Identity (Leary & Tangney), 224
Hanks, Tom, 236
Hanson, R., 67
Hardwiring for Happiness (Hanson), 67
Harrison, Ford, 236

Heart strategies:
Connect the "I's," 206–213
Find the Human "Why," 191–199
Show Hope, 199–206
Heath, C., 203, 222, 259, 270–271
Heath, D., 203, 222, 259, 270–271
Helping (Schein), 234
"Helping" Versus "Being a Helper" (Bryan, Master, Walton), 224–225
Henderson, M., 197
Heuristic judgments, 29
Hickman, Homer, 211
Higgins, E. T., 260–261
Homosexuality incident, 9–10, 11–14, 18–19
Hoosiers, 250
Howard, R., 236
How Stories Change the Brain (Zak), 273
How to Get People to Do Stuff (Weinschenk), 140, 224
Hughes, L., 205

IKEA effect, 230, 235
IKEA Effect, The (Norton), 235
I Love Lucy, 147
Improving the Academic Performance of College Freshmen (Wilson & Linville), 204
Incredible, The, 266
Influence (Cialdini), 160, 208–209, 222, 261
Influence guides tenet:
Building Community Spirit in Schools, 138–139, 282–283
checklist for, 282–283
Influencer (Patterson, Grenny, Maxfield, McMillan, Switzler), 195, 233
Integrated practice tenet:
Building Community Spirit in Schools, 135, 280–281
checklist for, 280–281
Internet websites:
Free to Learn blog, 251
Greater Good Magazine, 263
mind-sets, 148
Pixar Studios, 147
TED Talks, 102–103
See also YouTube
Intrinsic motivation, 103–104, 105, 108, 110

Jardine, D., 38
Johnson, D., 148–149
Johnston, J., 211
Join the Club (Rosenberg), 234–235

Kahneman, D., 29
Kanat-Maymon, Y., 250
Keltner, D., 195–196
Kennedy, John F., 126, 127, 187
Keyes, T. S., 148–149
Kramer, S., 202–203, 209

Lauber, John, 12
Leaders Eat Last (Sinek), 248
Lead With a Story (Smith), 271–272
Leary, M. R., 224
Legal approach to bullying, 45–49
Lewis, Damian, 251
Linville, P., 204
Luce, Clare Booth, 187

Made to Stick (Heath & Heath), 270–271
Make It Safe To Play strategy:
    activities for, 251–253
    anecdote, 242
    Autonomy Supportive Teaching
        (AST), 250
    defined, 243–245
    "do" strategy, 241–253
    process for, 245–247
    recommendations for, 252–253
    resources for, 247–250
    self-determination theory (SDT), 250
    text-based discussion, 251
    video clip discussion, 250–251
Marsh, J., 195–196
Martin Luther King (Washington), 198
Marwick, A., 262
Master, A., 224–225
Maxfield, D., 195, 233, 259
McMillan, R., 195, 233, 259
Melton, G. D., 211
Mental frames:
    frame/game of schools, 33–34
    question-and-answer topics, 290–291
Mere Belonging (Walton, Cohen, Cwir,
    Spencer), 210–211
Miller, B., 204
Mind-sets:
    academic mindset, 95–96
    activity for, 148–149
    Building Community Spirit in
        Schools, 148–149
    bullying prevention application,
        99–100
    bullying prevention implications, 101
    Change Identity strategy, 218
    question-and-answer topics, 296–297

reframing bullying prevention, 95–101
reframing challenges, 96–97
reframing effects, 97–98
reframing impact on educators, 97
reframing limitations, 98–99
Modern Times, 147
Moneyball, 204
Moral education:
    Building Community Spirit in
        Schools, 124–126
    Change Identity strategy, 220–221
Motivation:
    autonomous motivation, 105, 106
    controlled motivation, 104–105, 106
    intrinsic motivation, 103–104, 105,
        108, 110
Multiplier Effect, The (Wiseman, Allen,
    Foster), 234
My Kid Would Never Bully, 263–265

Nagaoka, J., 148–149
Negative messages, 119–121
Negativity bias, 68–69
New Yorker, 277
No Place for Bullying (Dillon), 46–48, 134
Norton, M., 235
Novogratz, J., 273

October Sky, 211
*One Teacher's Brilliant Strategy to Stop
    Bullying* (Melton), 211
Organizational reframing:
    bullying prevention implications, 95
    dominant parent frame, 90–91
    empirical research, 91–93
    execution frame, 93
    factory frame, 90–91
    fear factor, 91, 93
    learning frame, 93
    psychological safety, 93–95
Origins and Pawns in Classrooms
    (Ryan & Grolnick), 273
Out of Our Minds (Robinson), 36–37

Patterson, K., 195, 233, 259
Paunesku, D., 197, 224
Pawn or Origin? (Charms), 226
Pedagogy of the Oppressed (Freire), 37
*Peer Influences and Positive Cognitive
    Restructuring* (Tate), 236–237
Pink, D., 149, 195, 210, 271
Pitt, Brad, 204
Pixar Studios, 147–148, 266

Positive Behavior Interventions and
  Supports (PBIS), 287–289
Positive emotions, 118–119
Practical Wisdom (Schwartz & Sharpe), 196
Practice Change guideline:
  Adaptive Schools, 176
  Appreciative Inquiry (AI), 175
  bullying prevention implications,
    174–177
  coaching, 176–177
  Five Truths of Helping, 177
  group decision-making, 171–174
  obstacles, 173–174
  recommendations for, 174–177
  reframing bullying prevention, 171–177
Prevention of School Bullying (Roth,
  Kanat-Maymon, Bibi), 250
Principle-based tenet:
  Building Community Spirit in Schools,
    133–134, 279–280
  checklist for, 279–280
Progress Principle, The (Amabile & Kramer),
  202–203, 209
Psychological safety:
  Building Community Spirit in
    Schools, 149–150
  organizational reframing, 93–95
  T-Chart activity, 251–253

Question-and-answer topics:
  character education programs, 292–293
  cyberbullying, 285–286
  differing mental frames, 290–291
  in-place bullying prevention programs,
    286–287, 293–294
  limitations of school criticism, 291
  mind-sets, 296–297
  Positive Behavior Interventions and
    Supports (PBIS), 287–289
  reframing obstacles, 294–295
  status-quo leadership, 289–290

Raising a Moral Child (Grant), 226
Ratatouille, 266
Reader's Digest, 211
Reclaiming Children and Youth, 236–237
Re-Direct (Wilson), 203–204, 222–223
Reducing the Racial Achievement Gap
  (Cohen, Garcia, Apfel, Master), 225
Reframing bullying prevention:
  anecdote, 83–85
  bullying incidents, 22–23
  controlled behavior, 83–85
  frame/game of schools, 42–43
  frame/game of student identity, 80
  game board of bullying, 85
  mind-sets, 95–101
  obstacles to, 294–295
  optimistic goals for, 86–89
  organizational reframing, 89–95
  self-determination theory (SDT), 101–111
  See also Building Community Spirit
    in Schools
Reframing guidelines:
  activities for, 184–189
  change process, 157–158
  Fundamental Attribution Error
    (FAE), 158–170
  Practice Change, 171–177
  self-affirmation theory, 178–182
Relatedness, 104
Relationships central tenet:
  Building Community Spirit in Schools,
    135–138, 281–282
  checklist for, 281–282
Remember the Titans, 197–198
Require Assembly strategy:
  activities for, 236–238
  anecdote, 229–230
  defined, 230–231
  IKEA effect, 230, 235
  process for, 231–233
  recommendations for, 237–238
  resources for, 233–235
  text-based discussion, 236–237
  video clip discussion, 236
  "who" strategy, 228–238
*Revisiting "The Culture of School and the
  Problem of Change"* (Sarason), 44
Robinson, K., 36–37
Roderick, M., 148–149
Rodkin, P., 58–59
Romney, Mitt, 11–14
Rosenberg, T., 234–235
Roth, G., 250
RSA Animation, 149
Ryan, R., 273

Sarason, S., 44
Schein, E., 234
School bus incident (2012):
  analysis of, 14–17
  bullying characteristics, 18–19
  description of, 10–11
  rationalization for, 25–26
  YouTube review, 10, 14, 25

Schwartz, B., 196
Seed, David, 12
Self-affirmation theory:
   Change Identity strategy, 221
   defined, 178–179
   recommendations for, 181–182
   reframing bullying prevention, 178–182
   statements about educators, 180
Self-determination theory (SDT):
   autonomous motivation, 105, 106
   autonomy, 104
   autonomy support, 105–106
   autonomy-supportive instruction, 108–109, 250
   basic concepts, 102–103, 103
   Building Community Spirit in Schools, 149–150
   bullying prevention implications, 110–111
   competence, 104
   controlled instruction, 109–110
   controlled motivation, 104–105, 106
   intrinsic motivation, 103–104, 105, 108, 110
   Make It Safe To Play strategy, 250
   origins of, 103
   reframing bullying prevention, 101–111
   relatedness, 104
   teaching styles, 106–110
Sharpe, K., 196
Show Hope strategy:
   anecdote, 199–200
   defined, 201
   heart strategy, 199–206
   process of, 201–202
   resources for, 202–204
   text-based discussion, 205
   video clip discussion, 204
Simmons, A., 272
Sinek, S., 196, 248
Slow thinking systems:
   frame/game of schools, 29–30, 32, 42, 43–44, 49–50
   Fundamental Attribution Error (FAE), 161
Smith, J. A., 195–196
Smith, P., 271–272
Social-Psychological Intervention in Education (Yeager & Walton), 97
Social stratification:
   frame/game of bullying, 56–59
   low tier, 58
   middle tier, 58
   top tier, 58

Spencer, S., 210–211
Spitzer, B., 197
Spotlight effect, 30
Start with Why (Sinek), 196
Stereotype threat, 166
Sticks and Stones (Bazelon), 20
Stossel, John, 185
Strangers to Ourselves (Wilson), 260
Student-centered tenet:
   Building Community Spirit in Schools, 132–133, 278–279
   checklist for, 278–279
Student empowerment approach:
   Building Community Spirit in Schools, 116
   frame/game of bullying, 63–64
Student in Distress, A (Thornberg), 262–263
Sullivan, L., 250–251
Suriowiecki, J., 171–172
Switch (Heath & Heath), 203, 222, 259
Switzler, A., 195, 233, 259

Tangney, J. P., 224
Tate, T. F., 236–237
Taylor, Frederick, 38
Teaching Adolescents to Become Learners (Farrington, Roderick, Allensworth, Nogaoka, Keyes, Johnson, Beechum), 148–149
Teaching styles:
   autonomy-supportive instruction, 108–109, 250
   controlled instruction, 109–110
   examples, 106–108
   self-determination theory (SDT), 106–110
Teaming (Edmondson), 90–95, 209–210, 247–248
TED Talks, 102–103, 273
Tell The *Right* Story strategy:
   activities for, 274–275
   anecdote, 265–267
   defined, 267–268
   "do" strategy, 265–275
   listening skills, 270
   process for, 268–269
   recommendations for, 275
   resources for, 270–273
   text-based discussion, 273
   video clip discussion, 273
Thank You Ma'am (Hughes), 205
Thinking, Fast and Slow (Kahneman), 29
Thornberg, R., 262–263

Ties strengthened tenet:
   Building Community Spirit in Schools, 140, 283
   checklist for, 283
To Sell Is Human (Pink), 210
Touch of Greatness, A, 250–251
Toy Story, 266
Train First Responders strategy:
   activities for, 263–265
   anecdote, 253–254
   defined, 254–257
   "do" strategy, 253–265
   external training, 258
   internal training, 258
   process for, 257–259
   recommendations for, 264–265
   resources for, 259–263
   text-based discussion, 263
   video clip discussion, 263
21st Century Learning and Learners (Friesen & Jardine), 38
20/20, 185
Two Questions That Can Change Your Life, 186–187

Unsolicited Evaluation is the Enemy of Creativity (Gray), 251
Up, 266

Wall-E, 266
Walton, G., 97, 197, 210–211, 224–225
Washington, Denzel, 197–198
Washington, J. M., 198
Weinschenk, S., 140, 224
Weir, P., 236
Whoever Tells the Best Story Wins (Simmons), 272
Whole New Mind, A (Pink), 271
"Who" strategies:
   Change Identity, 215–228
   Require Assembly, 228–238
Why We Do What We Do (Deci & Flaste), 102, 249
Willard, N., 286
Wilson, T., 203–204, 222–223, 260
Wisdom of Crowds, The (Suriowiecki), 171–172
Wiseman, L., 234
Witness, 236
WWSIATI approach, 30

Yakin, B., 197–198
Yeager, D., 97, 197
YouTube:
   Born to Learn, 251
   Moneyball, 204
   My Kid Would Never Bully, 263–265
   Remember the Titans, 197–198
   school bus incident (2012), 10, 14, 25
   TED Talks, 102–103
   20/20, 185

Zak, P., 273
Zimbardo, P., 263

CORWIN
A SAGE Company

Corwin is committed to improving education for all learners by publishing books and other professional development resources for those serving the field of PreK–12 education. By providing practical, hands-on materials, Corwin continues to carry out the promise of its motto: **"Helping Educators Do Their Work Better."**